AS-Level

Physics

The ... uide

Editors:
Claire Thompson, Julie Wakeling.
Contributors
Tony Alldridge, Abraham Baravi, Jane Cartwright, Peter Cecil, Martin Chester, Peter Clarke,
Sharon Keeley, Simon Little, Kate Manson, Barbara Mascetti, John Myers, Zoe Nye,
Katherine Reed, Emma Singleton, Sharon Watson, Andy Williams.

Proofreaders:
Stuart Barker, Ian Francis, Les Hearn, Steve Parkinson.

Published by Coordination Group Publications Ltd.

This book is suitable for:

Edexcel(core), AQA A and OCR A.

It also covers the major topics for:
AQA B, Edexcel Salters Horners and OCR B.

There are notes at the tops of double pages to tell you if
there's a bit you can ignore for your syllabus.

Many thanks to the HST programme at CERN and the University of Birmingham for their kind
permission to reproduce the photographs used on p104 & 105.

ISBN-10: 1 84146 974 2
ISBN-13: 978 1 84146 974 4

Groovy website: www.cgpbooks.co.uk
Jolly bits of clipart from CorelDRAW®
Printed by Elanders Hindson Ltd, Newcastle upon Tyne.

Contents

Scalars and Vectors

Mechanics is one of those things that you either love or hate. I won't tell you which side of the fence I'm on.

Scalars only have Size, but Vectors have Size and Direction

1) A **scalar** has **no direction** — it's **just an amount** of something, like the **mass** of a **sack of meaty dog food**.

2) A **vector** has magnitude (**size**) and **direction** — like the **speed and direction** of next door's **cat** running away.

3) **Force** and **velocity** are both **vectors** — you need to know **which way** they're going as well as **how big** they are.

4) Here's a few examples to get you started:

Scalars	Vectors
mass, temperature, time, length, speed, energy	displacement, force, velocity, acceleration, momentum

Adding Vectors involves Pythagoras and Trigonometry

Adding two or more vectors is called finding the **resultant** of them.

Example   Jemima goes for a walk. She walks 3 m North and 4 m East. She has walked 7 m but she isn't 7 m from her starting point. Find her displacement.

Start by drawing a **triangle**:
You get the **magnitude** of the resultant vector using Pythagoras:

$R^2 = 3^2 + 4^2 = 25$

So $R = 5$ m   You knew that.

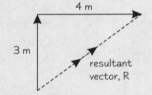

Jemima

Now find the **bearing** of Jemima's new position from her original position.

You use the triangle again, but this time you need to use trigonometry. It's a right-angled triangle, and you know the opposite and the adjacent sides, so you need to use:

$\tan \theta = 4 / 3$

$\theta = 53.1°$

All this SOH CAH TOA stuff is really useful in Physics — so make sure you're completely OK with it.

Use the Same Method for Resultant Forces or Velocities

Always start by drawing a diagram.

Example

You know the resultant force is at 45° to the horizontal with this one.

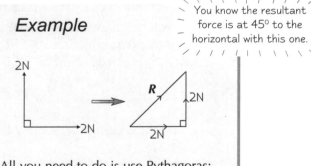

All you need to do is use Pythagoras:

$R^2 = 2^2 + 2^2 = 8$

which gives you $R = 2.83$N.
Remember to take the square root.

Example

If the vectors aren't at right angles, you'll need to use the cosine rule or do a scale drawing.

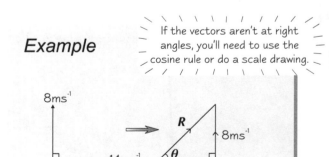

Start with: $R^2 = 14^2 + 8^2 = 260$
so you get: $R = 16.1$ ms^{-1}.
Then: $\tan \theta = 8/14 = 0.5714$

$\theta = 29.7°$

Scalars and Vectors

Sometimes you have to do it backwards.

It's Useful to Split a **Vector** into **Horizontal** and **Vertical Components**

This is the opposite of finding the resultant — you start from the resultant vector and split it into two components at right angles to each other. You're basically **working backwards** from the examples on the other page.

Resolving a vector v into horizontal and vertical components

You get the **horizontal** component v_x like this:

$$\cos \theta = v_x / v$$

$$\boxed{v_x = v \cos \theta}$$

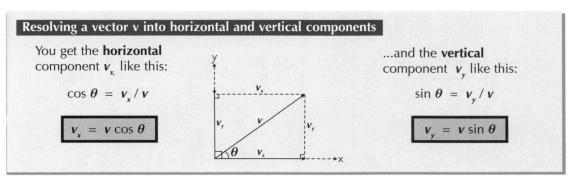

...and the **vertical** component v_y like this:

$$\sin \theta = v_y / v$$

$$\boxed{v_y = v \sin \theta}$$

Example

Charley's amazing floating home is travelling at a speed of 5 ms⁻¹ at an angle of 60° to the horizontal. Find the vertical and horizontal components.

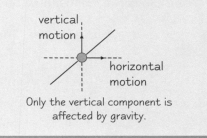

Charley's mobile home was the envy of all his friends.

The **horizontal** component v_x is:

$v_x = v \cos \theta = 5 \cos 60° = 2.5$ ms⁻¹

The vertical component v_y is:

$v_y = v \sin \theta = 5 \sin 60° = 4.33$ ms⁻¹

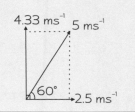

4.33 ms⁻¹ 5 ms⁻¹ 60° 2.5 ms⁻¹

Resolving is dead useful because the two components of a vector **don't affect each other**. This means you can deal with the two directions **completely separately**.

vertical motion

horizontal motion

Only the vertical component is affected by gravity.

Practice Questions

Q1 Explain the difference between a scalar quantity and a vector quantity.

Q2 Jemima has gone for a swim in a river which is flowing at 0.35 ms⁻¹. She swims at 0.18 ms⁻¹ at right-angles to the current. Show that her resultant velocity is 0.39 ms⁻¹ at an angle of 27.2° to the current.

Q3 Jemima is pulling on her lead with a force of 40 N at an angle of 26° below the horizontal. Show that the horizontal component of this force is about 36 N.

Exam Questions

Q1 The wind is creating a horizontal force of 20 N on a falling rock of weight 75 N. Calculate the magnitude and direction of the resultant force. [2 marks]

Q2 A glider is travelling at a velocity of 20.0 ms⁻¹ at an angle of 15° below the horizontal. Find the horizontal and vertical components of the glider's velocity. [2 marks]

His Dark Vectors Trilogy — displacement, velocity and acceleration...

Well there's nothing like starting the book on a high. And this is nothing like... yes, ok. Ahem. Well, good evening folks. I'll mostly be handing out useful information in boxes like this. But I thought I'd not rush into it, so this one's totally useless.

Motion with Constant Acceleration

Displacement is the vector quantity of distance. So when you're asked about displacement, think of both the distance and the direction. Acceleration is the rate of change of velocity, so it's a vector quantity just like velocity is.

Uniform Acceleration *is* Constant Acceleration

Uniform means **constant** here. It's nothing to do with what you wear.

There's **four main equations** that you use for **uniform acceleration**.

You need to be able to use them and if you're doing OCR A, you need know how they're **derived**.

1) **Acceleration is the rate of change of velocity**

$$a = \frac{(v-u)}{t} \quad \text{so} \quad \boxed{v = u + at}$$

where:

u = initial velocity a = acceleration
v = final velocity t = time taken

Acceleration could mean a change in speed or direction or both.

2) s = average velocity × time

$$\boxed{s = \frac{(u+v)}{2} \times t} \quad s = \text{displacement}$$

3) Substitute the expression for v from equation 1 into equation 2 to give:

$$s = \frac{(u+u+at) \times t}{2} = \frac{2ut+at^2}{2} \qquad \boxed{s = ut + \frac{1}{2}at^2}$$

4) You can **derive** the fourth equation from equations **1** and **2**:

Use equation **1** in the form:
$$a = \frac{v-u}{t}$$

Multiply both sides by s, where:
$$s = \frac{(u+v)}{2} \times t$$

This gives us:
$$as = \frac{(v-u)}{t} \times \frac{(u+v)t}{2}$$

The t's on the right cancel so:
$$2as = (v-u)(v+u)$$
$$2as = v^2 - uv + uv - u^2$$

so:
$$\boxed{v^2 = u^2 + 2as}$$

Example

A tile falls from a roof 25 m high. Calculate its speed when it hits the ground and how long it takes to fall.

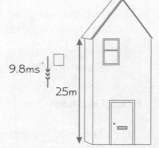

First of all, write out what you know:

$s = 25$ m

$u = 0$ ms^{-1} since the tile's stationary to start with

$a = 9.8$ ms^{-2} due to gravity

$v = ?$ $t = ?$

Usually you take upwards as the positive direction. In this question it's probably easier to take downwards as positive, so you get $g = +9.8$ ms^{-2} instead of $g = -9.8$ ms^{-2}.

9.8ms^{-2} 25m

Then, choose an equation with only **one unknown quantity**.

So start with $v^2 = u^2 + 2as$

$v^2 = 0 + 2 \times 9.8 \times 25$

$v^2 = 490$

$v = 22.1$ ms^{-1}

Now, find t using:

$s = ut + \frac{1}{2}at^2$

$25 = 0 + \frac{1}{2} \times 9.8 \times t^2 \implies$

$t^2 = \dfrac{25}{4.9}$

Final answer:

$t = 2.3s$

Motion with Constant Acceleration

Example

A car accelerates steadily from rest at a rate of 4.2 ms⁻² for 6 seconds.

a)   Calculate the final speed.

b)   Calculate the distance travelled in 6 seconds.

Remember — always start by writing down what you know.

a) a = 4.2 ms⁻²   choose the right equation... $v = u + at$

   u = 0 ms⁻¹ $v = 0 + 4.2 × 6$

   t = 6s   *Final answer:* $v = 25.2$ ms⁻¹

   v = ?

b) s = ?   you can use: $s = \dfrac{(u+v)t}{2}$ or: $s = ut + \frac{1}{2}at^2$

   t = 6s

   u = 0 ms⁻¹

   a = 4.2 ms⁻¹ $s = \dfrac{(0+25.2)×6}{2}$ $s = 0 + \frac{1}{2} × 4.2 × (6)^2$

   v = 25.2 ms⁻¹

   Final answer: $s = 75.6$m $s = 75.6$m

You have to Learn the Constant Acceleration Equations

Make sure you learn the equations. There's only four of them and these questions are always dead easy marks in the exam, so you'd be dafter than Ant and Dec in drag not to learn them...

Practice Questions

Q1   Write out the four constant acceleration equations.

Q2   Show how the equation s = ut + ½ at² can be derived.

Exam Questions

Q1   A sky diver jumps from an aeroplane. She accelerates due to gravity for 5 s. Assume no air resistance.
   (a)   Calculate her maximum velocity.   [2 marks]
   (b)   How far does she fall in this time?   [2 marks]

Q2   A motorcyclist slows down uniformly as he approaches a red light. He takes 3.2 seconds to
   come to a halt and travels 40 m in this time.
   (a)   How fast was he travelling initially?   [2 marks]
   (b)   Calculate his acceleration. (N.B. a negative value shows a deceleration)   [2 marks]

Constant acceleration — it'll end in tears...

If a question refers to uniform or constant acceleration, they'll almost always want you to use one of these equations.
It can be a bit tricky working out which one to use — start by writing out what you know and what you need to know.
That makes it much easier to see which equation you need. To be sure. Arrr.

6

Displacement-Time Graphs

Drawing graphs by hand — oh joy. You'd think examiners had never heard of the graphical calculator.
Ah well, until they manage to drag themselves out of the dark ages, you'll just have to grit your teeth and get on with it.

Acceleration Means a Curved D-T Graph

A graph of displacement against time for an **accelerating object** always produces a **curve**.
If the object is accelerating at a **uniform rate**, then the **rate of change** of the **gradient** will be constant.

Example

Plot a displacement-time graph for a lion who accelerates constantly from rest at 2 ms^{-2} for 5 seconds.

Do a **table of values** first:

...then plot the **graph**:

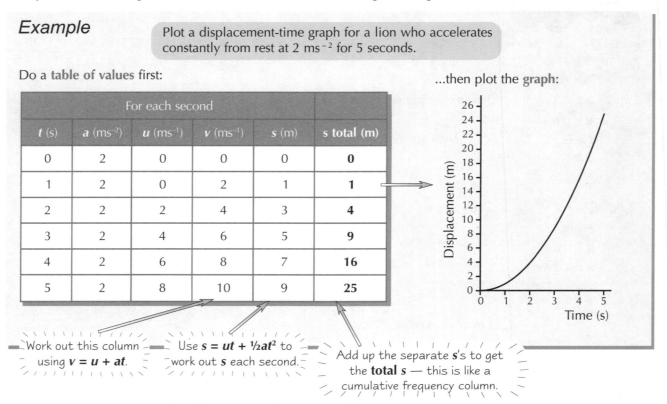

For each second					
t (s)	a (ms^{-2})	u (ms^{-1})	v (ms^{-1})	s (m)	s total (m)
0	2	0	0	0	**0**
1	2	0	2	1	**1**
2	2	2	4	3	**4**
3	2	4	6	5	**9**
4	2	6	8	7	**16**
5	2	8	10	9	**25**

Work out this column using $v = u + at$.

Use $s = ut + \frac{1}{2}at^2$ to work out s each second.

Add up the separate s's to get the **total s** — this is like a cumulative frequency column.

Different Accelerations have Different Gradients

In the example above, if the lion accelerates at a **different rate** it'll change the **gradient** of the curve like this:

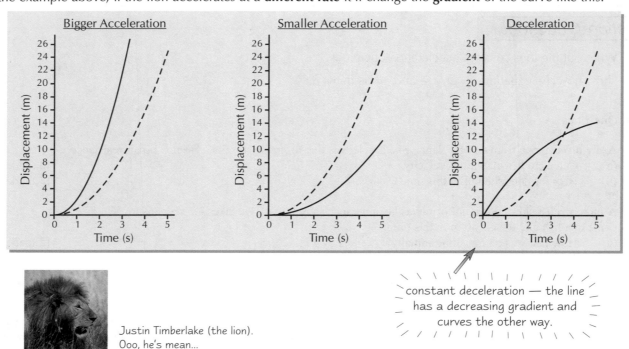

constant deceleration — the line has a decreasing gradient and curves the other way.

Justin Timberlake (the lion).
Ooo, he's mean...

SECTION ONE — MECHANICS

Displacement-Time Graphs

The **Gradient** of a **Displacement-Time Graph** Tells You the Velocity

When the velocity is constant, the D-T graph's a **straight line**.
Velocity is defined as...

$$velocity = \frac{change\ in\ displacement}{time\ taken}$$

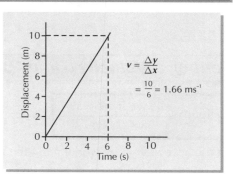

On the D-T graph, this is $\frac{change\ in\ y}{change\ in\ x}$, i.e. the gradient.

So to get the velocity from a D-T graph, just find the gradient.

It's the same with curved graphs

If the gradient **isn't constant** (i.e. if it's a curved line), it means the object is **accelerating**.

To find the **velocity** at a certain point you need to draw a **tangent** to the curve at that point and find its gradient.

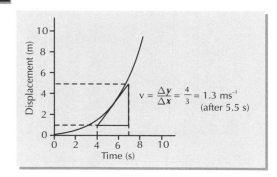

Practice Questions

Q1   What is given by the slope of a D-T graph?

Q2   Sketch a displacement-time graph to show: a) constant velocity,   b) acceleration,   c) deceleration

Exam Questions

Q1   Describe the motion of the cyclist as shown by the graph below.   [4 marks]

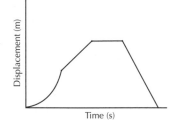

Q2   A baby crawls 5 m in 8 seconds at a constant velocity.   She then rests for 5 seconds before crawling a further
       3 m in 5 seconds. Finally, she makes her way back to her starting point in 10 seconds, travelling at a constant
       speed all the way.
       (a)   Draw a displacement — time graph to show the baby's journey.   [4 marks]
       (b)   Calculate her velocity at all the different stages of her outward journey.   [2 marks]

Some curves are bigger than others...

Whether it's a straight line or a curve, the steeper it is, the greater the velocity. There's nothing difficult about these graphs — the main problem is that it's easy to get them muddled up with velocity-time graphs (next page). If in doubt, think about the gradient — is it velocity or acceleration, is it changing (curve), is it constant (straight line), is it 0 (horizontal line)...

Velocity-Time and Acceleration-Time Graphs

*Speed-time graphs and velocity-time graphs are pretty similar.
The big difference is that velocity-time graphs can have a
negative part to show something travelling in the opposite direction:*

The **Gradient** of a **Velocity-Time Graph** tells you the **Acceleration**

1) $$\text{acceleration} = \frac{\text{change in velocity}}{\text{time taken}}$$ ➡   *likewise for a speed-time graph*

So you get the acceleration by working out the **gradient** of a **velocity-time graph**.

2)   **Uniform** acceleration is always a **straight line**.

3)   The **steeper** the **gradient**, the **greater** the **acceleration**.

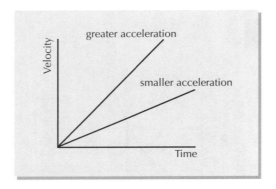

Example

A lion strolls along at 1.5 ms⁻¹ for 4 s and then accelerates uniformly at a
rate of 2.5 ms⁻² for 4 s. Plot this information on a velocity-time graph.

The values have all been calculated
here using a **constant acceleration equation**.

Donny Osmond (the lion)...

t (s)	a (ms⁻²)	u (ms⁻¹)	v (ms⁻¹)
0 to 4	0	1.5	**1.5**
5	2.5	1.5	**4.0**
6	2.5	4.0	**6.5**
7	2.5	6.5	**9.0**
8	2.5	9.0	**11.5**

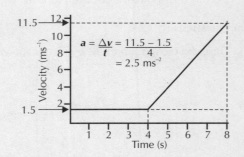

$$a = \frac{\Delta v}{t} = \frac{11.5 - 1.5}{4}$$
$$= 2.5 \text{ ms}^{-2}$$

You can see that the **gradient of the line** is **constant** and has a value of 2.5 ms⁻² representing the **acceleration of the lion**.

Distance Travelled = Area under Speed-Time Graph

You know that:

distance travelled = average speed × time

So you can find the distance travelled by working out the **area under a speed-time graph**.

Velocity-Time and Acceleration-Time Graphs

Non-Uniform Acceleration is a Curve on a V-T Graph

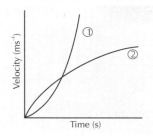

1) If the acceleration is changing, the gradient of the velocity-time graph also changes — so you **won't** get a **straight line**.
2) **Increasing acceleration** is shown by an **increasing gradient**.
3) **Decreasing acceleration** is shown by a **decreasing gradient**. Simple enough...

Example

A racing car accelerates uniformly from rest to 40 ms⁻¹ in 10 s. It maintains this speed for a further 20 s before coming to rest by decelerating at a constant rate over the next 15 s. Draw a velocity-time graph for this journey and use it to calculate the total distance travelled by the racing car.

Split the **graph** up into **sections**: A, B & C
Calculate the **area** of each and **add** the three results together.
A: Area = ½ base × height = ½ × 10 × 40 = 200 m
B: Area = b × h = 20 × 40 = 800 m
C: Area = ½ b × h = ½ × 15 × 40 = 300 m
Total distance travelled = 1300 m

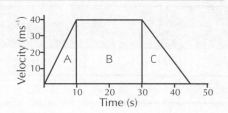

Acceleration-Time Graphs show Constant Acceleration as a Horizontal Line

These aren't used very often, but you need to know how to read them if they do come up.

1) **Constant acceleration** is a **horizontal line** — just read off the acceleration axis to find the acceleration.
2) The **gradient** represents the **rate of increase/decrease** of acceleration.
3) The **area under the graph** represents the **velocity**.

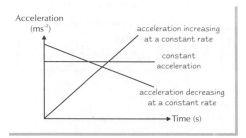

Practice Questions

Q1 How do you calculate velocity from a displacement-time graph?
Q2 How do you calculate the distance travelled from a speed-time graph?
Q3 Sketch displacement-time graphs for constant velocity and constant acceleration.

Exam Questions

Q1 A lion accelerates uniformly from rest at 2 ms⁻² along a straight track.
    (a) Sketch a velocity-time graph for the first 5 s of his journey. [2 marks]
    (b) Use a constant acceleration equation to calculate his displacement each second and plot this information onto a displacement-time graph. [5 marks]
    (c) Suggest another method of calculating the lion's displacement after each second and use this to check your answers to part (b). [2 marks]

Still awake — I'll give you five more minutes...

There's a really nice sunset outside my window. It's one of those ones that makes the whole landscape go pinky-yellowish. And that's about as much interest as I can muster on this topic. Normal service will be resumed on page 11, I hope.

Mass, Weight and Centre of Gravity

Weightlessness — that just seems like a very odd concept to me. Just imagine what your hair would do without gravity...

Mass is the Property of a Body that Resists Change in Motion

1) The 'mass' of an object means the **amount of matter** in it. It's measured in **kg**.

2) Mass is a measure of a body's **resistance to change in velocity** (its **inertia**).

3) The **mass** of an object **doesn't alter** if the strength of the **gravitational field** changes.

4) Weight is a **force**. It's measured in **newtons** (N), like all forces.

5) Weight is the **force experienced by a mass** due to the **effect of a gravitational field** acting on it.

6) The weight of an object **does vary** according to the size of the **gravitational field** acting on it.

> **weight = mass × gravitational field strength (W = mg)**   where g = 9.8 Nkg⁻¹ on Earth.

This table shows Cliff Richard (the lion*)'s mass and weight on the Earth and the Moon.

Weight
240 N

Weight
1470 N

Name	Quantity	Earth (g = 9.8 Nkg⁻¹)	Moon (g = 1.6 Nkg⁻¹)
Mass	Mass (scalar)	150 kg	150 kg
Weight	Force (vector)	1470 N	240 N

Density is Mass per Unit Volume

Density is a measure of the 'compactness' (for want of a better word) of a substance. It relates the mass of a substance to how much space it takes up.

> $$density = \frac{mass}{volume} \qquad \rho = \frac{m}{V}$$

The symbol for density is a Greek letter rho (ρ) — it looks like a p but it isn't.

The **units** of **density** are **g cm⁻³** or **kg m⁻³**
N.B. 1 g cm⁻³ = 1000 kg m⁻³

1) The density of an object depends on what **substance** it's made of. Density **doesn't vary** with **size or shape**.

2) The **density** of a body determines whether it **floats** or **sinks**.

3) A solid object will **float** on a fluid if it has a **lower density** than the **fluid**.

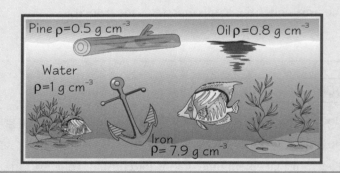

Pine ρ=0.5 g cm⁻³
Oil ρ=0.8 g cm⁻³
Water ρ=1 g cm⁻³
Iron ρ=7.9 g cm⁻³

Centre of Gravity — Assume All the Mass is in One Place

1) The **centre of gravity** (or centre of mass) of a body is the **single point** that you can consider its **whole weight** to **act through** (whatever the orientation of the body).

2) The **weight** of a body behaves as a **single force** acting through the **centre of gravity**.

3) The object will **balance** around this **point**, although in some cases the **centre of gravity** will **fall outside** the object.

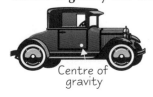
Centre of gravity

Centre of gravity

Centre of gravity

Mass, Weight and Centre of Gravity

Find the Centre of Gravity either by Symmetry or Experiment

Experiment to find the Centre of Gravity of an Irregular Object

1) Hang the object freely from a point (e.g. one corner).
2) Draw a vertical line downwards from point of suspension.
3) Hang the object from a different point.
4) Draw a vertical line down from point of suspension.
5) The centre of gravity is at the intersection of the two lines.

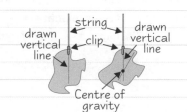

drawn vertical line — string — clip — drawn vertical line

Centre of gravity

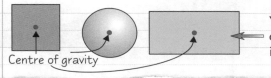

Centre of gravity

You can easily work out that the centre of gravity for a regular object is at its centre by symmetry.

How High the Centre of Gravity is tells you How Stable the Object is

1) An object will be nice and **stable** if it has a **low centre** of **gravity** and a **wide base area**. This idea is used a lot in design, e.g. Formula 1 racing cars.

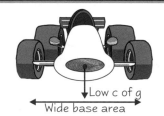

Low c of g
Wide base area

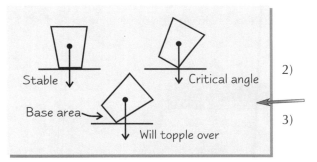

Stable

Critical angle

Base area

Will topple over

2) The **higher** the **centre of gravity**, and the **smaller** the **base area**, the **less stable** the object will be. Think of unicyclists...

3) An object will topple over if a **vertical line** drawn **downwards** from its **centre of gravity** falls **outside** its **base area**.

Practice Questions

Q1 A lioness has a mass of 200 kg. What would be her mass and weight on the Earth (where $g = 9.8$ Nkg^{-1}) and on the Moon (where $g = 1.6$ Nkg^{-1})?

Q2 What is meant by the centre of gravity of an object?

Exam Questions

Q1 (a) Define **density**. [1 mark]
   (b) A cylinder of aluminium, radius 4 cm and height 6 cm, has a mass of 820 g. Calculate its density. [3 marks]
   (c) Use the information from part (b) to calculate the mass of a cube of aluminium of side 5 cm. [1 mark]

Q2 (a) Explain what is meant by the **centre of gravity** of a body. [1 mark]
   (b) Explain, using diagrams, why a double-decker bus is less stable if all the passengers are on the top floor than if all the passengers are on the bottom floor. [4 marks]

The centre of gravity of this book should be round about page 62...

This is a really useful area of physics. To would-be nuclear physicists it might seem a little dull — but if you want to be an engineer, something a bit more useful (no offence Einstein), then things like centre of gravity and density are dead important things to understand. You know, for designing things like cars and submarines... yep, pretty useful I'd say.

Forces and Equilibrium

If you jump out of a plane at 2,000 ft, you want to know that you're not going to be accelerating all the way.

Free-Body Force Diagrams show All Forces on a Single Body

1) **Free-body force** diagrams show a **single body** on its own.
2) All the **forces** which **act on** that body are added to the diagram, but the **forces exerted by** that body are **not** included
3) Remember **forces** are **vector quantities** and so the **arrow labels** should show the **size** and **direction** of the forces.
4) If a body is in **equilibrium** (i.e. not accelerating) the **forces** acting on it will be **balanced**.

Drawing free body force diagrams isn't too hard — you just need lots of practice. Here's a few **examples**:

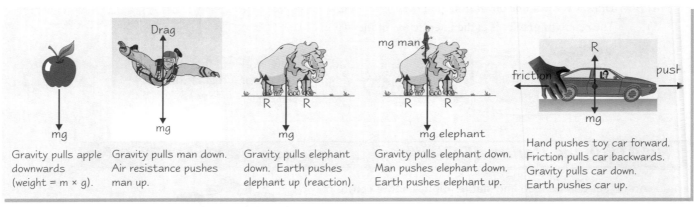

Gravity pulls apple downwards (weight = m × g).

Gravity pulls man down. Air resistance pushes man up.

Gravity pulls elephant down. Earth pushes elephant up (reaction).

Gravity pulls elephant down. Man pushes elephant down. Earth pushes elephant up.

Hand pushes toy car forward. Friction pulls car backwards. Gravity pulls car down. Earth pushes car up.

And here's a few **easy rules** to remember with these diagrams:
1) It only needs to be a **simple sketch** (often just a box will do).
2) The **object** should be **separate** from everything else (though it sometimes helps to show where the ground is).
3) Draw **only** the **forces** acting **directly** on the body.
4) Remember to include both **size** and **direction** for each **force**.

Resolving a Force means Splitting it into Components

1) Forces can be in **any direction**, so they're not always at right angles to each other. This is sometimes a bit **awkward** for **calculations**.

2) To make an 'awkward' force easier to deal with, you can think of it as **two separate forces**, acting at **right angles** to **each other**.

Example

Here, the force **F** has exactly the same effect as the horizontal and vertical forces, F_H and F_V. Expressing **F** as F_H and F_V is called **resolving the force** F.

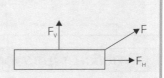

3) To find the size of a component force in a particular direction, you need to use trigonometry (see page 3). Forces are vectors, so you can deal with them like that and put them end to end.

So this...

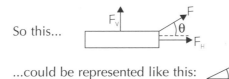

...could be represented like this:

Using trig. you get:

$$\frac{F_H}{F} = \cos\theta \quad \text{or} \quad F_H = F\cos\theta$$

And:

$$\frac{F_V}{F} = \sin\theta \quad \text{or} \quad F_V = F\sin\theta$$

Example

A tree trunk is pulled along the ground by an elephant exerting a force of 1200 N at an angle of 25° to the horizontal. Calculate the components of this force in the horizontal and vertical directions.

Horizontal force = 1200 × cos 25° = **1088 N**
Vertical force = 1200 × sin 25° = **507 N**

Forces and Equilibrium

You **Add** the **Components Back Together** to get the **Resultant Force**

1)   If **two forces** act on an object, you find the **resultant** (total) **force** by adding the **vectors** together and creating a **closed triangle**, with the resultant force represented by the **third side**.

2)   Forces are vectors (as you know) so you use **vector addition** — draw the forces as vector arrows put 'tail to top'.

3)   Then it's yet more trigonometry to find the **angle** and the **length** of the third side.

Example

Two dung beetles roll a dung ball along the ground at constant velocity. Beetle A applies a force of 0.5 N Northwards while beetle B exerts a force of only 0.2 N Eastwards. What is the resultant force on the dungball?

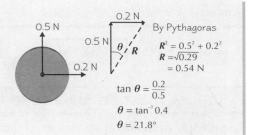

By Pythagoras
$R^2 = 0.5^2 + 0.2^2$
$R = \sqrt{0.29}$
$= 0.54$ N

$\tan\theta = \dfrac{0.2}{0.5}$

$\theta = \tan^{-1} 0.4$

$\theta = 21.8°$

Choose sensible **Axes** for **Resolving**

Use directions that **make sense** for the situation you're dealing with. If you've got an object on a slope, choose your directions **along the slope** and **at right-angles to it**. You can turn the paper to an angle if that helps.

Examiners like to call a slope an "inclined plane".

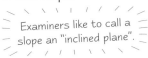

The component of the bone's weight down the slope is 2.5N so you'd need 2.5N of friction to stop it sliding away.

Practice Questions

Q1   Sketch a free body force diagram for an ice hockey puck moving across the ice (assuming no friction).

Q2   What are the horizontal and vertical components of the force F?

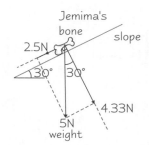

Exam Questions

Q1   A picture is suspended from a hook as shown in the diagram. Calculate the tension force, *T*, in the string.

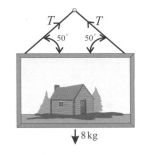

[2 marks]

Q2   Two elephants pull a tree trunk as shown in the diagram. Calculate the resultant force on the tree trunk.

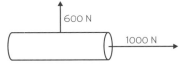

[2 marks]

Free body force diagram — sounds like something you'd get with a dancemat...

Remember those F cos θ and F sin θ bits. Write them on bits of paper and stick them to your wall. Scrawl them on your pillow. Tattoo them on your brain. Whatever it takes — you just **have to learn them**.

Moments and Torques

This is not a time for jokes. There is not a moment to lose. The time for torquing is over. Oh ho ho ho ho *bang*. (Ow.)

A **Moment** is the **Turning Effect** of a **Force**

The **moment**, or **torque**, of a **force** depends on the **size** of the force and **how far** the force is applied from the **turning point**:

> **moment of a force** (in Nm) = **force** (in N) × **perpendicular distance from pivot** (in m)

In symbols, that's: $M = F \times d$

Moments must be **Balanced** or the **Object** will **Turn**

The **principle of moments** states that for a body to be in **equilibrium**, the **sum of the clockwise moments** about any point **equals** the **sum of the anticlockwise moments** about the same point.

Example

Two children sit on a see saw as shown in the diagram. An adult balances the see-saw at one end. Find the size and direction of the force that the adult needs to apply.

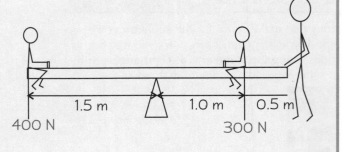

1.5 m 1.0 m 0.5 m

400 N 300 N

In equilibrium, $\sum$ anticlockwise moments = $\sum$ clockwise moments

$$400 \times 1.5 = 300 \times 1 + 1.5F$$
$$600 = 300 + 1.5F$$

Final answer: $F = 200$ N downwards

$\sum$ means "the sum of"

Example

A builder wants to move a large rock of mass 250 kg. He has a metal rod 2 m long, which he uses as a lever. He pivots the rod around a smaller rock placed 40 cm from the large rock. Calculate the size of the force he must use to push down on the rod.

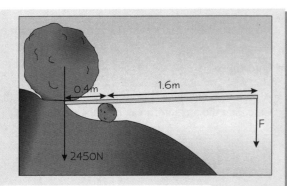

0.4m 1.6m

2450N

F

In equilibrium, $\sum$ clockwise moments = $\sum$ anticlockwise moments

$$1.6F = (250 \times 9.8) \times 0.4$$
$$1.6F = 980$$
$$F = 612.5 \text{ N}$$

Final answer: The builder needs to exert a force **greater than 612.5 N** to shift the rock.

Moments and Torques

A *Couple* is a *Pair* of *Forces*

1)   A couple is a **pair** of **forces** of **equal size** which act
parallel to each other, but in **opposite directions**.

2)   A couple doesn't cause any resultant linear force, but **does** produce
a **turning force** (usually called a **torque** rather than a moment).

The **size** of this **torque** depends on the **size** of the **forces** and the
distance between them.

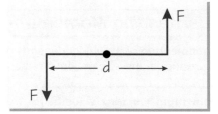

> **Torque of a couple** (in Nm) = **size of one of the forces** (in N) × **perpendicular distance between the forces** (in m)

In symbols, that's: $T = Fd$

Example

A cyclist turns a sharp right corner by applying equal but
opposite forces of 20N to the ends of the handlebars.

The length of the handlebars is 0.6m.
Calculate the torque applied to the handlebars

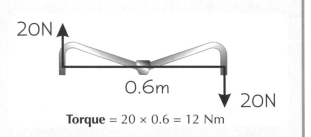

Torque = 20 × 0.6 = 12 Nm

Practice Questions

Q1   A girl of mass 40 kg sits 1.5 m from the middle of a see-saw.
Show that her brother, mass 50 kg, must sit 1.2 m from
the middle if the see-saw is to balance

Q2   What is meant by the word 'couple'?

Exam Questions

Q1   A driver is changing his flat tyre. The torque required to undo the nut is 60 Nm.
He uses a 0.4 m long double-ended wheel wrench.
Calculate the force that he must apply at each end of the spanner.   [2 marks]

Q2   A diver of mass 60 kg stands on the end of a diving board 2 m from the pivot point.
Calculate the upward force exerted on the retaining spring 30 cm from the pivot.

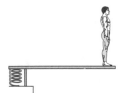

[2 marks]

It's all about balancing — just ask a tightrope walker...

*They're always see-saw questions aren't they. It'd be nice if once, **just once**, they'd have a question on... I don't know,
rotating knives or something. Just something unexpected... anything. It'd make physics a lot more fun, I'm sure. *sigh**

Momentum

Ignore all this momentum stuff if you're doing AQA B or OCR.

This section is about linear momentum — that's momentum in a straight line (not a circle). Whoop de do.

Understanding **Momentum** helps Physicists do **Calculations** on **Collisions**

The **momentum** of an object depends on two values — **mass** and **velocity**.
The **product** of these two values is the momentum of the object.

Remember velocity is a vector quantity, which means it has size and direction.

| **momentum = mass × velocity** | or in symbols: | p (in kg ms^{-1}) = m (in kg) × v (in ms^{-1}) |

Momentum is always **Conserved**

1) Assuming **no external forces** act, momentum is always **conserved**.

2) This means the **total momentum** of two objects **before** they collide will **equal** the total momentum **after** the collision.

3) This is very handy for working out the **velocity** of objects after a collision (as you do...):

Example A skater of mass 75 kg and velocity 4 ms^{-1} collides with a stationary skater of mass 50 kg.
The two skaters join together and move off in the same direction. Calculate their velocity after impact.

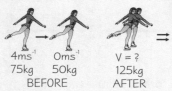

4ms^{-1} 0ms^{-1} V = ?
75kg   50kg   125kg
BEFORE   AFTER

Momentum of skaters before = momentum of skaters after
$(75 × 4) + (50 × 0) = 125 v$
$300 = 125 v$
So $v = 2.4$ ms^{-1}

Before you start a momentum calculation, always draw a quick sketch.

4) The same principle can be applied in **explosions**. E.g. when you fire an **air rifle**, the **forward momentum** gained by the pellet **equals** the **backward momentum** of the rifle, and you feel the rifle recoiling into your shoulder.

Example A bullet of mass 0.005 kg is shot from a rifle at a speed of 200 ms^{-1}.
The rifle has a mass of 4 kg. Calculate the velocity at which the rifle recoils.

4kg × v 0.005kg × 200ms^{-1}

Momentum before explosion = Momentum after explosion
$0 = (0.005 × 200) + (4 × v)$
$0 = 1 + 4v$
$v = -0.25$ ms^{-1}

Rocket Propulsion can be Explained by Momentum

For a **rocket** to be **propelled forward** it must expel **exhaust gases**. The momentum of the rocket in the forward direction is **equal** to the momentum of the exhaust gases in a backward direction.

Example A rocket of mass 500 kg is completely stationary in an area of space a long way from any gravitational fields. It starts its engines. The rocket ejects 2.0 kg of gas per second at a speed of 1000 ms^{-1}. Calculate the velocity of the rocket after 1 second.
(For the purpose of this calculation ignore the loss of mass due to fuel use.)

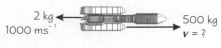

2 kg
1000 ms^{-1} 500 kg
v = ?

The total momentum before launch = 0 kg ms^{-1} as initially the rocket is stationary, the total momentum after the launch must also = 0 kg ms^{-1}.
Total momentum after launch = $(500 × v) + (2 × 1000) = 0$
$500 v = -2000$
$v = -4$ ms^{-1}

The minus sign shows that the rocket moves in the opposite direction to the exhaust gases.

Momentum

Collisions can be Elastic or Inelastic

See page 29 for more on this.

An **elastic collision** is one where **momentum** is **conserved** and **kinetic energy** is conserved — i.e. no energy is dissipated as heat, sound, etc.
If a collision is **inelastic** it means that some of the kinetic energy has been converted into other forms during the collision. But **momentum is always conserved.**

Example   A toy lorry (mass 2 kg) travelling at 3 ms⁻¹ crashes into a smaller toy car (mass 800 g), travelling in the same direction at 2 ms⁻¹. The velocity of the lorry after the collision is 2.6 ms⁻¹ in the same direction. Calculate the new velocity of the car and the kinetic energy before and after the collision.

Momentum before collision   = Momentum after collision

$$(2 \times 3) + (0.8 \times 2) = (2 \times 2.6) + (0.8\ v)$$
$$7.6 = 5.2 + 0.8\ v$$
$$2.4 = 0.8\ v$$
$$v = 3\ ms^{-1}$$

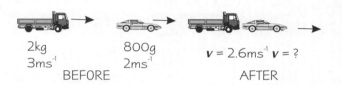

2kg   800g
3ms⁻¹   2ms⁻¹ $v = 2.6ms^{-1}$ $v = ?$
BEFORE   AFTER

Kinetic Energy before collision = k.e of lorry + k.e of car
$$= \tfrac{1}{2}mv^2 \text{ (lorry)} + \tfrac{1}{2}mv^2 \text{ (car)}$$
$$= \tfrac{1}{2}(2 \times 3^2) + \tfrac{1}{2}(0.8 \times 2^2)$$
$$= 9 + 1.6$$
$$= 10.6\ J$$

The difference in the two values (10.6 J – 10.36 J = 0.24 J) represents the amount of kinetic energy dissipated as heat or sound, or in damaging the vehicles.

Kinetic Energy after collision = $\tfrac{1}{2}(2 \times 2.6^2) + \tfrac{1}{2}(0.8 \times 3^2)$
$$= 6.76 + 3.6$$
$$= 10.36\ J$$

Impulse = Change in Momentum

Edexcel only.

1) **Impulse** is defined as **force × time**, *Ft*. The units are **newton seconds**, Ns.
2) Newton's second law says **force = rate of change of momentum** (see pages 20-21), or $F = (mv - mu) \div t$
3) Rearranging this gives:

$$Ft = mv - mu$$
or **impulse = change of momentum**

Practice Questions

Q1   Give two examples of conservation of momentum in practice.

Q2   Explain briefly how rocket propulsion works.

Q3   Describe what happens when a tiny object makes an elastic collision with a massive object, and why.

Exam Questions

Q1   A ball of mass 0.6 kg moving at 5 ms⁻¹ collides with a larger stationary ball of mass 2 kg.
The smaller ball rebounds in the opposite direction at 2.4 ms⁻¹. What is the velocity of the larger ball?   [3 marks]

Q2   A toy train of mass 0.7 kg, travelling at 0.3 ms⁻¹ collides with a stationary toy carriage of mass 0.4 kg.
The two toys couple together. What is their new velocity?   [3 marks]

Who fancies fish and chips...

It seems a bit of a contradiction to say that momentum's always conserved then tell you that impulse is change in momentum. The difference is that impulse is only talking about the change of momentum of one of the objects, whereas conservation of momentum is talking about the whole system.

Newton's Laws of Motion

If you're doing AQA B or OCR you can skip these pages too.

Sir Isaac Newton (1642-1727) said: **"If I have seen further than other men, it is because I have stood on the shoulders of giants."** And then fallen off again due to the Earth's gravitational field...

Newton's **1st Law** Says You're Going Nowhere unless I **Push** You (well, kinda)

1) **Newton's 1st Law of motion** states the **velocity** of an object will **not change** unless a **resultant force** acts on it.

2) In plain English this means a body will remain at rest or moving in a **straight line** at a **constant speed**, unless acted on by a **resultant force**.

3) If the forces **aren't balanced**, the **overall resultant force** will cause the body to **accelerate**. This may involve a change in **direction**, or **speed**, or both. (See Newton's 2nd Law, pages 20-21).

4) Take an apple sitting on a table, for example. As a general rule, an apple sitting on a table won't go anywhere (unless the table's wonky, of course. Anyway...). It doesn't move because the **forces** on it are **balanced**.

reaction (R)   =   **weight** (mg)
(force of table pushing apple up)   =   (force of gravity pulling apple down)

The two examples below show **moving objects** obeying **Newton's 1st Law**.
Both have **balanced forces** acting on them and in each case their **velocity** remains **constant**.

Example

A coal truck is moving with constant velocity.
thrust = drag
(forward force provided by person pushing) = (frictional forces: air resistance & friction at wheels)

Friction   Thrust

Example

A sky-diver falling at terminal (maximum) velocity.
weight = lift

(force of gravity pulling   (air resistance pushing
sky-diver downwards)   sky-diver upwards)

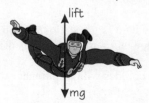

The faster the sky-diver falls, the more air particles he brushes past each second and so the greater the drag or lift. The sky-diver will continue to accelerate until the upward force of air resistance is the same as his weight. Forces are now in equilibrium and he has reached 'terminal velocity'.

Newton's Laws of Motion

Newton's 3rd Law of Motion:

Each Force has an Equal, Opposite Reaction Force

There's a few different ways of stating Newton's 3rd Law, but the clearest way is:

> **If an object A EXERTS A FORCE on object B, then object B exerts THE EXACT OPPOSITE FORCE on object A**

You'll also hear the law as "every action has an equal and opposite reaction".
But this confuses people who wrongly think the forces are both applied to the same object.
(If that were the case, you'd get a resultant force of zero and nothing would ever move anywhere...)
So remember — the pair of forces **act on different objects**.

The best way to get it is by looking at loads of examples:

1) If you **push against a wall**, the wall will **push back** against you, **just as hard**. As soon as you stop pushing, so does the wall. Amazing...

2) If you think about it, there must be an **opposing force** when you lean against a wall — otherwise you (and the wall) would **fall over**.

3) If you **pull a cart**, whatever force **you exert** on the rope, the rope exerts the **exact opposite** pull on you.

4) When you **sit** on a large **ill-tempered mutated** goose, your weight exerts a **downwards** force on the goose, while you feel the **equal force** of the goose **pushing upwards** on you.

Newton's 3rd law applies in **all situations** and to all **types of force**. But the pairs of forces are always the **same type**, e.g. both gravitational or both electrical.

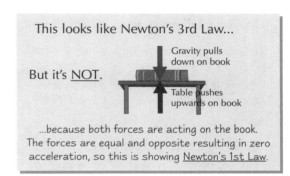

This looks like Newton's 3rd Law...

But it's NOT.

Gravity pulls down on book

Table pushes upwards on book

...because both forces are acting on the book. The forces are equal and opposite resulting in zero acceleration, so this is showing Newton's 1st Law.

Practice Questions

Q1 State Newton's 1st and 3rd laws and explain what they mean.

Q2 Draw a diagram to show the forces acting on an aeroplane travelling at constant velocity. Label the forces.

Q3 What are the pair of forces acting between an orbiting satellite and the Earth?

Exam Questions

Q1 a) Draw diagrams to show the forces acting on a parachutist

   (i) at the moment of jumping from the plane
   (ii) accelerating downwards
   (iii) having reached terminal velocity   [3 marks]

   b) List two things a parachutist could do to reduce his terminal velocity.   [2 marks]

Vader felt a great disturbance in the force (and Yoda felt an equal but opposite one)...

These equations may not really fill you with a huge amount of excitement (and I'd hardly blame you if they didn't)... but it was pretty fantastic at the time — suddenly people actually understood how forces work, and how they affect motion. I mean arguably it was one of the most important discoveries, like, ever. Bigger than Quantum Theory, even. Maybe.

Newton's Second Law

There are several reasons why Michael Schumacher consistently enters a Grand Prix <u>not</u> driving a bus. One of them is that a bus is dead heavy, so it takes a lot of force to make it accelerate. Which is what Newton's 2nd Law says, in a nutshell.

At GCSE You Learn Newton's 2nd Law as: F = ma

...which, as you'll have been rightly told, stands for:

resultant force (F) = mass (m) × acceleration (a)

Learn that equation — it crops up all over the place in AS Physics. And learn what it means:

1)   It says that the **more force** you have acting on a certain mass, the **more acceleration** you get.

2)   It says that for a given force the **more mass** you have, the **less acceleration** you'll get.

REMEMBER:

1)   The **resultant force** is the **vector sum** of all the forces.

2)   The force is **always** measured in **newtons**. **Always.** Or the equation **doesn't work** (see bottom of page).

3)   The **mass** is always measured in **kilograms**.

4)   **a** is the **acceleration** of the object as a result of **F**. It's **always** measured in **metres per second per second** (ms^{-2}).

5)   The **acceleration** is always in the **same direction** as the **resultant force**.

The Formal Statement of the Law talked about Rate of Change of Momentum

Newton didn't just write down that equation. What he discovered was this:

> "The **rate of change of momentum** of an object is **directly proportional** to the **resultant force** which acts on the object."

(You need to **learn** that formal statement unless you're doing AQA B.)

It **looks** a lot **different from the equation** you know, but both statements are actually saying the same thing.

Think about it in terms of this snooker ball. $\Longrightarrow$

The ball has mass **m** kg and it's travelling initially at a constant velocity **u** ms^{-1}.
It's acted on by a resultant force **F** N for **t** seconds, after which time its new velocity is **v** ms^{-1}.

Momentum = mass × velocity, so:

initial momentum = **mu**, and momentum after **t** seconds = **mv**

Hence, change in momentum = **mv − mu**

This change happened over time **t**, so rate of change of momentum = $\dfrac{mv - mu}{t}$

... which Newton says is proportional to F: $\dfrac{mv - mu}{t} \propto \boldsymbol{F}$, or: $\dfrac{mv - mu}{t} = kF$ where **k** is a constant.

Taking **m** out as a factor gives: $m\left(\dfrac{v - u}{t}\right) = kF$

But since $a = \dfrac{v - u}{t}$ (const. acc^{n} formulas, p4): $ma = kF$ where **k** is a constant.

That's **almost** the equation you're used to. You get it by making **k** = 1, i.e. by defining 1 newton as the force needed to accelerate a 1 kg mass by 1 ms^{-2}.

You need to Learn the Definition of the Newton and its Relationship to F = ma

1)   This is what a newton is:

1 N is the force needed to accelerate a 1 kg mass by 1 ms^{-2}.

2)   And the reason is to give a constant of **k = 1** in the equation **kF = ma**.
So that you just get a **nice simple summary** of **Newton's Second Law**: F = ma.

Newton's Second Law

As you may remember from GCSE , if you drop any two objects from the top of Blackpool Tower together, they'll hit the ground at the same time. Galileo came up with that. The idea, not the Blackpool Tower bit. It hadn't even been built.

Galileo said: All Objects Fall at the Same Rate (if you Ignore Air Resistance)

You need to understand **why** this is true. Newton's 2nd law explains it neatly — consider two balls dropped at the same time — ball **1** being heavy, and ball **2** being light. Then use Newton's 2nd Law to find their acceleration.

mass = m_1
resultant force = F_1
acceleration = a_1

 ↓ W_1

By Newton's Second Law:

$$F_1 = m_1 a_1$$

Ignoring air resistance, the only force acting on the ball is weight, given by $W_1 = m_1 g$ (where g = gravitational field strength = 9.81 N/kg).

So: $F_1 = m_1 a_1 = W_1 = m_1 g$

So: $m_1 a_1 = m_1 g$, then m_1 cancels out to give: $a_1 = g$

mass = m_2
resultant force = F_2
acceleration = a_2

 ↓ W_2

By Newton's Second Law:

$$F_2 = m_2 a_2$$

Ignoring air resistance, the only force acting on the ball is weight, given by $W_2 = m_2 g$ (where g = gravitational field strength = 9.81 N/kg).

So: $F_2 = m_2 a_2 = W_2 = m_2 g$

So: $m_2 a_2 = m_2 g$, then m_2 cancels out to give: $a_2 = g$

... in other words, the **acceleration** is **independent of the mass**. It makes **no difference** whether the ball's **heavy or light**. And I've kindly **hammered home the point** by showing you two almost identical examples.

You can Only Ignore Air Resistance with Small, Heavy Objects (or on the Moon)

1) On Earth, **air resistance** affects some objects much more than others. The **larger an object**, the **more air resistance** it causes. The **lighter an object** is, the **more effect air resistance has** (because there's less weight to cancel it out).

2) Experiments done in a **vacuum** (or on the **Moon**) do show that the **theory works** in places where there's **no air**.

3) And for **very dense objects** on the Earth, the effect of **air resistance** is **very small, so** you can normally **ignore** it. That's usually what they'll give you in **exam questions**. Hurrah.

Practice Questions

Q1 State Newton's Second Law in two different ways. (Only one if you're doing AQA B.)

Q2 Write down the definition of the newton.

Q3 State the acceleration of a mass of 37.2 kg if you dropped it off a cliff. Take g = 9.81 ms^{-2} and ignore air resistance.

Exam Questions

Q1 A boat is moving across a river at a right angle to the flow of the river. The engines provide a force of 500N and the boat experiences a drag of 100N. The force on the boat due to the flow of the river is 300N. The mass of the boat is 250kg.

    a) Calculate the magnitude of the resultant force acting on the boat.   [2 marks]

    b) Calculate the magnitude of the acceleration of the boat.   [2 marks]

Q2 This question asks you to use Newton's second law to explain three situations.

    a) Two cars have different maximum accelerations.
    What are the only two overall factors that determine the acceleration a car can have?   [2 marks]

    b) Michael can always beat his younger brother Tom in a sprint, however short the distance.
    Give two possible reasons for this.   [2 marks]

    c) Michael and Tom are both keen on diving. They notice that they seem to take the same time to drop
    from the diving board to the water. Explain why this is the case.   [3 marks]

And another thing...

Newton's Second Law is one of the most useful ones you'll come across in mechanics. But remember — it was originally about rate of change of momentum. And they only got rid of the proportionality thing by creating a new unit. Cunning.

Free Fall and Projectile Motion

If you're doing AQA A, skip straight to page 23.
Here's a double page spread on how to calculate the air speed velocity of an unladen swallow. And stuff.

Free Fall is when there's Only Gravity and Nothing Else

Free fall is defined as the motion of an object undergoing an acceleration of '**g**'. You need to remember:-

1) Acceleration is a **vector quantity** — and '**g**' acts **vertically downwards**.
2) The magnitude of **g** is taken as **9.81ms⁻²**, though there's slight variation at different points on the Earth's surface.
3) The **only force** acting on an object in free fall is its **weight**.
4) Objects can have an initial velocity in any direction and still undergo **free fall** as long as the **force** providing the initial velocity is **no longer acting**.

You Need to Know How to Measure g by using an Object in Free Fall

You don't have to do it this way — but if you don't know a method of measuring **g** already, learn this one.
You need to be able to:
1) **Sketch** a diagram of the **apparatus**.
2) **Describe** the **method**.
3) **List** the **measurements** you made.
4) **Explain** how '**g**' was **calculated**.

Another gravity experiment.

Experiment to Measure Gravity

In this experiment you have to assume that the effect of air resistance on the ball bearing is negligible.

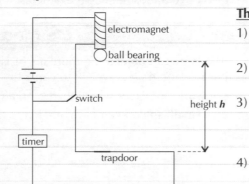

The Method:

1) Flick the switch to simultaneously start the timer and disconnect the electromagnet, releasing the ball bearing.
2) The ball bearing falls, knocking the trapdoor down and breaking the circuit — which stops the timer.
3) Use the time **t** measured by the timer, and the height **h** that the ball bearing has fallen, to calculate a value for **g**, using $h = \frac{1}{2}gt^2$ (see below for more on acceleration formulas).
4) You need to remember that the height **h** is measured from the **bottom** of the ball bearing to the **trap door**.

You can Just Replace a with g in the Equations of Motion

You need to be able to work out **speeds**, **distances** and **times** for objects moving vertically with an **acceleration of g**. As **g** is a **constant acceleration** you can use the **equations of motion**. But because **g** is downwards, you need to be careful about directions. To make it clear, there's a sign convention: **upwards is positive, downwards is negative**.

Case 1: No initial velocity (it's just falling)

Initial velocity **u** = 0
Acceleration **a** = **g** = −9.81ms⁻²
Hence the equations of motion become: ⟹

$$v = gt \qquad v^2 = 2gs$$
$$s = \frac{1}{2}gt^2 \qquad s = \frac{vt}{2}$$

Case 2: An initial velocity upwards (it's thrown up into the air)

The equations of motion are just as normal,
but with **a** = **g** = −9.81 ms⁻²

> Sign Conventions — Learn Them:
> **g** is always <u>downwards</u> so it's <u>usually negative</u>
> **t** is <u>always positive</u>
> **u** and **v** can be either <u>positive or negative</u>
> **s** can be either <u>positive or negative</u>

Case 3: An initial velocity downwards (it's thrown down)

Example: Alex throws a stone down a cliff. She throws it with a downwards velocity of 2 ms⁻¹. It takes 3s to reach the water below. How high is the cliff?

1) You know   **u** = -2 ms⁻¹, **a** = **g** = -9.81 ms⁻² and **t** = 3 s. You need to find **s**.

2) Use $s = ut + \frac{1}{2}gt^2 = (-2 \times 3) + \left(\frac{1}{2} \times -9.81 \times 3^2\right) = \underline{\mathbf{-50.15\ m}}$ ⟸ *Notice that **s** is negative because it's downwards from the start.*

Free Fall and Projectile Motion

Any object given an initial velocity and then left to move freely under gravity is a projectile.
If you're doing AS Maths, you've got all this to look forward to in M1 as well, quite likely. Fun for all the family.

You have to think of *Horizontal* and *Vertical* Motion *Separately*

Example: Alex fires a bullet horizontally with a velocity of 100 ms⁻¹ from a gun 1.5 m above the ground. How long does it take to hit the ground, and how far has it travelled?

Consider vertical motion:

1) It's **constant acceleration** under gravity...
2) You know $u = 0$ (no vertical velocity at first), $s = -1.5$ m and $a = g = -9.81$ ms⁻². You need to find t.
3) Use $s = \dfrac{1}{2}gt^2 \Rightarrow t = \sqrt{\dfrac{2s}{g}} = \sqrt{\dfrac{2 \times -1.5}{-9.81}} = 0.55$ s
4) So the bullet hits the ground after **0.55** seconds.

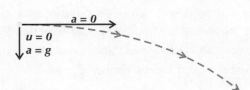

Consider horizontal motion:

1) The horizontal motion isn't affected by gravity or any other force (ignoring air resistance), so it moves at a **constant speed**.
2) That means you can just use good old **speed = distance / time**.
3) Now $v_h = 100$ ms⁻¹, $t = 0.55$ s and $a = 0$. You need to find s_h.
4) $s_h = v_h t = 100 \times 0.55 = \underline{\textbf{55 m}}$

Where v_h is the horizontal velocity, and s_h is the horizontal distance travelled (rather than the height fallen).

It's *More Tricky* if it *Starts Off* at an *Angle*   You won't have to do calculations like this for your AS exams though.

If something's projected at an angle (like, say, a javelin) you start off with both horizontal and vertical velocity. You can work these equations out using the ideas you've already used for vertical and horizontal motion:

Method:
1) Resolve the initial velocity into horizontal and vertical components
2) Use the vertical component to work out how long it is in the air and/or how high it goes.
3) Use the horizontal component to work out how far away it goes while it is in the air.

Practice Questions

Q1   What is the value of the acceleration of a free falling object?
Q2   What is the initial velocity of an object which is dropped?
Q3   What is the initial vertical velocity for a object projected horizontally with a velocity of 5ms⁻¹?
Q4   How does the horizontal velocity of a free falling object change with time?

Exam Questions

Q1   In an experiment to measure the value of the gravitational acceleration 'g', this apparatus is used. The card is dropped vertically through the light gate and interrupts the beam twice. Data from the light gate is processed by the computer to give a value for the acceleration of the card.
   (a)   What three pieces of data will the computer need to obtain from the light gate?   [3 marks]
   (b)   The width of the piece of card needs to be entered on the computer. Explain how this value and the measurements from the light gate can be used to calculate 'g'.   [3 marks]

Q2   Charlene is bouncing on a trampoline. She reaches her highest point a height of 5 m above the trampoline.
   (a)   Calculate the speed with which she leaves the trampoline surface.   [2 marks]
   (b)   How long does it take her to reach the highest point?   [2 marks]
   (c)   What will her velocity be as she lands back on the trampoline?   [2 marks]

Is that an African swallow or a European swallow...

Right. That's enough. No more of this silliness.

Terminal Velocity

You don't need to know the stuff on these pages if you're doing Edexcel.
Terminal velocity is the maximum velocity you can reach. It's when the air resistance balances out the force that's trying to accelerate you. As soon as the forces acting on you balance out, there's no resultant force — and hence no acceleration.

Friction *is a* Force *that* Opposes Motion

There are two main types of friction:

1) **contact friction** between **solid surfaces** (which is what we usually mean when we just use the word 'friction')

2) **fluid friction** (known as drag or fluid resistance or air resistance).

Things you need to remember about frictional forces:

1) They **always** act in the **opposite direction** to the **motion** of the object.

2) They can **never** speed things up or start something moving.

3) They convert **kinetic energy** into **heat**.

> In a bit more detail then:
>
> **The friction contact force**
>
> 1) is **greater** for **rougher** surfaces
>
> 2) is **directly proportional** to the normal **reaction** force, so it's greater for a heavy object than for a light one
>
> 3) **doesn't depend** on the **area** of contact (I know, you'd kinda think it would, wouldn't you...)
>
> 4) **doesn't vary** (much) with **speed**.
>
> **Fluid resistance (or fluid friction):**
>
> 1) 'Fluid' is a word which means either a **liquid or a gas** — something which can **flow**.
>
> 2) The force depends on the thickness (or **viscosity** of the fluid).
>
> 3) It **increases** as **speed increases** (for simple situations it's directly proportional, but you don't need to worry about the mathematical relationship).

Terminal Velocity *— when the* Friction *Force* Equals *the* Driving Force

You will reach a **terminal velocity** at some point, if you have:

1) a **driving force** which stays the **same** all the time

2) a **frictional** or **resistance force** (or collection of forces) that will increase with speed

There are **three main stages** to reaching terminal velocity:

The car **accelerates** from **rest** using a constant driving force.

As the **velocity increases**, the **resistance forces increase** (because of things like turbulence — you don't need the details). This **reduces the resultant force** on the car and hence **reduces its acceleration**.

Eventually the car reaches a velocity at which the **resistance forces are equal to the driving force**. There is now **no resultant force** and **no acceleration**, so the car carries on at **constant velocity**.

Sketching a *Graph* for Terminal Velocity

You need to be able to **recognise** and **sketch** the graphs for **velocity against time** and **acceleration against time** for the **terminal velocity** situation.

Nothing for it but practice — shut the book and sketch them from memory. Keep doing it till you get them right every time.

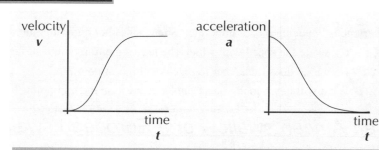

Terminal Velocity

Things *Falling* through *Air* or *Water* Reach a *Terminal Velocity* too

When something's falling through **air**, the **weight** of the object is a **constant force** accelerating the object.
Air resistance is a **frictional force** opposing this motion, which **increases** with **speed**.
So before a parachutist opens the parachute, exactly the same thing happens as with the car example:

1) A skydiver leaves a plane and will **accelerate** until the **air resistance** equals his **weight**.

2) He will then be travelling at a **terminal velocity**.

But... the terminal velocity of a person in freefall is too great to land without dying a horrible death.
The **parachute increases** the **air resistance massively**, which slows them down to a lower terminal velocity:

3) Before reaching the ground he will **open his parachute** which immediately **increases the air resistance** so it is now **bigger** than his **weight**.

4) This **slows him down** until his speed has dropped enough for the **air resistance** to be **equal to his weight** again. This new terminal velocity is small enough to survive landing.

The graphs are a bit different, because you have a new terminal velocity being reached after the parachute is opened:

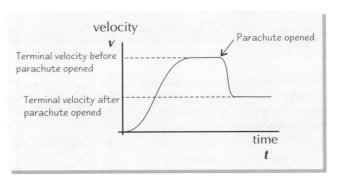

Practice Questions

Q1 What forces limit the speed of a skier going down a slope?

Q2 What conditions cause a terminal velocity to be reached?

Q3 Sketch a graph to show how the velocity changes with time for an object falling through air.

Exam Questions

Q1 A space probe free falls towards the surface of a planet.
The graph on the right shows the velocity data recorded by the probe as it falls.

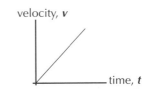

(a) The planet does not have an atmosphere. Explain how you can tell this from the graph. [2 marks]

(b) Sketch the velocity-time graph you would expect to see if the planet did have an atmosphere. [2 marks]

(c) Explain the shape of the graph you have drawn. [3 marks]

You'll never understand this without going parachuting...

When you're doing questions about terminal velocity, remember the frictional forces reduce acceleration not speed.
They usually don't slow an object down, apart from the parachute example, where the skydiver is travelling faster
when the parachute opens than the terminal velocity for the parachute-skydiver combination.

* No. 37 in a series of 100 least convincing excuses for an interesting holiday.

SECTION ONE — MECHANICS

Work and Power

If you're doing AQA B, skip these pages.

As everyone knows, work in Physics isn't like normal work. It's harder. Work also has a specific meaning that's to do with movement and forces. You'll have seen this at GCSE — it just comes up in more detail for AS level.

Work is Done Whenever Energy is Transferred

This table gives you some examples of **work being done** and the **energy changes** that happen.

1) Usually you need a force to move something because you're having to **overcome another force**.

2) The thing being moved has **kinetic energy** while it's **moving**.

3) The kinetic energy is transferred to **another form of energy** when the movement stops.

ACTIVITY	WORK DONE AGAINST	FINAL ENERGY FORM
Lifting up a box.	gravity	gravitational potential energy
Pushing a chair across a level floor.	friction	heat
Pushing two magnetic north poles together.	magnetic force	magnetic energy
Stretching a spring.	stiffness of spring	elastic potential energy

The word **'work'** in Physics means the **amount of energy transferred** from one form to another when a force causes a movement of some sort.

Work = Force × Distance

When a car tows a caravan, it applies a force to the caravan and moves it to where you want it to go. To **find out** how much **work** has been **done**, you need to use the **equation**:

> **work done (W) = force causing motion (F) × distance moved (s)**
> ...where W is measured in joules (J), F is measured in newtons (N) and s is measured in metres (m).

Points to remember:

1) **Work** is the **energy** that's been **changed** from one form to another — it's not necessarily the **total** energy. E.g. moving a book from a low shelf to a higher one will increase its gravitational potential energy, but it had some potential energy to start with. Here, the **work done** would be the **increase** in potential energy, **not the total** potential energy.

2) Remember the distance needs to be measured in metres — if you have **distance in centimetres or kilometres**, you need to **convert** to metres first.

3) The force F will be a **fixed** value in any calculations, either because it's **constant** or because it's the **average** force.

4) The equation assumes that the **direction of the force** is the **same** as the **direction of movement**.

5) The equation gives you the **definition** of the joule (symbol J): 'one joule is the work done when a force of 1 newton moves an object through a distance of 1 metre'

The Force isn't always in the Same Direction as the Movement

Sometimes the **direction of movement** is **different** from the **direction of the force**.

Example

1) To **calculate the work done** in a situation like this, you need to consider the **horizontal** and **vertical components** of the **force**.

2) The only **movement** is in the **horizontal** direction. This means the **vertical force** is not causing any motion (and hence not doing any work) — it's just **balancing** out some of the **weight**, meaning there's a **smaller reaction force**.

direction of force on sledge

rosebud

direction of motion

3) The horizontal force is causing the motion — so to **calculate** the **work done**, this is the **only force** you need to consider. Which means we get:

> $W = Fs \cos \theta$

Where θ is the **angle** between the **direction of the force** and the **direction of motion**. See pages 12-13 for more on resolving forces.

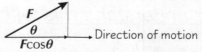

Direction of motion

Work and Power

Power = Work Done per Second

Power means many things in everyday speech, but in physics (of course!) it has a special meaning. Power is the **rate of doing work**, in other words it is the **amount of energy transformed** from one form to another **per second.**

You **calculate power** from this equation:

> **Power (P) = work done (W) / time (t)**
> ...where **P** is measured in watts (W), **W** is measured in joules (J) and **t** is measured in seconds (s)

The **watt** (symbol W) is defined as a **rate of energy transfer** equal to **1 joule per second**.

Yep, that's another **equation and definition** for you to **learn**.

Power is also Force × Velocity (P = Fv)

Sometimes, it's **easier** to use **this version** of the power equation. This is how you get it:

1) You **know P = W/t**
2) You also **know W = Fs**, which gives **P = Fs/t** (if the object is moving at constant velocity).
3) But **v = s/t**, which you can substitute into the above equation to give **P = Fv**
4) It's easier to use this if you're given the **speed** in the question.
   Learn this equation as a **shortcut** to link **power** and **speed**.

Example

A car is travelling at a speed of $10\,ms^{-1}$ which is kept going against the frictional force by a driving force of 500 N in the direction of motion. Find the power supplied by the engine to keep the car moving.

Use the shortcut **P = Fv**, which gives:

$P = 500 \times 10 = 5000$ W

If the force and motion are in different directions, you can replace **F** with **Fcosθ** to get: $\boxed{P = Fv\cos\theta}$

You **aren't** expected to **remember** this equation, but it's made up of bits that you **are supposed to know**, so be ready for the possibility of calculating **power** in a situation where the **direction of the force and direction of motion are different**.

Practice Questions

Q1 Write down the equation used to calculate work if the force and motion are in the same direction.

Q2 Write down the equation for work if the force is at an angle to the direction of motion.

Q3 Write down the equations relating (i) power and work and (ii) power and speed.

Exam Questions

Q1 A traditional narrowboat is drawn by a horse walking along the towpath.
The horse pulls the boat at a constant speed between two locks which are
1500 m apart. The tension in the rope is 100 N at 40° to the direction of motion.

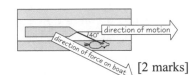

    a) How much work is done on the boat? [2 marks]
    b) The boat moves at $0.8\,ms^{-1}$. Calculate the power supplied to the boat in the direction of motion. [2 marks]

Q2 A motor is used to lift a 20 kg load a height of 3 m. (Take $g = 9.81\,Nkg^{-1}$)

    a) Calculate the work done in lifting the load. [2 marks]
    b) The speed of the load during the lift is $0.25\,ms^{-1}$. Calculate the power delivered by the motor. [2 marks]

Work — there's just no getting away from it...

Loads of equations to learn. Well, that's what you came here for, after all. Can't beat a good bit of equation-learning, as I've heard you say quietly to yourself when you think no one's listening. Aha, can't fool me. Ahahahahahahahahahahahahaha.

Conservation of Energy

*Energy can never be **lost**. I repeat — **energy** can **never** be lost. Which is basically what I'm about to take up two whole pages saying. But that's, of course, because you need to do exam questions on this as well as understand the principles.*

Learn the **Principle** of **Conservation** of **Energy**

The **principle of conservation of energy** says that:

> Energy **cannot be created** or **destroyed**. Energy **may be transferred** from one form to another but the total amount of energy in a system will not change.

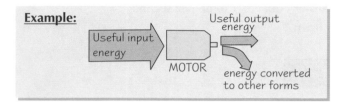

Example:

You Need it for **Questions** about **Kinetic** and **Potential Energy**

The Principle of Conservation of Energy nearly always comes up when you're doing questions about changes between kinetic and potential energy.

A quick reminder:

1) **Kinetic energy** is energy of anything **moving** which you work out from $KE = \frac{1}{2}mv^2$ where **v** is the velocity it's travelling at and **m** is its mass.

2) There are **different types of potential energy** — e.g. gravitational, elastic, etc.

3) **Gravitational potential energy** is the energy something gains if you lift it up. You work it out using: **PE = mgh**, where **m** is the mass of the object, **h** is the height it is lifted and **g** is the gravitational field strength ($9.81\,\text{Nkg}^{-1}$ on Earth).

4) **Elastic potential energy** is the energy you get in, say, a stretched rubber band or spring. You work this out using $E = \frac{1}{2}ke^2$, where **e** is the extension of the spring and **k** is the spring constant (see p35).

Examples

These pictures show you three **examples** of changes between kinetic and potential energy.

1) As Becky throws the **ball upwards**, **kinetic energy** is converted into **gravitational potential energy**. When it **comes down** again, that **gravitational potential** energy is **converted back** into **kinetic** energy.

2) As Dominic goes **down the slide**, **gravitational potential energy** is converted to **kinetic energy**.

3) As Simon bounces upwards from the trampoline, **elastic potential energy** is converted to **kinetic energy**, to **gravitational potential energy**. As he comes back down again, that **gravitational potential** energy is **converted back** to **kinetic** energy, to **elastic potential** energy, and so on.

In **real life** there are also **frictional forces** — Simon would have to use some **force** from his **muscles** to keep **jumping** to the **same height** above the trampoline each time. You're usually told to **ignore friction** in exam questions — this means you can **assume** that the **only forces** are those which provide the **potential energy** (in this example that's **Simon's weight** and the **tension** in the springs and trampoline material). If you're ignoring friction, you can say that the **sum of the kinetic and potential energies is constant**.

Conservation of Energy

In a **Collision**, **Kinetic Energy** is **Conserved** — But **Only** If it's **Elastic**

1) As long as there's **no friction**, you know that **momentum is always conserved** in a collision (you have the **same total momentum after** a collision **as you had before**) (see pages 16 and 17).

2) **After** a collision, objects sometimes **stick together**, and sometimes **bounce apart**. Either way the momentum is still **conserved**.

3) But the **kinetic energy** is **not** always conserved as kinetic energy. Usually, some of it gets converted into **sound or heat** energy.

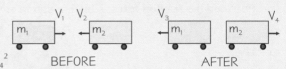
In the real world, some energy's always lost in a collision. Sometimes, if the energy loss is small, it's okay to assume the collision is elastic.

A collision where the **total kinetic energy** is the **same** after a collision is called an **elastic collision**.

A collision where the **total kinetic energy** is **less** after a collision is called an **inelastic collision**.

In the diagram on the right, given no friction,

1) it is **always true** that $m_1v_1 + m_2v_2 = m_1v_3 + m_2v_4$

2) it is **sometimes true** that $\frac{1}{2}m_1v_1^2 + \frac{1}{2}m_2v_2^2 = \frac{1}{2}m_1v_3^2 + \frac{1}{2}m_2v_4^2$

BEFORE   AFTER

Example

A cart of mass 50 g hurtles at 20 ms⁻¹ towards a stationary cart of mass 60 g.
After the collision, both carts move forward in the same direction.

$m_1 = 50g$ $m_2 = 60g$
$V_1 = 20ms^{-1}$ $V_2 = 0$
BEFORE

a) If the first cart moves forward at 8 ms⁻¹ after the collision, calculate the speed of the second cart.

b) Calculate the kinetic energy before and after the collision.

c) State whether the collision was elastic or inelastic, giving a reason for your answer.

a) Using Conservation of Momentum (pages 16-17):
total momentum before = total momentum after
$(0.05 \times 20) + (0.06 \times 0) = (0.05 \times 8) + (0.06 \times v_2)$
$1 = 0.4 + 0.06v_2 \Rightarrow v_2 = 0.6 \div 0.06 = $ **10 ms⁻¹**

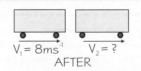
$V_1 = 8ms^{-1}$ $V_2 = ?$
AFTER

Remember — it's not lost, just converted into other forms of energy (heat and sound most likely).

b) kinetic energy = ½mv^2
Before: $KE = ½ \times 0.05 \times 20^2 = $ **10 J**
After: $KE = (½ \times 0.05 \times 8^2) + (½ \times 0.06 \times 10^2) = 1.6 + 3 = $ **4.6 J**

c) The collision must be inelastic, because the total kinetic energy is reduced in the collision.

Practice Questions

Q1 State the Principle of Conservation of Energy.

Q2 What are the equations for calculating kinetic energy and gravitational potential energy?

Q3 What's always conserved in a collision (if there's no friction going on)?

Q4 What's the difference between elastic and inelastic collisions?

Exam Questions

Q1 A skateboarder is on a half pipe. He lets the board run down one side of the ramp and up the other. The height of the ramp is 2 m. Take **g** as 9.81 Nkg⁻¹

a) If you assume that there is no friction, what would be his speed at the lowest point of the ramp? [3 marks]

b) How high will he rise up the other side? [1 mark]

c) Real ramps are not frictionless, so what must the skater do to reach the top on the other side? [1 mark]

Q2 A railway truck of mass 10 000 kg is travelling at 1 ms⁻¹ and collides with a stationary truck of mass 15 000 kg. The two trucks stay together after the collision.

a) What can you say about the total kinetic energy before and after the collision? [1 mark]

b) Calculate the final velocity of the two trucks. [2 marks]

c) Calculate the total kinetic energy before and after the collision. [2 marks]

Energy is never lost — it just sometimes prefers the scenic route...

Remember to check your answers — I can't count the number of times I've forgotten to square the velocities or to multiply by the ½... I reckon it's definitely worth the extra minute to check.

Forces on Vehicles and Car Safety

These pages are for OCR A only.
Real collisions now — how to avoid them and how car manufacturers try to make sure you survive.

The **Motive Force** is the **Force** that **Makes You Move**

A car's a good enough example to be starting with:

1) A **car's engine** creates a **force** which gives the car its **acceleration**. That force is called the **motive force** (sometimes also known as the driving force).

2) The **bigger the motive** force, the **greater the acceleration** for a particular car. (Remember $F = ma$)

3) The force is transferred to the wheels and causes the **wheel to push backwards on the ground**.

4) The **ground pushes forwards** on the wheel.

5) Provided the **friction force** is **big enough** to **stop** the wheel **slipping**, the car **moves forward**.

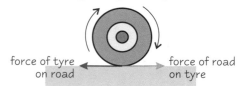

force of tyre
on road

force of road
on tyre

Learn what is meant by motive force
Make sure you know what forces are
acting on the wheels.

Motive Power is **Rate of Work** done by the **Motive Force**

The **motive power** of a **vehicle** is defined as the **rate of working** of a **motive force**.

$P = W/t$ can also be written as $P = Fv$ (see page 27) — and that's usually the easiest equation to use to find motive power, because you're normally given the motive force in the question.

So... learn this:

> **motive power** = **motive force** × **velocity**

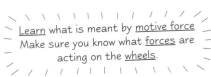

You use **Friction** to **Stop** as well as to **Start**

There are two sources of resistance to movement of a car:

1) **Drag** (fluid resistance, air resistance, fluid friction):
    - **increases** as the **speed** of the car **increases**,
    - acts **against** the **motive force** and **reduces the resultant force** and the **acceleration**,
    - eventually **equals the motive force** to cause the car to have a **constant terminal speed**,
    - will make the car **slow down** if the motive force is **reduced**,
    - is **less** on streamlined things than on big fat blocky things.

2) **Friction** (solid friction, frictional contact force):
    - makes the **tyres grip** to the road, so the car moves forward...
      - the motive force turns the wheels, so the tyres push **backwards** on the road.
      - the friction force opposes this by pushing **forwards** (like in the diagram above).
    - is also used in the **brakes**...
      - when a car brakes, the brake pads make **contact** with discs on the wheels.
      - the **friction force** created makes the wheels (and car) slow down.

Example

Giles's car bumps into the back of a stationary bus. The car was travelling at 2 ms⁻¹ and comes to a stop in 0.2 s. Giles was wearing his seatbelt and takes 0.8 s to stop. The mass of the car is 1000 kg and Giles's mass is 75 kg.

a) Find the decelerations of Giles and the car.

b) Calculate the average force acting on Giles during the accident.

c) Work out the force that would have acted on Giles if he had stopped in as short a time as the car.

> a) Use $v = u + at$:
> For the car: $u = 2$ ms⁻¹, $v = 0$, $t = 0.2$ s
> Which gives: $0 = 2 + 0.2a \Rightarrow 0.2a = -2 \Rightarrow a = -10$ ms⁻² so the **deceleration = 10 ms⁻²**
> For Giles: $u = 2$ ms⁻¹, $v = 0$, $t = 0.8$ s
> Which gives: $0 = 2 + 0.8a \Rightarrow 0.8a = -2 \Rightarrow a = -2.5$ ms⁻² so the **deceleration = 2.5 ms⁻²**
>
> b) Use $F = ma = 75 \times 2.5 =$ **187.5 N**
>
> c) Use $F = ma$ again, but with 10 ms⁻² instead of 2.5 ms⁻²: $F = ma = 75 \times 10 =$ **750 N**

Forces on Vehicles and Car Safety

Car Safety Features are Usually Designed to Slow You Down Gradually

Modern cars have **safety features** built in. **Air bags**, for example, make use of the idea of slowing the collision down so it **takes you longer to stop**, so your **deceleration is less** and there is **less force** on you.

Safety features you need to know about are:

1) **Seatbelts** keep you in your seat and also give a little so that you are brought to a stop in a longer time.

2) **Airbags** inflate when you have a collision and are squishy so they bring you to rest in a longer time. They also act over quite a big surface area, which reduces the pressure on any one particular part of your body.

3) **Crumple zones** at the front and back of the car are designed to give way more easily and absorb some of the energy of the collision.

4) **Safety cages** are designed to prevent the area around the occupants of the car from being crushed in.

Many Factors Affect How Quickly You Stop

Braking distance and thinking distance together make the **total distance you need to stop** after you see a problem. Remember this as:

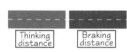

Thinking distance + Braking distance = Stopping distance

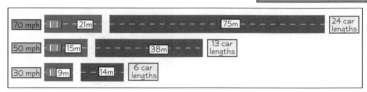

In an exam you might need to list factors that affect the thinking and braking distances.

thinking distance = speed × reaction time

Reaction time is increased by **tiredness**, **alcohol** or other **drug** use, **illness**, **distractions** such as noisy children and Wayne's World-style headbanging.

Braking distance depends on **braking force**, **friction** between tyres and road, **mass** and **speed**

Braking force is reduced by **reduced friction** between the brakes and the wheels (**worn** or **badly adjusted brakes**).

Friction between the tyres and the road is reduced by **wet** or **icy** roads, **leaves or dirt** on the road, **worn-out tyre treads**, etc.

Mass is affected by the size of the car and what you put in it.

Practice Questions

Q1 What is meant by the term 'motive force'?

Q2 What forces help a car to accelerate and to decelerate?

Q3 What equation can you use to work out the force you experience during a collision?

Q4 What factor affects both thinking distance and braking distance?

Exam Questions

Q1 Sarah sees a cow step into the road 30 m ahead of her. Sarah's reaction time is 0.5 s. She is travelling at 20 ms⁻¹. Her maximum braking force is 10 000 N and her car (with her in it) has a mass of 850 kg.
   (a) How far does she travel before applying her brakes? [2 marks]
   (b) Calculate her braking distance. [3 marks]
   (c) Does Sarah hit the cow? Justify your answer with a suitable calculation. [1 mark]

Q2 In a crash test a car slams into a solid barrier at 20 ms⁻¹. The car comes to a halt in 0.1 s. The crash test dummy goes through the windscreen and hits the barrier with a speed of 18 ms⁻¹ and then also comes to a stop in 0.1 s. The mass of the car is 900 kg and the mass of the dummy is 50 kg.
   (a) Calculate the forces on the car and the dummy as they are brought to a stop. [4 marks]
   (b) The car is modified to include crumple zones and an airbag. Explain what difference this will make and why. [3 marks]

Crumple zone — the heap of clothes on my bedroom floor...

Being safe in a car is mainly common sense — don't drive if you're stoned up to the eyeballs and don't drive a car with dodgy brakes. But you still need to cope with exam questions, so don't go on till you're sure you know this all off by heart.

Hooke's Law

If you're doing AQA B, you can skip this whole section — it's not a very long one though, sorry.
Hooke's Law doesn't apply to all materials, and only works for any material up to a certain point.

Hooke's Law Says that Extension is Proportional to Force

If a **metal wire** is supported at the top and then a weight attached to the bottom, it **stretches**.
The weight pulls down with force **F** producing an equal and opposite force at the support.

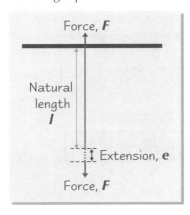

1) **Robert Hooke** discovered in 1676 that the extension of a stretched wire, **e**, is proportional to the load or force, **F**.
   This relationship is now called **Hooke's law**.

2) Hooke's law can be written:

$$F = ke$$

Where **k** is a constant that depends on the material being stretched.
k is called the **stiffness constant**.

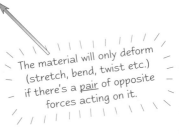

The material will only deform (stretch, bend, twist etc.) if there's a pair of opposite forces acting on it.

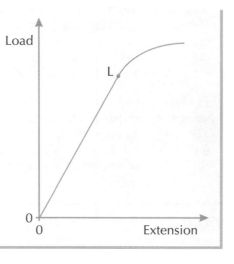

I'm a bit irrelevant on this page — bungee ropes don't obey Hooke's Law. Do you think I need to get out more?

Hooke's law Also Applies to Springs

A metal spring also changes length when you apply a **pair of opposite forces**.

1) The **extension** or **compression** of a spring is **proportional** to the **force** applied — so Hooke's Law applies.

2) For springs, **k** in the formula **F = ke** is usually called the **spring stiffness** or **spring constant**.

> Hooke's Law works just as well for **compressive** forces as **tensile** forces. For a spring, **k** has the **same value** whether the forces are tensile or compressive (that's not true for all materials).

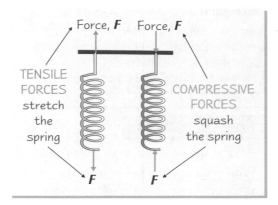

Hooke's law Stops Working at the Elastic Limit

There's a **limit** to the force you can apply for Hooke's law to stay true.

1) The graph shows load against extension for a **typical metal wire**.

2) The first part of the graph shows Hooke's law being obeyed — there's a **straight-line relationship** between **load** and **extension**.

3) When the load becomes great enough, the graph starts to **curve**. The point marked E on the graph is called the **elastic limit**.

4) If you increase the load past the elastic limit, the material will be **permanently stretched**. When all the force is removed, the material will be **longer** than at the start.

5) **Metals** generally obey Hooke's law up to the elastic limit.

6) Be careful — there are some materials, like **rubber**, that don't obey Hooke's Law at all.

Hooke's Law

So basically...

A Stretch can be Elastic or Plastic

Elastic

If a **deformation** is **elastic**, the material returns to its **original shape** once the forces are removed.

1) When the material is put under **tension**, the **atoms** of the material are **pulled apart** from one another.

2) Atoms can **move** small distances relative to their **equilibrium positions**, without actually changing position in the material.

3) Once the **load** is **removed**, the atoms **return** to their **equilibrium** distance apart.

For a metal, elastic deformation happens as long as **Hooke's Law** is obeyed.

Plastic

If a deformation is **plastic**, the material is **permanently stretched**.

1) Some atoms in the material move position relative to one another.

2) When the load is removed, the **atoms don't return** to their original positions.

A metal stretched **past its elastic limit** shows plastic deformation.

Practice Questions

Q1 State Hooke's Law.

Q2 Define tensile forces and compressive forces.

Q3 Explain what is meant by the elastic limit of a material.

Q4 From studying the force-extension graph for a material as it is loaded and unloaded, how can you tell:

(a) if Hooke's law is being obeyed,

(b) the elastic limit has been reached?

Q5 What is plastic behaviour of a material under load?

Exam Questions

Q1 A metal guitar string stretches 4.0 mm when a 10 N force is applied.

(a) If the string obeys Hooke's Law, how far will the string stretch with a 15 N force? [1 mark]

(b) Calculate the stiffness constant for this string in Nm^{-1}. [2 marks]

(c) The string is tightened beyond its elastic limit. What would be noticed about the string? [1 mark]

Q2 A rubber band is 6.0 cm long. When it is loaded with 2.5 N, its length becomes 10.4 cm. Further loading increases the length to 16.2 cm when the force is 5.0 N.

Does the rubber band obey Hooke's law? Justify your answer with a suitable calculation. [2 marks]

Sod's Law — if you don't learn it, it'll be in the exam...

Okay, so this isn't the most riveting stuff in the world — but at least it's fairly simple. I promise you, Physics does get more interesting than this. You always get the boring stuff near the beginning of a book. Wait till page 98 — you'll be longing for a bit of 17th century tedium then. Come back Hooke, all is forgiven.

Stress and Strain

How much a material stretches for a particular applied force depends on its dimensions.
If you want to compare the properties of two different materials, you use stress and strain instead.
A stress-strain graph is the same for any sample of a particular material — the size of the sample doesn't matter.

A Stress Causes a Strain

A material subjected to a pair of **opposite forces** might **deform**, i.e. **change shape**. If the forces **stretch** the material, they're **tensile**. If the forces **squash** the material, they're **compressive**.

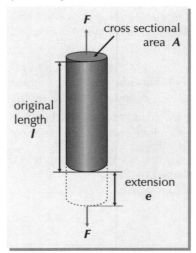

1) **Tensile stress** is defined as the **force applied**, *F*, divided by the **cross-sectional area**, *A*:

$$\text{stress} = \frac{F}{A}$$

The **units** of stress are **Nm⁻²** or pascals, **Pa**.

2) **Tensile strain** is defined as the **change in length**, e.g. the **extension**, divided by the **original length** of the material:

$$\text{strain} = \frac{e}{l}$$

Strain has **no units** — it's just a **number**.

3) It doesn't matter whether the forces producing **stress** and **strain** are **tensile** or **compressive** — the **same equations** apply.

A Stress Big Enough to Break the Material is Called the Breaking Stress

As a greater and greater **force** is applied to a material, the **stress** on it **increases**.

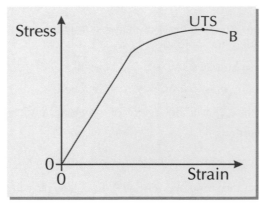

1) The effect of the **stress** is to start to **pull** the **atoms apart** from one another.

2) Eventually the stress becomes **so great** that atoms **separate completely**, and the **material breaks**. This is shown by point **B** on the graph. The stress at which this occurs is called the **breaking stress**.

3) The point marked **UTS** on the graph is called the **ultimate tensile stress**. This is the **maximum stress** that the material can withstand.

4) **Engineers** have to consider the **UTS** and **breaking stress** of materials when designing a **structure**.

Elastic Strain Energy is the Energy Stored in a Stretched Material

When a material is **stretched**, **work** has to be done in stretching the material.

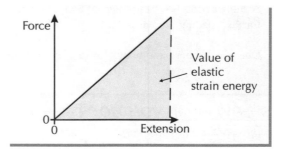

1) **Before** the **elastic limit**, **all** the **work done** in stretching is **stored** as **potential energy** in the material.

2) This stored energy is called **elastic strain energy**.

3) On a **graph** of **force against extension**, the elastic strain energy is given by the **area under the graph**.

Stress and Strain

You can Calculate the Energy Stored in a Stretched Wire

Provided a material obeys Hooke's law, the **potential energy** stored inside it can be **calculated** quite easily.

1) The work done on the wire in stretching it is equal to the energy stored.

2) **Work done** equals **force × displacement**.

3) However, the **force** on the material **isn't constant**. It rises from zero up to force **F**.
To calculate the **work done**, use the average force between zero and **F**, i.e. ½**F**.

$$\text{work done} = \tfrac{1}{2}F \times e$$

4) Then the **elastic strain energy**, **E**, is:

$$E = \tfrac{1}{2}Fe$$

5) Because Hooke's law is being obeyed, $F = ke$ and F
can be replaced in the equation to give:

$$E = \tfrac{1}{2}ke^2$$

6) If the material is stretched beyond the **elastic limit**, some work is done separating atoms.
This will **not** be **stored** as strain energy and so isn't available when the force is released.

Practice Questions

Q1 Write a definition for tensile stress.

Q2 Explain what is meant by the tensile strain on a material.

Q3 What is meant by the breaking stress of a material?

Q4 How can the elastic strain energy be found from the force against extension graph of a material under load?

Q5 The work done is usually calculated as force multiplied by displacement.
Explain why the work done in stretching a wire is ½Fe.

Exam Questions

Q1 A steel wire is 2.00 m long. When a 300 N force is applied to the wire, it stretches 4.0 mm. The wire has a circular cross-section with a diameter of 1.0 mm.

(a) What is the cross-sectional area of the wire? [1 mark]

(b) Calculate the tensile stress in the wire. [1 mark]

(c) Calculate the tensile strain of the wire. [1 mark]

Q2 A copper wire (which obeys Hooke's Law) is stretched by 3.0mm when a force of 50N is applied.

(a) Calculate the stiffness constant for this wire in Nm⁻¹. [2 marks]

(b) What is the value of the elastic strain energy in the stretched wire? [1 mark]

UTS a laugh a minute, this stuff...

Here endeth the proper physics for this section — the next four pages are materials science (and I don't care what your exam boards say). It's all a bit too "useful" and "applied" for my liking. Messy "real" things. What's wrong with an ideal system, I ask you? Calls itself a physics course... grumble... grumble... wasn't like this in my day...

The Young Modulus

Busy chap, Thomas Young. He did this work on tensile stress as something of a sideline. Light was his main thing.
He proved light was a wave, explained how we see in colour and worked out what causes astigmatism.

The **Young Modulus** is Stress ÷ Strain

When you apply a **load** to a material, it experiences a **tensile stress** and a **tensile strain**.

1) Up to a point called the **limit of proportionality**, the stress and strain
of a material are proportional to each other.

2) So, for a particular material, stress divided by strain is a constant.
This constant is called the **Young modulus**, *E*.

$$E = \frac{\text{tensile stress}}{\text{tensile strain}} = \frac{F/A}{e/l} = \frac{Fl}{eA}$$

Where, **F** = force in N, **A** = cross-sectional area in m²,
l = initial length in m and **e** = extension in m.

3) The **units** of the Young modulus are the same as stress (**Nm⁻²** or pascals), since strain has no units.

4) The Young modulus is used by **engineers** to make sure their materials can withstand sufficient forces.

To **Find** the Young Modulus, You need a **Very Long Wire**

This is the experiment you're most likely to do in class:

Mum moment: if you're doing this experiment, <u>wear safety goggles</u> — if the wire snaps, it could get very messy. And no 'it's all fun and games till...' jokes please.

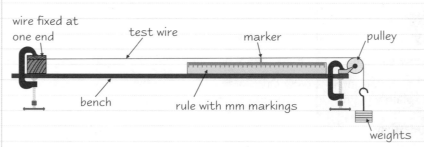

The Young Modulus

wire fixed at one end — test wire — marker — pulley — bench — rule with mm markings — weights

The test wire should be thin, and as long as possible. The **longer and thinner** the wire, the more it **extends** for the same force.

Start with the **smallest weight** necessary to straighten the wire.

Measure the **distance** between the **fixed end of the wire** and the **marker** — this is your unstretched length.

If you then increase the weight, the **wire stretches** and the **marker moves**.

Increase the **weight** by steps, recording the marker reading each time — the **extension** is the **difference** between this reading and the **unstretched length**.

Once you've taken all your readings, use a **micrometer** to measure the **diameter** of the wire in several places. Take an average of your measurements, and use that to work out the average **cross-sectional area** of the wire.

The other standard way of measuring Young's modulus in the lab is using **Searle's apparatus**. This is a bit more accurate, but it's harder to do and the equipment's more complicated.

The Young Modulus

Use a Stress-Strain Graph to Find E

You can plot a **graph** of **stress against strain** from your results.

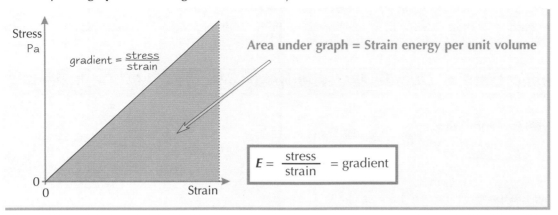

1) The **gradient** of the graph gives the Young modulus, **E**.
2) The **area under the graph** gives the **strain energy** (or energy stored) per unit volume i.e. the energy stored per 1 m³ of wire.
3) The stress-strain graph is a **straight line** provided that Hooke's law is obeyed, so you can also calculate the energy per unit volume as:

energy = ½ × stress × strain

Practice Questions

Q1 Define the Young modulus for a material.

Q2 What are the units for the Young modulus?

Q3 Explain why a thin test wire is used to find the Young modulus.

Q4 What is given by the area contained under a stress-strain graph?

Exam Questions

Q1 A steel wire is stretched elastically. For a load of 80 N, the wire extends by 3.6 mm.
The original length of the wire is 2.50 m and its average diameter is 0.6 mm.

    (a) Calculate the cross-sectional area of the wire in m².   [1 mark]

    (b) Find the tensile stress applied to the wire.   [1 mark]

    (c) Calculate the tensile strain of the wire.   [1 mark]

    (d) What is the value of the Young modulus for steel?   [1 mark]

Q2 The Young modulus for copper is 1.3×10^{11} Nm⁻².

    (a) If the stress on a copper wire is 2.6×10^{8} Pa, what is the strain?   [2 marks]

    (b) If the load applied to the copper wire is 100 N, what is the cross-sectional area of the wire?   [1 mark]

    (c) Calculate the strain energy per unit volume for this loaded wire.   [1 mark]

Learn that experiment — it's important...

And that wasn't all Young did with his life either. As if that wasn't enough, he was a well respected physician and an Egyptologist. He was one of the people who helped decipher the Rosetta stone. Makes you feel kind of inferior, doesn't it.

Interpreting Graphs of Different Materials

Stretch a material past its elastic limit and it'll either be permanently stretched if it's ductile, or break if it's brittle.
If you want to compare the properties of different materials, you should really use a stress-strain graph, rather than a force-extension one (since the force-extension graph depends on the shape of the material).
For your exam though, you only need to know the shapes of force-extension graphs.
[Detailed stress-strain graphs for materials like mild steel come up in the Edexcel Solid Materials Topic.]

Beyond the Elastic Limit, a Ductile Material will be Permanently Deformed

1) The **force-extension** graph is **linear** (i.e. obeys Hooke's Law) up to point **A** (the **limit of proportionality**).

2) Point **E** is the **elastic limit**. Within the region OE, if **all the force** is **removed**, the **extension** of the material returns to **zero**, i.e. the material goes back to the length it started at. This bit of the graph represents **elastic deformation**.

3) If enough **force** is applied to take the material **past** its elastic limit, the material is **permanently deformed**. The material will remain in whatever shape you've stretched it to.

4) **Y** is known as the **yield point**. At this point, the material suddenly **gives a bit**. **Engineers** often use **yield point** as a measure of the **strength** of the material.

5) Any material that **yields** like this is called **ductile**.

6) Most **metals** are ductile, e.g. copper, gold, iron, etc.

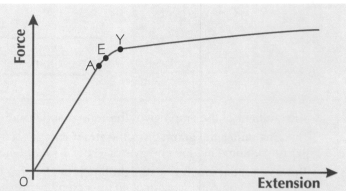

Beyond the Elastic Limit, a Brittle Material just Breaks

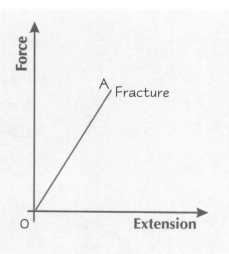

1) **A** is the **elastic limit**.

2) Beyond the **elastic limit**, there's **no plasticity** — the material just **fractures** (snaps).

3) A material that behaves this way is called **brittle**.

4) Materials such as **glass**, **perspex**, **cast iron** and **chocolate chip cookies** are brittle.

Mmmmmm... cookies.

Interpreting Graphs of Different Materials

Some Polymers are Brittle till you Warm them up a bit

1) How **polymers** behave depends on their **molecular structure** and **temperature**.

2) **Polythene's easy** to stretch, whereas **perspex** is very **brittle** at **room temperature**.
But **heat** it up and it becomes **plastic**.

3) The graphs below show **two different polymers** under stress (know how they feel).

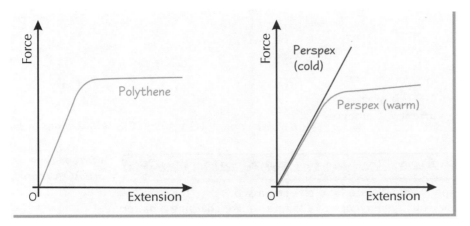

4) You can see that **polythene** experiences a **plastic deformation**.
Its behaviour is similar to **ductile materials**.

5) On the other hand, **perspex** behaves like a **brittle** material at **room temperature**.
If you **warm** it up a **bit**, it loses its **brittleness** and becomes **slightly bendy**.
Warm it up even more and it shows **plastic** behaviour — you can shape it however you like.

Practice Questions

Q1 Describe the properties of ductile materials under stress and give two examples.

Q2 Describe the properties of brittle materials under stress and give two examples.

Q3 Describe the properties of polymeric materials under stress and give two examples.

Exam Questions

Q1 The force-extension graphs below are for samples of two different brittle materials. Both samples had length 1 m and cross-sectional area 5 cm². The samples were stretched to their breaking points.

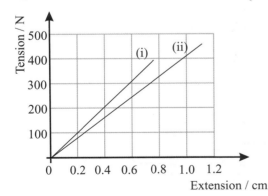

(a) What is a brittle material? [1 mark]

(b) Calculate the stiffness constant for each of the two samples. [3 marks]

(c) Compare the relative strengths of the two materials. [2 marks]

Hmm — all very useful, I'm sure...

Aaarghhh, I hate this stuff. I'm a physicist, not an engineer. You need to know it for your exam though, so I've gritted my teeth and got through it. Don't say I never do anything for you. Can we get back to some physics now? Can we, can we?

Charge, Current and Potential Difference

You wouldn't reckon there was that much to know about electricity, just plug something in, and bosh — electricity. Ah well, never mind the age of innocence — here are all the gory details...

Current is the Rate of Flow of Charge

The **current** in a **wire** is like **water** flowing in a **pipe**. The **amount** of water that flows depends on the **flow rate** and the **time**. It's the same with electricity — **current is the rate of flow of charge**.

$$Q = It \quad \text{or} \quad I = \frac{Q}{t}$$

Where **Q** is the charge in coulombs.

Remember that conventional current flows from + to -, the opposite way from electron flow.

The Coulomb is the Unit of Charge

One **coulomb** (**C**) is defined as the **amount of charge** that passes in **1 second** when the **current** is **1 ampere**.

If you're doing AQA A or OCR, skip straight to here.

The Total Charge is the Area Under a Current-Time Graph

Current-time graphs are AQA B only.

The **area** under a **current-time graph** is **equal** to the **total charge passed**. It's useful for those **awkward situations** where the **current changes** — like **charging a battery**.

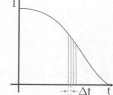

The current gets less as the battery charges up.

Explanation:
Split up the time into lots of little bits Δt. The charge for each bit ΔQ is IΔt which is the area of the strip — so the total charge is the total area.

Here, the total charge equals one rhino.

The Drift Velocity is the Average Velocity of the Electrons

When **current** flows through a wire, you might imagine the **electrons** all moving in the **same direction** in an orderly manner. Nope. In fact, they move **randomly** in **all directions**, but tend to **drift** one way. The **drift velocity** is just the **average velocity** and it's **much, much less** than the electron's **actual speed**. (Their average speed is about 10^6 ms^{-1}!)

The Current Depends on the Drift Velocity

The **current** is given by the equation: $\boxed{I = nAvq}$

You don't need to derive this for the exam but you do need to understand what it means.

where:
- **I** = electric current in A
- **n** = number of charge carriers per m^3
- **A** = cross-sectional area in m^2
- **v** = drift velocity in ms^{-1}
- **q** = charge in C carried by each charge carrier

See what the Equation Means by Changing One Variable at a Time

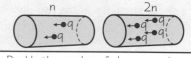

Double the number of charge carriers and the current doubles.

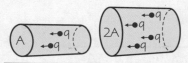

Doubling the area also doubles the current.

If the carriers move twice as fast you get twice the charge in the same time — twice the current.

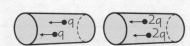

Doubling the charge carried by each carrier means you get twice the charge in the same time — twice the current.

Charge, Current and Potential Difference

Different Materials have Different Numbers of Charge Carriers

1) In a **metal**, the **charge carriers** are **free electrons** — they're the ones from the **outer shell** of each atom. Thinking about the formula $I = nAvq$, there are **loads** of charge carriers making n big. The **drift velocity** only needs to be **small**, even for a **high current**.

2) **Semiconductors** have **fewer charge carriers** than metals, so the **drift velocity** will need to be **higher** if you're going to have the **same current**.

3) A **perfect insulator** wouldn't have **any charge carriers**, so $n = 0$ in the formula and you'd get **no current**. **Real** insulators have a **very small** n.

Charge Carriers in Liquids and Gases are Ions

1) **Ionic crystals** like sodium chloride are **insulators**. Once **molten**, though, the liquid **conducts**. Positive and negative **ions** are the **charge carriers**. The **same thing** happens in an **ionic solution** like copper sulphate solution.

2) **Gases** are **insulators**, but if you apply a **high enough voltage** electrons get **ripped out** of **atoms**, giving you **ions** along a path. You get a **spark**.

Potential Difference is the Energy per Unit Charge

To make electric charge flow through a conductor, you need to do work on it. **Potential difference** (p.d.), or **voltage**, is defined as the **energy converted per unit charge moved**.

$$V = \frac{W}{Q}$$

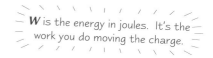

W is the energy in joules. It's the work you do moving the charge.

Back to the 'water analogy' again. The p.d. is like the pressure that's forcing water along the pipe.

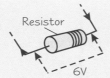

Resistor

6V

Here you do 6J of work moving each coulomb of charge through the resistor so the p.d. across it is 6V. The energy gets converted to heat.

Definition of the Volt

The **potential difference** across a conductor is **1 volt** when you convert **1 joule** of energy moving **1 coulomb** of charge through the conductor.

$$1\,\text{V} = 1\,\text{J\,C}^{-1}$$

Practice Questions

Q1 Describe in words how current and charge are related.

Q2 Define the coulomb.

Q3 What is represented by the area under a current-time graph?

Q4 Explain what drift velocity is.

Q5 Define potential difference.

Exam Questions

Q1 A battery delivers 4500 C of electric charge to a circuit in 10 minutes. Calculate the average current. [2 marks]

Q2 Copper has 1.0×10^{29} free electrons per m^3. Calculate the drift velocity of the electrons in a copper wire of cross-sectional area $5.0 \times 10^{-6}\,\text{m}^2$ when it is carrying a current of 13 A. (electron charge $= 1.6 \times 10^{-19}\,\text{C}$) [3 marks]

Q3 An electric motor runs off a 12 V d.c. supply and has an overall efficiency of 75%. Calculate how much electric charge will pass through the motor when it does 90 J of work. [3 marks]

I can't even be bothered to make the current joke...

Talking of currant jokes, I saw this bottle of wine the other day called 'raisin d'être' — 'raison d'être' of course meaning 'reason for living', but spelled slightly different to make 'raisin', meaning 'grape'. Ho ho. Chuckled all the way out of Tesco.

Resistance and Resistivity

"You will be assimilated. Resistance is futile."

Sorry, I couldn't resist it (no pun intended), and I couldn't think of anything useful to write anyway. This resistivity stuff gets a bit more interesting when you start thinking about temperature and light dependence, but for now, just learn this.

Everything has Resistance

1) If you put a **potential difference** (p.d.) across an **electrical component**, a **current** will flow.

2) **How much** current you get for a particular **p.d.** depends on the **resistance** of the component.

3) You can think of a component's **resistance** as a **measure** of how **difficult** it is to get a **current** to **flow** through it.

Mathematically, **resistance** is: $$R = \frac{V}{I}$$

This equation really **defines** what is meant by resistance.

4) **Resistance** is measured in **ohms** (Ω).

A component has a resistance of **1Ω** if a **potential difference** of **1V** makes a **current** of **1A** flow through it.

Three Things Determine Resistance

If you think about a nice, **simple electrical component**, like a **length of wire**, its **resistance** depends on:

1) **Length (l)**. The **longer** the wire the **more difficult** it is to make a **current flow**.

2) **Area (A)**. The **wider** the wire the **easier** it will be for the electrons to pass along it.

3) **Resistivity (ρ)**. This **depends** on the **material**. The **structure** of the material of the wire may make it easy or difficult for charge to flow. In general, resistivity depends on **environmental factors** as well, like **temperature** and **light intensity**.

The **resistivity** of a material is defined as the **resistance** of a **1m length** with a **1m² cross-sectional area**. It is measured in **ohm metres** (Ωm).

This is the Greek letter rho, the symbol for resistivity. $$\rho = \frac{RA}{l}$$ where A = area in m², l = length in m

You will more **usually** see the equation in the **form**: $$R = \rho\frac{l}{A}$$

Typical values for the **resistivity** of **conductors** are **really small**.

For example, the resistivity of **copper** (at 25°C) is just 1.72×10^{-8} Ωm.

If you **calculate** a **resistance** for a **conductor** and end up with something **really small** (e.g. 1×10^{-7} Ω), go back and **check** that you've **converted** your **area** into **m²**.

It's really easy to make mistakes with this equation by leaving the area in **cm²** or **mm²**.

Resistance and Resistivity

For an **Ohmic Conductor**, R is a **Constant**

A chap called **Ohm** did most of the early work on resistance. He developed a rule to **predict** how the **current** would **change** as the applied **potential difference increased**, for **certain types** of conductor. The rule is now called **Ohm's Law** and the conductors that **obey** it (mostly metals) are called **ohmic conductors**.

> Provided the **temperature** is **constant**, the **current** through an ohmic conductor is **directly proportional** to the **potential difference** across it.

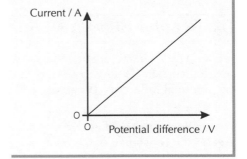

1) As you can see from the graph, **doubling** the **p.d. doubles** the **current**.
2) What this means is that the **resistance** is **constant**.
3) Often **external factors**, such as **light level** or **temperature** will have a **significant effect** on resistance, so you need to remember that Ohm's law is **only** true for **ohmic conductors** at **constant temperature**.

$$R = \frac{V}{I}$$

Superconductors are a **Very Special Case**   *AQA B only.*

Strange things sometimes happen when materials get **really cold**.

The **resistance gradually decreases**, until it reaches a **transition temperature**, when **all** of its resistance **suddenly disappears**. It has become a **superconductor**.

> **Below** their **transition temperature** superconductors have **no resistance**.

Practice Questions

Q1 Name one environmental factor likely to alter the resistance of a component.
Q2 What is special about an ohmic conductor?
Q3 What happens to a superconductor at its transition temperature?
Q4 What three factors does the resistance of a length of wire depend on?
Q5 What are the units for resistivity?

Exam Questions

Q1 Aluminium has a resistivity of $2.8 \times 10^{-8}\,\Omega$ m at 20 °C and a transition temperature of 1.2 K.

(a) Calculate the resistance of a pure aluminium wire of length 4 m and diameter 1 mm, at 20°C. [3 marks]

(b) The wire is cooled to a temperature of 1 K. What is its resistance now? Explain your answer. [2 marks]

Q2 The table below shows some measurements taken by a student during an experiment investigating an unknown electrical component.

Potential Difference (V)	Current (mA)
2.0	2.67
7.0	9.33
11.0	14.67

(a) Use the first row of the table to calculate the resistance of the component when a p.d. of 2V is applied. [2 marks]

(b) By means of further calculation, or otherwise, decide whether the component is an ohmic conductor. [3 marks]

Resistance and resistivity are NOT the same...

Superconductors are great. You can use a magnet to set a current flowing in a loop of superconducting wire. Take away the magnet and the current keeps flowing forever. A wire with no resistance never loses any energy. Pretty cool, huh.

I/V Characteristics

Woohoo — real physics. This stuff's actually kind of interesting.

I/V Graphs Show how Resistance Varies

The term '**I/V characteristic**' refers to a **graph** which shows how the **current** (**I**) flowing through a **component changes** as the **potential difference** (**V**) across it is increased.

The **shallower** the **gradient** of a characteristic **I/V** graph, the **greater** the **resistance** of the component.

A **curve** shows that the resistance is **changing**.

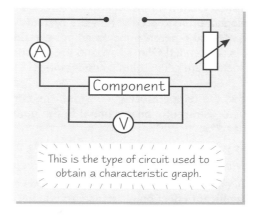

This is the type of circuit used to obtain a characteristic graph.

The I/V Characteristic for a Metallic Conductor is a Straight Line

At **constant temperature**, the **current** through a **metallic conductor** is **directly proportional** to the **voltage**. The fact that the characteristic graph is a **straight line** tells you that the **resistance doesn't change**. **Metallic conductors** are **ohmic** — they have **constant resistance provided** the temperature doesn't change.

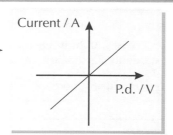

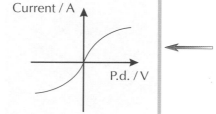

The characteristic graph for a **filament lamp** is a **curve**, which starts **steep** but gets **shallower** as the **voltage rises**. The **filament** in a lamp is just a **coiled up** length of **metal wire**, so you might think it should have the **same characteristic** as a **metallic conductor**. It doesn't because it **gets hot**. **Current** flowing through the lamp **increases** its **temperature**.

The **resistance** of a **metal increases** as the **temperature increases**.

The Temperature Affects the Charge Carriers   *AQA B and Edexcel.*

1) **Charge** is carried through **metals** by **free electrons** in a **lattice** of **positive ions**.
2) Heating up a metal doesn't affect how many electrons there are, but it does make it **harder** for them to **move about**. The **ions vibrate more** when heated, so the electrons **collide** with them more often, **losing energy**.

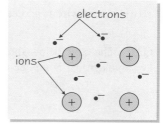

The **resistance** of most metallic conductors **goes up linearly** with **temperature**.

Semiconductors are Used in Sensors

Semiconductors are **nowhere near** as good at **conducting** electricity as **metals**. This is because there are far, far **fewer charge carriers** available. However, if **energy** is supplied to the semiconductor, **more charge carriers** are often **released**. This means that they make **excellent sensors** for detecting **changes** in their **environment**.

You need to know about **three** semiconductor components — **thermistors**, **LDRs** and **diodes**.

I/V Characteristics

The **Resistance** of a **Thermistor** Depends on **Temperature**

Thermistors are **resistors**, which have a **resistance** that depends on their **temperature**. You only need to know about **NTC** thermistors — NTC stands for 'Negative Temperature Coefficient'. This means that the **resistance decreases** as the **temperature goes up**. The characteristic graph for an NTC thermistor curves upwards.

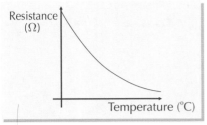
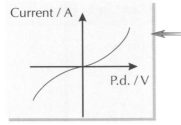

Increasing the current through the thermistor increases its temperature. The increasing gradient of this characteristic tells you that the resistance is decreasing.

Warming the thermistor gives more **electrons** enough **energy** to **escape** from their atoms. This means that there are **more charge carriers** available, so the resistance is lower.

The Resistance of an **LDR** depends on **Light Intensity**

LDR stands for **Light Dependent Resistor**. The **greater** the intensity of **light** shining on an LDR, the **lower** its **resistance**.

The explanation for this is similar to that for the thermistor. In this case, **light** provides the **energy** that releases more electrons. More charge carriers means a lower resistance.

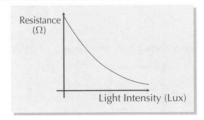

Large Dayglow Rabbit

Diodes Only Let **Current Flow** in **One Direction**

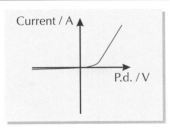

Diodes are designed to let **current flow** in **one direction** only. You don't need to be able to explain how they work, just what they do.

1) **Forward bias** is the **direction** in which the **current** is **allowed to flow**.

2) **Most** diodes require a **threshold voltage** of about **0.6V** in the **forward direction** before they will conduct.

3) In **reverse bias**, the **resistance** of the diode is **very high** and the current that flows is **very tiny**.

Practice Questions

Q1 Sketch the circuit used to determine the *I/V* characteristics of a component.

Q2 Draw an *I/V* characteristic graph for a diode.

Q3 What is an LDR?

Q4 If an *I/V* graph is curved, what does this tell you about the resistance?

Exam Questions

Q1 (a) Sketch a characteristic *I/V* graph for a filament lamp. [1 mark]

(b) State how the resistance changes as the temperature increases. [1 mark]

(c) Explain why this happens. [2 marks]

Thermistor man — temperature-dependent Mr Man...

Learn the graphs on this page, and make sure you can explain them. Whether it's a light dependent resistor or a thermistor, the same principle applies. More energy releases more charge carriers, more charge carriers means a lower resistance.

Electrical Energy and Power

Power and energy are pretty familiar concepts — and here they are again. Same principles, just different equations.

Power is the Rate of Transfer of Energy

Power (P) is **defined** as the **rate** of **transfer** of **energy**.
It's measured in **watts (W)**, where **1 watt** is equivalent to **1 joule per second**.

or $$P = \frac{E}{t}$$

There's a really simple formula for **power** in **electrical circuits**:

$$P = VI$$

This makes sense, since:

1) **Potential difference (V)** is defined as the **energy transferred** per **coulomb**.
2) **Current (I)** is defined as the **number** of **coulombs** transferred per **second**.
3) So **p.d.** × **current** is **energy transferred per second**, i.e. **power**.

You know from the definition of **resistance** that:

$$V = IR$$

Combining the **two equations** gives you loads of **different ways** to **calculate power**.

$$P = VI \qquad P = \frac{V^2}{R} \qquad P = I^2R$$

Obviously, which equation you should use depends on what **quantities** you're given in the **question**.

Energy is Easy to Calculate if you Know the Power

Sometimes it's the **total energy** transferred that you're interested in. In this case you simply need to **multiply** the **power** by the **time**. So:

$$E = VIt \qquad \left(or \ E = \frac{V^2}{R}t \quad or \ E = I^2Rt \right)$$

You've got to make sure that the time is in seconds.

Electricity Companies don't use Joules and Watts

OCR A only.

Electricity companies charge their customers for '**units**' of electricity. Another name for a unit is a **kilowatt hour (kWh)**. If you know the **power** of an **appliance** and the **length of time** it's used for you can work out the **energy** it uses in kWh.

$$\begin{array}{ccc} \textbf{Energy} & = & \textbf{Power} \ \times \ \textbf{Time} \\ \textbf{(kWh)} & & \textbf{(kW)} \qquad \textbf{(h)} \end{array}$$

1 kW = 1000 W
1 hour = 60 minutes = 3600 seconds

The **joule** is the **SI unit** of **energy**, but a joule is such a **small amount** of energy compared with the amount a typical household uses every month that it's **impractical**.

Example

A **1500W** hairdryer is on for **10 minutes**. How much energy does it use in J and kWh?

$E = Pt = 1500 \times 10 \times 60 = \boxed{900\ 000\ J}$ $E = Pt = 1.5 \times 1/6 = \boxed{0.25\ kWh}$

1 kWh = 3.6 million joules

Electrical Energy and Power

Hot Wires mean Noisy Signals

Copper wires carrying electrical signals still play an important role in **information transmission**. Some parts of a telephone system, for example, will almost certainly involve **analogue electrical signals** travelling down a **wire**. These signals get badly affected by noise.

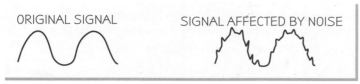

ORIGINAL SIGNAL   SIGNAL AFFECTED BY NOISE

Electrical noise arises mainly from the **random motion** of electrons and atoms in the wire. This type of random motion increases as the **temperature** of the wire goes up.

The **resistance** of the wire affects the **amount of noise** in a signal:

1) The **power dissipated** by a **resistor** (as heat) is given by $P = I^2R$

2) So, for a given current, the **greater** the **resistance** the **more energy** is converted to **heat** each second.

3) So a **bigger** resistance means **more heat**, which means **more noise**.

Reducing the resistance of the wire helps reduce this kind of noise. This is usually done by making the **wire thicker**.

Practice Questions

Q1   Write down the equation linking power, current and resistance.

Q2   How many joules is 1kWh?

Q3   How does 'random noise' in a wire depend on the temperature of the wire?

Q4   Power is measured in watts. What is 1 watt equivalent to?

Exam Questions

Q1   This question concerns a mains powered hairdryer, the circuit diagram for which is given below.

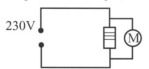

230V

    (a)   The heater has a power of 920 W in normal operation. Calculate the current in the heater.   [2 marks]

    (b)   The motor has a resistance of 190 Ω. What current will flow when the hairdryer is switched on? [2 marks]

    (c)   Show that the total power of the hairdryer in normal operation is just under 1.2 kW.   [3 marks]

    (d)   Calculate the number of kilowatt hours of electrical energy converted if the hairdryer is used for 15 minutes.   [1 mark]

Q2   A 12 V car battery supplies a current of 48 A for 2 seconds to the car's starter motor. The total resistance of the connecting wires is 0.01 Ω.

    (a)   Calculate the energy transferred from the battery.   [2 marks]

    (b)   Calculate the energy wasted as heat in the wires.   [2 marks]

The thicker the better — as far as electrical wires are concerned...

Whenever you get equations in this book, you know you're gonna have to learn them. Fact of life.
I used to find it helped to stick big lists of equations all over my walls in the run up to the exams. But as that's
possibly the least cool wallpaper imaginable, I don't advise inviting your friends round till after the exams...

E.m.f. and Internal Resistance

There's resistance everywhere — inside batteries, in all the wires and in the components themselves.
No one's for giving current an easy ride.

Batteries have Resistance

From now on, I'm assuming that the resistance of the wires in the circuit is zero. In practice, they do have a small resistance.

Resistance comes from **electrons colliding** with **atoms** and **losing energy**.

In a **battery**, **chemical energy** is used to make **electrons move**. As they move, they collide with atoms inside the battery — so batteries **must** have resistance. This is called **internal resistance**.

Internal resistance is what makes **batteries** and **cells warm up** when they're used.

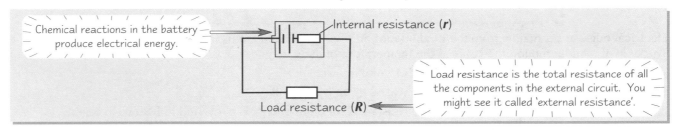

Chemical reactions in the battery produce electrical energy.

Internal resistance (*r*)

Load resistance is the total resistance of all the components in the external circuit. You might see it called 'external resistance'.

Load resistance (*R*)

1) The amount of **electrical energy** the battery produces for each **coulomb** of charge is called its **electromotive force or e.m.f.** (*E*). Be careful — e.m.f. **isn't** actually a force. It's measured in **volts**.

2) The **potential difference** across the **load resistance** (*R*) is the **energy transferred** when **one coulomb** of charge flows through the **load resistance**. This potential difference is called the **terminal p.d.** (*V*).

3) If there was **no internal resistance**, the **terminal p.d.** would be the **same** as the **e.m.f.** However, in **real** power supplies, there's **always some energy lost** overcoming the internal resistance.

4) The **energy wasted per coulomb** overcoming the internal resistance is called the **lost volts** (*v*).

Conservation of energy tells us:

energy per coulomb supplied by the source	=	energy per coulomb used in load resistance	+	energy per coulomb wasted in internal resistance

There are Loads of Calculations with E.m.f. and Internal Resistance

Examiners can ask you to do **calculations** with **e.m.f.** and **internal resistance** in loads of **different** ways. You've got to be ready for whatever they throw at you.

$$E = V + v \qquad E = I(R + r)$$
$$V = E - v \qquad V = E - Ir$$

Learn these equations for the exam. Only one of them will be on your formula sheet.

These are all basically the **same equation**, just written differently. If you're given enough information you can calculate e.m.f. (*E*), terminal p.d. (*V*), lost volts (*v*), current (*I*), load resistance (*R*) or internal resistance (*r*). Which equation you should use depends on what information you've got, and what you need to calculate.

This bottom bit's for AQA B only.

The Size of the Terminal P.d. Depends on the Size of the Load Resistance

A **smaller load resistance** means that the **internal** resistance is a **bigger fraction** of the **total resistance**. So more voltage will be **lost** across the internal resistance, and the **terminal p.d.** will be **smaller**.

The **energy dissipated** in the external circuit also depends on the load resistance, but it's slightly more complicated.

energy dissipated = *IVt*

The **extreme cases** are:

1) If the load resistance is **zero**, there'll be **no voltage**, and so **no energy** dissipated in the load.

2) If the load resistance is **infinite**, there'll be **no current**, and so **no energy** is dissipated.

In **between** these values the **energy increases**.
The **maximum energy dissipated** is when the **load resistance** is the **same** as the **internal resistance**.

E.m.f. and Internal Resistance

Use this **Circuit** to **Measure Internal Resistance** and **E.m.f.**

By **changing** the value of **R** (**load resistance**) in this circuit and **measuring** the **current** (**I**) and **p.d.** (**V**), you can work out the **internal resistance** of the source.

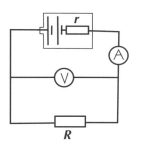

Start with the equation:

$$V = E - Ir$$

Plot a graph of **V** against **I**.

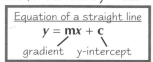

1) Rearrange the equation:
   $$V = -rI + E$$

2) Since **E** and **r** are constants, that's just the equation of a **straight line** (in the form: **y = mx + c**).

   Equation of a straight line
   $$y = mx + c$$
   gradient   y-intercept

3) So, the intercept on the **y** axis is **E**.

4) And, the gradient is **–r**.

An **easier** way to **measure** the **e.m.f.** of a **power source** is by connecting a high resistance **voltmeter** across its **terminals**. A **small current flows** through the **voltmeter**, so there must be some **lost volts** — this means you measure a value **very slightly less** than the **e.m.f.** In **practice** the difference **isn't** usually **significant**.

Most Power Supplies Need Low Internal Resistance

A **car battery** has to deliver a **really high current** — so it needs to have a **low internal resistance**. The cells used to power a **torch** or a **personal stereo** are the **same**. **Generally**, **batteries** have an **internal resistance** of **less than 1Ω**. Since **internal resistance** causes **energy loss**, you'd think **all** power supplies should have a **low internal resistance**. **High voltage power supplies** are the **exception**. **HT** (high tension) and **EHT** (extremely high tension) **supplies** are designed with **very high** internal resistances. This means that if they're **accidentally short circuited** only a **very small current** can flow. Much **safer**.

Practice Questions

Q1   What causes internal resistance?

Q2   What is meant by 'lost volts'?

Q3   What is the difference between e.m.f. and terminal p.d.?

Q4   Write the equation used to calculate the terminal p.d. of a power supply.

Exam Questions

Q1   A large battery with an internal resistance of 0.8Ω and e.m.f. 24V is used to power a dentist's drill with resistance 4Ω.

    (a)   Calculate the current in the circuit when the drill is connected to the power supply.   [2 marks]

    (b)   Calculate the voltage across the drill while it is being used.   [1 mark]

Q2   A student mistakenly connects a 10Ω resistance ray box to an HT power supply of 500V.
The ray box does not light, and the student measures the current flowing to be only 50mA.

    a)   Calculate the internal resistance of the HT power supply.   [3 marks]

    b)   Explain why this is a sensible internal resistance for an HT power supply.   [2 marks]

You're UNBELIEVABLE... [Frantic air guitar]... Ueuuurrrrghhh... Yeah...

"The things. You say. Dum-dum-de-de-duh-duh-duh-duh. The things. You say. DUM. You're unbelievable..."

[Sorry, just having a bit of a 90s nostalgia trip. Back to physics...]

Conservation of Energy & Charge in Circuits

There are some things in Physics that are so fundamental that you just have to accept. Like the fact that there's loads of Maths in it. And that energy is conserved. And that Physicists get more homework than everyone else.

Charge Doesn't 'Leak Away' Anywhere — it's **Conserved**

1)   As **charge flows** through a circuit, it **doesn't** get **used up** or **lost**.

2)   This means that whatever **charge flows into** a junction will **flow out** again.

3)   Since **current** is **rate of flow of charge**, it follows that whatever **current flows into** a junction is the same as the current **flowing out** of it. It's easier to see with an example:

e.g.

> CHARGE
> $Q_1 = 6$ C $\rightarrow$ $Q_2 = 2$ C
> $Q_3 = 4$ C
> $Q_1 = Q_2 + Q_3$

> CHARGE FLOWING IN 1 SECOND
> $Q_1 = 6$ C => $I_1 = 6$ A $\longrightarrow$ $Q_2 = 2$ C => $I_2 = 2$ A
> $Q_3 = 4$ C => $I_3 = 4$ A
> $I_1 = I_2 + I_3$

Kirchhoff's first law says:

> The total **current entering a junction** = the total **current leaving it**.

Energy conservation is vital.

Energy *is* Conserved too

1)   **Energy is conserved.** You already know that. In **electrical circuits**, **energy** is **transferred round** the circuit. Energy **transferred to** a charge is **e.m.f.**, and energy **transferred from** a charge is **potential difference**.

2)   In a **closed loop**, these two quantities must be **equal** if energy is conserved (which it is).

Kirchhoff's second law states just that:

> The **total e.m.f.** around a **series circuit** = the **sum** of the **p.d.s** across each component.   (or $E = \Sigma IR$ in symbols)

Exam Questions get you to Apply **Kirchhoff's Laws** to Combinations of **Resistors**

A **typical exam question** will give you a **circuit** with bits of information missing, leaving you to fill in the gaps. You need to remember the **following rules**:

SERIES Circuits

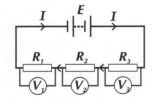

1)   **same current** in **all points** of the circuit (since there are no junctions)

2)   **e.m.f. split** between **components** (by Kirchhoff's 2nd law), so:
$E = V_1 + V_2 + V_3$

3) $V = IR$, so if I is constant:
$IR = IR_1 + IR_2 + IR_3$

4)   cancelling the Is gives:

> $R = R_1 + R_2 + R_3$

PARALLEL Circuits

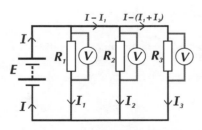

1)   **current** is **split** at each **junction**, so:
$I = I_1 + I_2 + I_3$

2)   **same p.d.** across **all components** (three separate loops — within each loop the e.m.f. equals sum of individual p.d.s)

3)   so, $V/R = V/R_1 + V/R_2 + V/R_3$

4)   cancelling the Vs gives:

$1/R = 1/R_1 + 1/R_2 + 1/R_3$

...and there's an example on the next page to make sure you know what to do with all that...

Conservation of Energy & Charge in Circuits

Worked Exam Question

A battery of e.m.f. 16 V and negligible internal resistance is connected in a circuit as shown:

a)   Show that the group of resistors between X and Y could be replaced by a
single resistor of resistance 15 Ω.

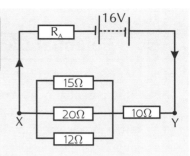

You can find the **combined resistance** of the 15Ω, 20Ω and 12Ω resistors using:

$1/R = 1/R_1 + 1/R_2 + 1/R_3 = 1/15 + 1/20 + 1/12 = 1/5 \Rightarrow R = 5\ \Omega$

So **overall resistance** between **X** and **Y** can be found by $R = R_1 + R_2 = 5 + 10 = \mathbf{15\ \Omega}$

b)   If $R_A = 20\ \Omega$:
(i)   calculate the potential difference across R_A,

Careful — there are a few steps here. You need the p.d. across R_A, but you don't know the current through it. So start there:
total resistance in circuit = 20 + 15 = 35 Ω, **so** current through R_A can be found using $I = V/R$:

$I = 16/35$ A

then you can use $V = IR$ to find the p.d. across R_A: $V = 16/35 \times 20 = \mathbf{9.1\ V}$

(ii)   calculate the current in the 15 Ω resistor.

You know the **current flowing** into the group of three resistors and out of it, but not through the individual branches.
But you know that their **combined resistance** is 5Ω (from part a) so you can work out the p.d. across the group:

$V = IR = 16/35 \times 5 = 16/7$ V

The p.d. across the **whole group** is the same as the p.d. across each **individual resistor**, so you can use this to find the
current through the 15Ω resistor:

$I = V/R = (16/7) / 15 = \mathbf{0.15\ A}$

Practice Questions

Q1   State Kirchhoff's laws.

Q2   Find the current through and potential difference across each of two 5 Ω resistors when they are placed in a
circuit containing a 5V battery, and are wired: a) in series, b) in parallel.

Exam Questions

Q1   For the circuit on the right:

(a) Calculate the total effective resistance for all three resistors in this combination.   [3 marks]

(b) Calculate the main current, I_3.   [2 marks]

(c) Calculate the potential difference across the 4 Ω resistor.   [1 mark]

(d) Calculate the potential difference across the parallel pair of resistors.
[1 mark]

(e) Using your answer from 1 (d), calculate the currents I_1 and I_2.   [2 marks]

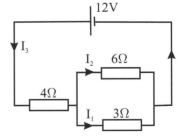

This is a very purple page — needs a bit of yellow I think...

*V = IR is the formula you'll use most often in these questions. Make sure you know whether you're using it on the overall
circuit, or just one specific component. It's amazingly easy to get muddled up — you've been warned.*

The Potential Divider

I remember the days when potential dividers were pretty much the hardest thing they could throw at you.
Then along came AS Physics. Hey ho.
Anyway, in context this doesn't seem too hard now, so get stuck in.

Use a *Potential Divider* to get a *Fraction* of a *Source Voltage*

1) At its simplest, a **potential divider** is a circuit with a **voltage source** and a couple of **resistors** in series.

2) The **potential** of the voltage source (e.g. a power supply) is **divided** in the **ratio** of the **resistances**. So, if you had a **2 Ω** resistor and a **3 Ω** resistor, you'd get **2/5** of the p.d. across the **2 Ω** resistor and **3/5** across the **3 Ω**.

3) That means you can **choose** the **resistances** to get the **voltage** you **want** across one of them.

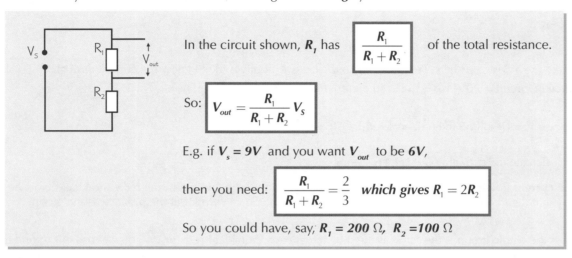

In the circuit shown, R_1 has $\dfrac{R_1}{R_1 + R_2}$ of the total resistance.

So: $V_{out} = \dfrac{R_1}{R_1 + R_2} V_s$

E.g. if $V_s = 9V$ and you want V_{out} to be $6V$,

then you need: $\dfrac{R_1}{R_1 + R_2} = \dfrac{2}{3}$ *which gives* $R_1 = 2R_2$

So you could have, say, $R_1 = 200\ \Omega$, $R_2 = 100\ \Omega$

4) This circuit is mainly used for **calibrating voltmeters**, which have a **very high resistance**.

5) If you put something with a **relatively low resistance** across R_1 though, you start to run into **problems**. You've **effectively** got **two resistors** in **parallel**, which will **always** have a **total** resistance **less** than R_1. That means that V_{out} will be **less** than you've calculated, and will depend on what's connected across R_1. Hrrumph.

If you're doing AQA A you can leave the rest of this and go straight to the questions now.

Add an *LDR* or *Thermistor* for a *Light* or *Temperature Switch*

1) A **light-dependent resistor** (LDR) has a very **high resistance** in the **dark**, but a **lower resistance** in the **light**.

2) An **NTC thermistor** has a **high resistance** at **low temperatures**, but a much **lower resistance** at **high temperatures** (it varies in the opposite way to a normal resistor, only much more so).

3) Either of these can be used as one of the **resistors** in a **potential divider**, giving an **output voltage** that **varies** with the **light level** or **temperature**.

4) Add a **transistor** and you've got yourself a **switch**, e.g. to turn on a light or a heating system.

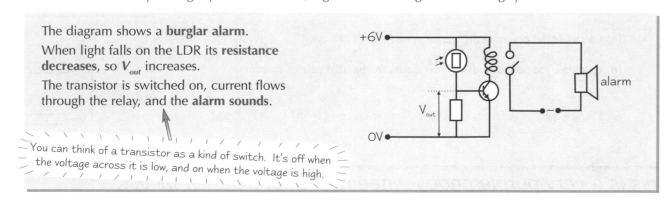

The diagram shows a **burglar alarm**.
When light falls on the LDR its **resistance decreases**, so V_{out} increases.
The transistor is switched on, current flows through the relay, and the **alarm sounds**.

You can think of a transistor as a kind of switch. It's off when the voltage across it is low, and on when the voltage is high.

The Potential Divider

A *Potentiometer* uses a *Variable Resistor* to give a *Variable Voltage*

1) A **potentiometer** has a variable resistor replacing R_1 and R_2 of the potential divider, but it uses the **same idea** (it's even sometimes **called** a potential divider just to confuse things).

2) You move a **slider** or turn a knob to **adjust** the **relative sizes** of R_1 and R_2. That way you can vary V_{out} from **0V** up to the source voltage.

3) This is dead handy, when you want to be able to **change** a **voltage continuously**, like in the **volume control** of a stereo.

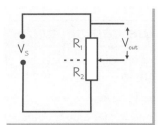

Here, V_s is replaced by the input signal (e.g. from a CD player) and V_{out} is the output to the amplifier and loudspeaker.

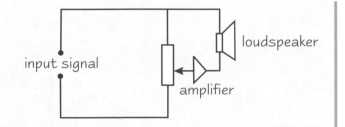

Practice Questions

Q1 Look at the burglar alarm circuit on page 52. How could you change the circuit so that the alarm sounds when the light level falls?

Q2 The LDR in the burglar alarm circuit has a resistance of 300 Ω when light and 900 Ω when dark. The fixed resistor has a value of 100 Ω. Show that V_{out} (light) = 1.5 V and V_{out} (dark) = 0.6 V.

Exam Questions

Q1 In the circuit on the right, all the resistors have the same value. Calculate the p.d. between:

    (i)   A and B.   [1 mark]

    (ii)   A and C.   [1 mark]

    (iii) B and C.   [1 mark]

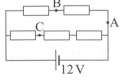

Q2 Look at the circuit on the right.

    (a)   Calculate the p.d. between A and B as shown by a high resistance voltmeter placed between the two points.

    (b)   A 40 Ω resistor is now placed between points A and B. Calculate the p.d. across AB and the current flowing through the 40 Ω resistor.

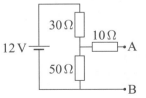

Variable voltage — it's, like, dead useful and that...

You'll probably have to use a potentiometer in every experiment you do with electricity from now on in, so you'd better get used to them. I never really got the hang of the things myself, but then lab and me don't mix — far too technical.

Alternating Current

If you're not doing AQA A, you can skip these pages.

Just when you think you've got the hang of this electricity lark, they spring alternating current on you. Here's where it all gets way more complicated. You can't use a normal voltmeter and ammeter any more — enter 'the oscilloscope'.

An **Oscilloscope** can show the **Waveform** of an **Alternating Current**

An **alternating** current or voltage is one that **changes with time**. The voltage goes up and down in a **regular pattern** — some of the time it's **positive** and some of the time it's **negative**.

1) An **oscilloscope** is basically, a snazzy **voltmeter**.

2) The **trace** you see is made by an **electron beam** moving across a screen.

3) The **time base** controls how **fast** the beam moves. You can **set** this using a **dial** on the **front** of the oscilloscope.

4) The **vertical height** of the trace at any point shows the **input voltage** at that point.

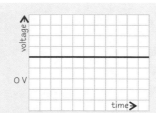

A **direct current** (d.c.) source is always at the same voltage, so you get a **horizontal line**.

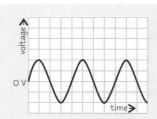

An **alternating current** (a.c.) source gives a regularly **repeating waveform**.

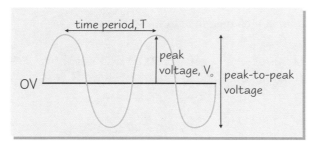

Measuring the **distance** between successive **peaks** along the time axis gives you the **time period** (as long as you know the time base setting). You can use this to calculate the **frequency**:

$$frequency = \frac{1}{time\ period}$$

$$f = \frac{1}{T}$$

This is the same for any type of wave.

The **peak voltage** is useful to know, though it's often **easier** to measure the **peak-to-peak voltage** and **halve** it.

V_{rms} and I_{rms} are often the **best ways** to Describe an **Alternating Current**

1) An **a.c. supply** with a **peak voltage** of **2V** will be **below 2V**, most of the time. That means it won't have as high a power output as a **2V d.c. supply**.

2) To **compare** them properly, you need to **average** the a.c. voltage somehow.

3) A **normal average won't work**, because the **positive** and **negative** bits **cancel out**. It turns out that something called the **root mean square (r.m.s.) voltage** does the trick.

4) For a **sine wave**, you get this by **dividing** the **peak voltage**, V_o, by $\sqrt{2}$. And it's the **same** for the **current**:

Even though this is only strictly true for a sine wave, that's what you get from a generator. It's also the only one on your syllabus, so I wouldn't worry about it.

$$V_{rms} = \frac{V_o}{\sqrt{2}} \qquad I_{rms} = \frac{I_o}{\sqrt{2}}$$

5) If you want to work out the **power**, just replace **I** and **V** in the power formula with the **r.m.s. values**.

$$Power = V_{rms} \times I_{rms}$$

Alternating Current

For the **resistance** it doesn't matter, as the **peak values** will give you the same answer:

$$\textbf{Resistance, } R = \frac{V_{rms}}{I_{rms}} = \frac{V_o}{I_o}$$

It's usually the **r.m.s. value** that's stated on a **power supply**.

For example, the value of **230V** stated for the **UK mains electricity supply** is the **r.m.s. value**.
Just use the equation above to get the **peak** value, or double that to get the **peak-to-peak** value:

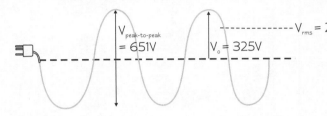

$V_{peak\text{-}to\text{-}peak}$ = 651V V_o = 325V V_{rms} = 230V

$$V_{peak} = \sqrt{2} \times V_{rms} = \textbf{325V}$$

$$V_{peak\text{-}to\text{-}peak} = 2 \times V_{peak} = \textbf{651V}$$

Practice Questions

Q1   Define the terms 'time period' and 'frequency' for an alternating signal.

Q2   Define the r.m.s. voltage of an alternating signal in terms of the peak voltage.

Q3   Why are the r.m.s. values for current and voltage used for a.c. supplies rather than the peak values?

Exam Questions

Q1   A CRO is used to study the waveform of a sinusoidal alternating voltage of frequency 100 Hz
and peak voltage of 2.0 V. The time base is set to 2.0 ms cm^{-1} horizontally and the voltage sensitivity
vertically is 0.5 V cm^{-1}.
Draw the trace you expect on a 10cm square grid and show all your working.   [4 marks]

Q2   An oscilloscope is set so that there is a horizontal line at zero volts, produced by a time base of 5.0 ms per
division. The Y-input voltage sensitivity is set at 1.0 volt per division.
Sketch the traces you would expect for each of the following cases.

   (a)   A 2.0V cell.

   (b)   An a.c. signal of 1.5V peak value and frequency 50Hz.   [5 marks]

Q3   Five cycles of a.c. are observed on a 10 division squared screen of a CRO.
The frequency of the signal is 2500Hz.
Work out :

   (a)   The time period of the signal.   [1 mark]

   (b)   The horizontal time-base in both seconds per div and ms per div.   [1 mark]

Yay, oscilloscopes — cool...

*If you do the electronics option for A2 you'll do a.c. in more detail. For now, though, all you need to know are the
equations on these two pages. Remember, any current or voltage you read off an a.c. power supply will be r.m.s.*

Magnetic Effects of Current

These pages are just for OCR A.

Electromagnetism's great, isn't it. Just keep telling yourself that and it'll all be fine.

Any **Wire** Carrying a **Current** will have a **Magnetic Field** Around It

The **three magnetic field shapes** you need to know for AS are:

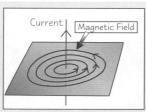 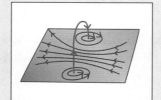 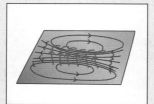

Long wire. You can work out the **direction** of the arrows using the 'Corkscrew Rule': imagine twisting a corkscrew **along** the wire in the **direction** of the **current** and the arrows on the **field lines** are in the **direction** of **rotation** of your hand.

Circular wire. There's a **circular magnetic field** round the wire (like with a straight wire) and **parallel lines** going through the circle.

Long solenoid (long coil). There's a **uniform magnetic field** down the **centre** of the coil where the **lines** are **parallel**, while elongated **ovals** sweep round **outside**.

The lines represent **magnetic flux lines**, and are drawn **increasingly close together** with **increasing field strength**.

If you Put a **Wire** Carrying a **Current** in a **Magnetic Field**, it'll **Experience** a **Force**

In a **uniform magnetic field** as shown in the diagram:

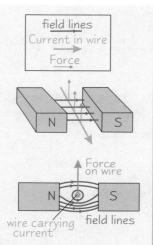

1) The **direction** of the **magnetic field** between the magnetic poles is **from N to S**.
2) The **force acts** as the wire carrying the current **cuts** through the magnetic flux lines **at right angles**. If current is **parallel**, **no** force acts.
3) The **direction** of the **force** is **perpendicular** to **both** the **current** direction **and** to the lines of **magnetic flux**.
4) The **direction** of the **force** is found using **Fleming's Left hand Rule**:

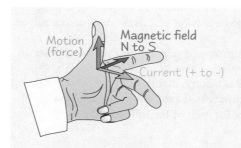

Fleming's Left Hand Rule

The **F**irst finger points in the direction of the uniform magnetic **F**ield, the se**C**ond finger points in the direction of the conventional **C**urrent. Then your thu**M**b points in the direction of the force (in which **M**otion takes place).

Field Strength is also called **Flux Density**, and it's measured in **Tesla (T)**

1) The size of the **force** on a current-carrying wire is **proportional** to the **current flowing** through it (**I**) — if you double the current, you get double the force.
2) It's also proportional to the **length of wire** in the **field** (**I**) — if you double the length, there's double the force.
3) To make it into a nice equation, someone introduced '**B**' as the **constant** of **proportionality** — this represents the **strength** of the **magnetic field**. The formula is:

$$F = BIl$$

4) So, the **magnetic field strength**, **B**, is defined as:

> The **size** of the **force** per **metre of length** per **unit of current** flowing in a wire **at right angles** to a magnetic field.

This makes the unit of magnetic field strength the **NA⁻¹m⁻¹** or (more conveniently) the **tesla (T)**. Phew...

Magnetic Effects of Current

Use **Fleming's Left Hand Rule** to **Predict Forces** on *Two Long Wires*

This is easier with an **experiment** to show you what I'm on about.

Two Long Wires in a Magnetic Field

1) **Clamp two wires** near to each other like in the picture.

2) Set a **current** going through them — I've got the currents both going the same way, but they could be in opposite directions. Up to you.

3) Each wire cuts the magnetic field of the other at right angles. You can use **Fleming's Left Hand Rule** to work out the **direction** of the **force**.

4) In my experiment the **left hand wire** creates a **magnetic field**, which puts a **left**wards (is that a word?) **force** on the right hand wire. Likewise the **right hand wire** puts a **right**wards **force** on the left wire — so the wires are **attracted** to each other.

5) It doesn't take a huge leap of faith to see that if the **currents** are in **opposite directions** then the wires will be **repelled** instead of attracted.

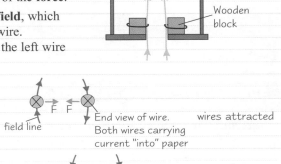

Elastic bands to hold wire

Wooden block

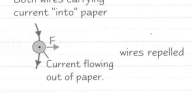

field line   End view of wire.   wires attracted
Both wires carrying
current "into" paper

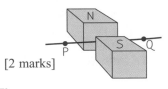

Current flowing   Current flowing   wires repelled
into paper.   out of paper.

The less well known 'Two Short Criers in a Field' experiment.

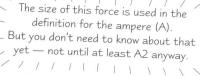

The size of this force is used in the definition for the ampere (A). But you don't need to know about that yet — not until at least A2 anyway.

Practice Questions

Q1 Write a definition for magnetic field strength.

Q2 Sketch out the magnetic field diagram for a flat coil and a solenoid with the current travelling in the opposite direction to that in the diagrams on page 56.

Q3 There is a force on a wire in a magnetic field. What will happen to the direction of this force if you
(i) swap over the N and S poles of the field; (ii) swap the poles **and** reverse the current direction?

Exam Questions

Q1 A wire lies perpendicular across a uniform magnetic field of strength 0.02T, so that 0.3 m of the wire is inside the length of the field. If the force exerted on this length of wire due to the current in it is 0.03N downwards, what is the magnitude and direction of the conventional current in the wire? [2 marks]

Q2 (a) The force on a current-carrying conductor in a magnetic field is given by $F = BIl$. State the condition for which this equation is valid. [1 mark]

(b) Will there be a force acting on a wire carrying 2 amps running parallel to a magnetic field? [1 mark]

(c) A wire carrying a current of 10 A passes at right angles through a field where B = 0.15T. Calculate the force acting on a wire of length 0.2 m. [2 marks]

(d) Two current-carrying wires are held close to each other and parallel. Explain what forces will act on the wires when they carry currents flowing in the **same** direction. [3 marks]

Field strength = flux density = field strength = flux density = field strength = f

For those of you who are burning with curiosity... the definition of an ampere is the current which when flowing through two parallel, infinitely long wires, 1 metre apart will produce a force of 2×10^{-7} N on each of the wires. Thrilling stuff, and as I say, you don't need to know it. Just in here for a bit of random interest, that's all.

Specific Heat Capacity and Specific Latent Heat

If you're doing one of the OCR specifications or AQA B you can miss out this whole section. Woo hoo!

You need energy to heat things up, and to change their state. It all comes down to energy, doesn't it. Pretty much always.

Specific Heat Capacity is how much Energy it Takes to Heat Something

When you heat something, its molecules get more **kinetic energy** and its **temperature** rises.

> The **specific heat capacity** (c) of a substance is the amount of **energy** needed to **raise** the **temperature** of **1 kg** of the substance by **1°C** (or 1K).

or put it another way: **energy = mass × specific heat capacity × change in temperature**

in symbols: $\Delta Q = mc\Delta\theta$ ΔT is sometimes used instead of $\Delta\theta$ for the change in temperature.

ΔQ is the energy change in J, m is the mass in kg and $\Delta\theta$ is the temperature rise in °C or K. Units of c are J kg^{-1} °C^{-1} or J kg^{-1} K^{1}.

You can Measure Specific Heat Capacity in the Laboratory

The **method's** the same for **solids** and **liquids**, but the **set-up's** a little bit different:

Specific Heat Capacity of a Solid

Electric heater, Solid, e.g. metal cylinder, Digital thermometer, Insulating material

Specific Heat Capacity of a Liquid

Insulating lid, Digital thermometer, Heating coil, Liquid, Insulating material

Method for Both

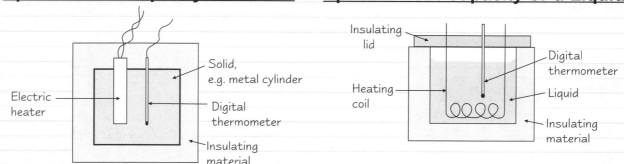

1) **Heat** the substance with the heater. You need a **temperature rise** of about 10 °C to get an **accurate** value of **c**. [NB. The insulation **reduces** the heat loss, but it's far from perfect. If you're really keen, start **below** and finish **above** room temperature to **cancel out** gains and losses.]

2) With an ammeter and voltmeter attached to your **electric heater** you can work out the energy supplied. Here's the circuit:

   Calculate the energy (ΔQ) using: $\Delta Q = VI\Delta t$

   where V is the heater voltage, I is the current and Δt is the time in seconds. (see p46)

3) Plug your data into: $\Delta Q = mc\Delta\theta$ to calculate **c**.   The value you end up with for c will probably be too high by quite a long way. That's because some of the energy from the heater gets absorbed by the air and the container.

Example

> You heat 0.25 kg of water from 12.1 °C to 22.9 °C with an electric immersion heater. The heater has a voltage of 11.2 V and a current of 5.3 A, and is switched on for 205 s.

Electrical energy supplied = $VI\Delta t$ = 11.2 × 5.3 × 205 = 12 170 J

Temperature rise = 22.9 − 12.1 = 10.8 °C

So $c = \dfrac{12170}{0.25 \times 10.8} = 4510$ Jkg^{-1}°C^{-1} The actual value for water is 4180 J kg^{-1} °C^{-1}. This result's too big, because ΔQ is bigger than it should be (like I said before).

Specific Heat Capacity and Specific Latent Heat

It takes **Energy** to **Change State**

You don't need this bit for Edexcel Salters Horners.

To **melt** a **solid**, you need to **break the bonds** that hold the molecules in place. The **energy** needed for this is called the **latent heat of fusion**. Similarly, when you **evaporate a liquid**, you have to **put in energy** to **pull the molecules apart** completely. This is the **latent heat of vaporisation**.

Specific Latent Heat is Defined as the Latent Heat **per kg**

The **larger** the **mass** of the substance, the **more energy** it takes to **change** its **state**. The **specific latent heat** is defined per kg to get around that problem:

> The **specific latent heat** (*l*) of **fusion** or **vaporisation** is the quantity of **thermal energy** required to **change the state** of **1 kg** of a substance.

which gives: **energy = specific latent heat × mass of substance changed**

or in symbols: $\Delta Q = l\Delta m$ ← You'll usually see the latent heat of vaporisation written l_v and the latent heat of fusion written l_f.

Where ΔQ is the energy in J, Δm is the mass in kg. The units of *l* are J kg^{-1}.

Measuring **Specific Latent Heat** is Similar to Measuring **c**

Specific Latent Heat of Vaporisation

Heating coil
boiling liquid
Condensed vapour collected

Specific Latent Heat of Fusion

heating coil
melting ice
funnel
insulation
water collected

Again you use an electric heater, so calculate the energy (ΔQ) with: $\Delta Q = VI\Delta t$
The **mass of liquid collected** is the Δm in the equation $\Delta Q = l\Delta m$ so stick in Δm and ΔQ to work out *l*.

Practice Questions

Q1   Define specific heat capacity.

Q2   Describe how you would measure the specific heat capacity of olive oil.

Q3   Show that the thermal energy needed to heat 2 kg of water from 20°C to 50°C is about 250 kJ.

Q4   Explain why energy is needed to evaporate a liquid and define the specific latent heat of vaporisation.

Exam Questions

Q1   In an experiment to measure the specific heat capacity of a metal, a 2 kg metal cylinder is heated from 4.5°C to 12.7°C in 3 minutes. The electric heater used is rated at 12V, 7.5A.
Assuming that heat losses were negligible, calculate the specific heat capacity of the metal.   [3 marks]

Q2   A 3 kW electric kettle contains 0.5 kg of water already at its boiling point. Neglecting heat losses, how long will it take to boil dry? (Specific latent heat of vaporisation of water = 2.26×10^6 J kg^{-1})   [3 marks]

My specific eat capacity — 24 pies...

You may be wondering (I would) why on earth you're learning this. Well, sorry, I don't know. Because it's in the exams, I guess. I mean, it kinda has its uses — water has a really big specific heat capacity, so it absorbs heat dead well, which is handy in cooling systems. But basically it's just a dead boring topic whose only real saving grace is that it's quite easy... (yawn)

Pressure in Fluids

This double page is for Edexcel only.

Ooo, pressure — bet you weren't expecting that in a thermal physics section. You need to know about pressure before you can do all the gas laws stuff on the next few pages — so this seemed as good a place to put it as any.

Pressure means **Concentration** of **Force**

If a force **F** is spread over an area **A** the pressure is defined as:

$$p = \frac{F}{A}$$

with **F** in N and **A** in m².

The unit of pressure is pascals (Pa). 1 Pa = 1 Nm⁻².

Area, A
Force, F

Units: Suppose you've got a pressure of 5 N/cm² and you want it in Pa (ie Nm⁻²). You need to remember that 1m² is 100cm × 100cm = 10 000cm², so your pressure is:

5 × 10 000 = 50 000 Pa or 50 kPa.

Pressure in a **Liquid** Increases with **Depth**

Imagine you dive into a swimming pool — as you go deeper the pressure **increases**. This is caused by the **weight** of all that water on top of you. In a **denser** liquid, the pressure would be **greater**.

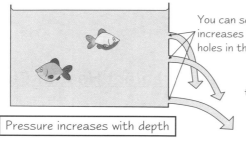

You can see that pressure increases with depth by drilling holes in the side of a fish tank*...

...because deeper in the tank, water is pushed out faster than at the top.

* ...not that I'd recommend this — it can be bad for the fish

Pressure increases with depth

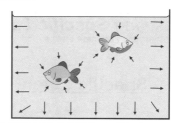

Liquid pressure acts in all directions

Upthrust is Caused by **Pressure Difference**

Upthrust is caused by the **pressure difference** between the bottom and the top of an object.

The resulting upward force on this block from the water pressure is greater than the block's weight, so it **rises** to the surface.

block rises

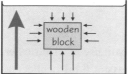

wooden block

Hydraulics Use Fluid Pressure

An important thing to remember with fluids is that they **transmit pressure, not force**. It's shown with this model hydraulic lift.

When you push the master piston you apply pressure to the liquid. The small area of the piston means you get lots of pressure.
p = F₁ / A₁

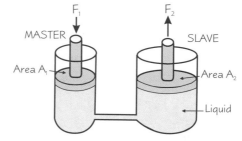

F₁
MASTER
Area A₁

F₂
SLAVE
Area A₂
Liquid

The liquid pressure acts on the large area of the slave piston, giving you a big force.
$F_2 = p \times A_2$

Example   A hydraulic system has a 4.0 × 10⁻³ m² master cylinder and a 5.0 × 10⁻² m² slave cylinder. What force will you get out when you push the master piston with a force of 100 N?

For the master $p = F_1 / A_1$ = 100 / 4.0 × 10⁻³ = 2.5 × 10⁴ Pa
So for the slave $F_2 = p \times A_2$ = 2.5 × 10⁴ × 5.0 × 10⁻² = 1250 N

This might sound like something for nothing, but remember that liquids are virtually **incompressible**. The volume of fluid displaced from the master cylinder is the same as the increase in volume of the fluid in the slave cylinder. If you have a bigger surface area, the piston won't **move** as far — so even with a bigger force, the **work done** will be the **same**.

Specific Heat Capacity and Specific Latent Heat

It takes **Energy** to **Change State**   *You don't need this bit for Edexcel Salters Horners.*

To **melt** a **solid**, you need to **break the bonds** that hold the molecules in place. The **energy** needed for this is called the **latent heat of fusion**. Similarly, when you **evaporate a liquid**, you have to **put in energy** to **pull the molecules apart** completely. This is the **latent heat of vaporisation**.

Specific Latent Heat is Defined as the Latent Heat **per kg**

The **larger** the **mass** of the substance, the **more energy** it takes to **change** its **state**. The **specific latent heat** is defined per kg to get around that problem:

> The **specific latent heat** (*l*) of **fusion** or **vaporisation** is the quantity of **thermal energy** required to **change the state** of **1 kg** of a substance.

which gives: **energy = specific latent heat × mass of substance changed**

or in symbols: $\Delta Q = l\Delta m$ ← You'll usually see the latent heat of vaporisation written l_v and the latent heat of fusion written l_f.

Where ΔQ is the energy in J, Δm is the mass in kg. The units of *l* are J kg^{-1}.

Measuring **Specific Latent Heat** is Similar to Measuring **c**

Specific Latent Heat of Vaporisation

Heating coil

boiling liquid

Condensed vapour collected

Specific Latent Heat of Fusion

heating coil

melting ice

funnel

insulation

water collected

Again you use an electric heater, so calculate the energy (ΔQ) with: $\Delta Q = VI\Delta t$

The **mass of liquid collected** is the Δm in the equation $\Delta Q = l\Delta m$ so stick in Δm and ΔQ to work out *l*.

Practice Questions

Q1 Define specific heat capacity.

Q2 Describe how you would measure the specific heat capacity of olive oil.

Q3 Show that the thermal energy needed to heat 2 kg of water from 20°C to 50°C is about 250 kJ.

Q4 Explain why energy is needed to evaporate a liquid and define the specific latent heat of vaporisation.

Exam Questions

Q1 In an experiment to measure the specific heat capacity of a metal, a 2 kg metal cylinder is heated from 4.5°C to 12.7°C in 3 minutes. The electric heater used is rated at 12V, 7.5A.
Assuming that heat losses were negligible, calculate the specific heat capacity of the metal.   [3 marks]

Q2 A 3 kW electric kettle contains 0.5 kg of water already at its boiling point. Neglecting heat losses, how long will it take to boil dry? (Specific latent heat of vaporisation of water = 2.26×10^6 J kg^{-1})   [3 marks]

My specific eat capacity — 24 pies...

You may be wondering (I would) why on earth you're learning this. Well, sorry, I don't know. Because it's in the exams, I guess. I mean, it kinda has its uses — water has a really big specific heat capacity, so it absorbs heat dead well, which is handy in cooling systems. But basically it's just a dead boring topic whose only real saving grace is that it's quite easy... (yawn)

Pressure in Fluids

This double page is for Edexcel only.

Ooo, pressure — bet you weren't expecting that in a thermal physics section. You need to know about pressure before you can do all the gas laws stuff on the next few pages — so this seemed as good a place to put it as any.

Pressure means **Concentration** of **Force**

If a force **F** is spread over an area **A** the pressure is defined as:

$$p = \frac{F}{A}$$

with **F** in N and **A** in m^2.

The unit of pressure is pascals (Pa). 1 Pa = 1 Nm^{-2}.

Units: Suppose you've got a pressure of 5 N/cm^2 and you want it in Pa (ie Nm^{-2}). You need to remember that $1m^2$ is 100cm × 100cm = 10 000cm^2, so your pressure is:

5 × 10 000 = 50 000 Pa or 50 kPa.

Pressure in a **Liquid** Increases with **Depth**

Imagine you dive into a swimming pool — as you go deeper the pressure **increases**. This is caused by the **weight** of all that water on top of you. In a **denser** liquid, the pressure would be **greater**.

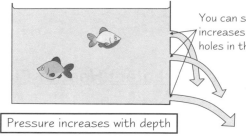

You can see that pressure increases with depth by drilling holes in the side of a fish tank*...

...because deeper in the tank, water is pushed out faster than at the top.

Pressure increases with depth

* ...not that I'd recommend this — it can be bad for the fish

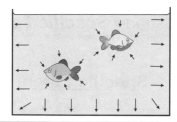

Liquid pressure acts in all directions

Upthrust is Caused by **Pressure Difference**

Upthrust is caused by the **pressure difference** between the bottom and the top of an object.

The resulting upward force on this block from the water pressure is greater than the block's weight, so it **rises** to the surface.

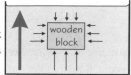

block rises

Hydraulics Use Fluid Pressure

An important thing to remember with fluids is that they **transmit pressure, not force**. It's shown with this model hydraulic lift.

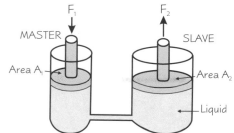

When you push the master piston you apply pressure to the liquid. The small area of the piston means you get lots of pressure.
$p = F_1 / A_1$

The liquid pressure acts on the large area of the slave piston, giving you a big force.
$F_2 = p × A_2$

Example A hydraulic system has a 4.0 × 10^{-3} m^2 master cylinder and a 5.0 × 10^{-2} m^2 slave cylinder. What force will you get out when you push the master piston with a force of 100 N?

For the master $p = F_1 / A_1 = 100 / 4.0 × 10^{-3} = 2.5 × 10^4$ Pa
So for the slave $F_2 = p × A_2 = 2.5 × 10^4 × 5.0 × 10^{-2}$ = 1250 N

This might sound like something for nothing, but remember that liquids are virtually **incompressible**. The volume of fluid displaced from the master cylinder is the same as the increase in volume of the fluid in the slave cylinder. If you have a bigger surface area, the piston won't **move** as far — so even with a bigger force, the **work done** will be the **same**.

Pressure in Fluids

There are Different Ways of Measuring Pressure

The simplest type of pressure gauge is a **manometer**. It's just a U-tube really.

Atmospheric pressure
(i.e. open to the air)

Gas pressure
to be measured

The difference in
levels, h, shows the
pressure difference.

h

liquid

You see these on **boilers** and **gas bottles**.

In a **Bourdon gauge**, the liquid or gas is forced into a **coiled tube**. As the pressure increases, the coil unwinds like one of those noisy things you get at parties.

Coiled tube

Pointer moves

Gas pressure

Tube uncoils

bar

Gas pressure

Front

Back

Barometers Measure Atmospheric Pressure

With a **mercury barometer**, the pressure of the atmosphere is balanced against a **column of mercury**. You get the pressure in mm of mercury (mm Hg). It's just pressure and **depth** again.

vacuum

mercury

h

trough

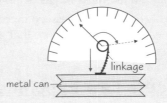

An adenoid barometer.

An **aneroid barometer** has a flexible metal can that expands and contracts with changes in air pressure.

linkage

metal can

They're often used as **altimeters** — atmospheric pressure goes down as you get higher above sea-level

You might meet pressure in various different units: 1 bar = 100 kPa.
1 atmosphere (roughly air pressure at sea level) is defined as 101.325 kPa.

You Get Electrical Pressure Sensors Nowadays

An **electrical pressure sensor** gives an **electrical output** which depends on the **pressure** applied to it. You don't need to know the details of how they work for the exam, but you need to know applications.

Pressure sensors have important **medical applications** e.g. the **ventilator**, used when a patient is too weak to breathe unaided. As the patient tries to take a breath, a pressure sensor detects the **slight reduction** in air pressure in the lungs. The ventilator then switches on automatically to inflate the lungs at just the right time.

Pressure sensors have many other uses like monitoring the **engine oil pressure** in a Formula One car.

Practice Questions

Q1 Explain the difference between force and pressure.

Q2 Explain in terms of liquid pressure why a boat floats.

Q3 Explain how liquid pressure can be used to magnify a force.

Q4 Describe two uses of pressure sensors.

Exam Questions

Q1 A circus performer of mass 62 kg is riding a unicycle of mass 3.5 kg. If the pressure exerted on the floor by the tyre is 310 kPa, find the area of contact between the tyre and the floor. (Take g = 9.8 N kg⁻¹) [2 marks]

Q2 An oil-filled hydraulic press has a master cylinder of area 4.2×10^{-4} m² and a slave cylinder of area 5.5×10^{-3} m². What force applied to the master piston will give a force of 3.0 kN in the press? [2 marks]

Pressure... Tension... Stress... Yep, that's Physics then...

The equation's pretty simple, but some of the concepts are a bit trickier. Any of them could come up in the exam, so you need to make sure you're totally happy with all the stuff on this page — how hydraulics systems control forces, how manometers, Bourdon gauges and different barometers work, and what you can use electrical pressure sensors for. Phew.

The Ideal Gas Equation

You only need to know the experiments if you're doing Edexcel. The rest of the page is for AQA A as well.

*Aaahh.. great... another one of those 'our gas equation doesn't work properly with **real gases**, so we'll invent an **ideal** gas that it **does work** for and they'll think we're dead clever' situations. Hmm. Physicists, eh...*

There's an **Absolute Scale** of **Temperature**

There is a **lowest possible temperature** called **absolute zero***.
This is given a value of **zero kelvin**, written **0 K** on the absolute temperature scale.

1)   The kelvin scale is named after Lord Kelvin who first suggested it.

2)   A change of **1 K** equals a change of **1 °C**.

3)   To change from degrees celsius into kelvin **add 273**.

$$K = C + 273$$

All equations in **thermal physics** use temperatures measured in kelvin.

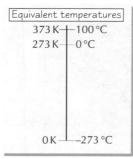

Equivalent temperatures
373 K —— 100 °C
273 K —— 0 °C

0 K —— –273 °C

*It's true. –273.15 °C is the lowest temperature theoretically possible. Weird, huh. You'd kinda think there wouldn't be a minimum, but there is.

The **Pressure Law** Gives **p/T = Constant** for an Ideal Gas

All the gas laws apply to a **fixed mass of gas**, so in any experiment it's important to make sure none escapes.

If a fixed volume of **gas** is **heated**, its **pressure increases**.
In this experiment, the water-bath makes sure that all the gas in the flask is thoroughly heated.

The Pressure Law Experiment

To keep the **volume** of the gas **constant**, the **mercury** in the left tube has to stay at the **same level** (shown by the marker).

When the gas is **heated**, the **pressure** in the flask **increases**. To keep the level of mercury in the **left hand tube** at the marker, increase the pressure on the **right hand tube** i.e. add more **mercury** to it.

From the amount of mercury **added**, you can work out how much the **pressure** must have **increased**. Add this to **atmospheric pressure** to get the **actual pressure** of the gas.

Measure the **temperature**, *T*, on the absolute scale.
Record the **pressure** for different values of *T*. You'll find that:

The value of **p/T** stays constant.

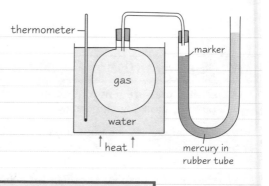

thermometer

marker

gas

water

↑ heat ↑

mercury in rubber tube

Boyle's Law Says **pV = Constant** for an Ideal Gas

At a **constant temperature** the **pressure** and **volume** of a gas are **inversely proportional**.
As the pressure goes up, the volume goes down and vice versa.

Boyle's Law Experiment

The **pump** pushes air into the **reservoir** applying pressure *p* to the oil, as measured by the gauge.

Increasing the pressure reduces the volume of the trapped gas, *V*, as measured by a scale.

The value **pV** stays constant.

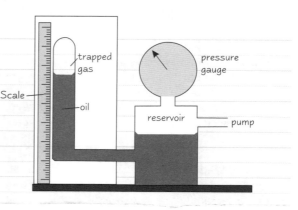

trapped gas

Scale

oil

pressure gauge

reservoir

pump

The Ideal Gas Equation

Combining the Gas Laws Gives pV/T = Constant

There's another gas law, called Charles' Law — you don't need to know the experiment for this one.

Charles' Law: At constant **pressure**, the **volume** V of a gas is **proportional** to its **absolute temperature** T, i.e. V/T is a **constant**.

Combining all three gas laws gives the equation:
$$\frac{pV}{T} = \text{constant}$$

Ello, ello...

Fiddle a bit more and you get the Ideal Gas Equation

1) The constant in the equation depends on the amount of gas used. ◄———— (Pretty obvious... if you have more gas it takes up more space.)
    The amount of **gas** can be **measured** in moles, n.

2) The constant then becomes $n\mathbf{R}$, where **R** is called the **molar gas constant**.
    Its value is $8.31 \, \text{J mol}^{-1} \text{K}^{-1}$.

3) Plugging this into the equation gives: $p\dfrac{V}{T} = n\mathbf{R}$ or rearranging, $pV = n\mathbf{R}T$

This equation works well for gases at **low pressure** and reasonably **high temperatures**.
Gases that obey this law are called **ideal gases**.

Practice Questions

Q1 What is 50 °C measured on the absolute scale?

Q2 A fixed mass of gas is at 300 K. If its temperature changes to 600 K and its volume stays the same, what happens to its pressure?

Q3 The pressure of a gas is 100 000 Pa and its temperature is 27 °C. The gas is heated — its volume stays fixed but the pressure rises to 150 000 Pa. Show that its new temperature is 40.5 °C.

Q4 The volume of a gas doubles whilst its temperature stays the same. What happens to its pressure?

Exam Questions

Q1 The mass of one mole of nitrogen gas is 0.028 kg. $R = 8.31 \, \text{J mol}^{-1} \text{K}^{-1}$.

  (a) A flask contains 0.014 kg of nitrogen gas. How many moles of nitrogen are in the flask? [1 mark]

  (b) If the flask is of volume 0.01 m³ and is at a temperature of 27 °C, what is the pressure inside it? [2 marks]

Q2 A large helium balloon has a volume of 10 m³ at ground level. The temperature of the gas in the balloon is 293 K and the pressure is 1×10^5 Pa. The balloon is released and rises to a height where its volume becomes 25 m³ and its temperature is 260 K.

  (a) Calculate the pressure inside the balloon at its new height. [3 marks]

  (b) State two assumptions you made in your calculations. [2 marks]

"Oh Jerry, why ask for the moon, when we can have the ideal gas..."

Ag... laws everywhere. And yep, you guessed it, you need to learn 'em all. Eeesh, sounding like a stuck record: 'learn this, learn that, give up your social life to learn equations'... Well don't blame me — you <u>chose</u> to do Physics. OK, end of rant, here's a useful tip: remember to change temperature into kelvin for the gas laws. (Loads of people forget that in exams.)

Finding the Pressure of an Ideal Gas

Kinetic theory tries to *explain* the *gas laws*. *It basically models a gas as a series of hard balls that obey Newton's Laws.*

You Need to be Able to **Derive** the **Pressure** of an **Ideal Gas**

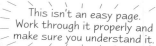
... unless you're doing Edexcel Salters Horners.

Start by **Deriving** the **Pressure** on **One Wall** of a Box, i.e. in the x direction

Imagine a cubic box with sides of length *l* containing *N* particles each of mass *m*.

This isn't an easy page. Work through it properly and make sure you understand it.

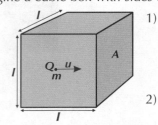

1) Say particle **Q** moves directly towards **wall A** with velocity *u*.
   Its **momentum** approaching the wall is *mu*. It strikes wall **A**.
   Assuming the **collisions** are perfectly **elastic**, it rebounds and heads
   back in the opposite direction with momentum –*mu*.
   So the **change in momentum** is *mu* – (–*mu*) = 2*mu*.

2) Assuming **Q** suffers no collisions the **time between collisions** of Q and
   wall A is 2*l/u*. The number of **collisions per second** is therefore *u/2l*.

3) This gives the **rate of change of momentum** as 2*mu* × *u/2l*.

4) Force equals the rate of change of momentum (Newton's Second Law),
   so the **force exerted on the wall** by this one particle = $2mu^2/2l = mu^2/l$.

5) Particle **Q** is only one of many in the cube. Each particle will have a different velocity u_1, u_2 etc.
   towards **A**. The total force, **F**, of all these particles on wall **A** is:

$$F = \frac{m(u_1^2 + u_2^2 + etc.)}{l}$$

6) You can define a quantity called the **mean square speed**, $\overline{u^2}$ as:

$$\overline{u^2} = \frac{u_1^2 + u_2^2 + etc.}{N}$$

7) If you put that into the equation above, you get:

$$F = \frac{Nm\overline{u^2}}{l}$$

8) So, the pressure of the gas on end **A** is given by:
   where *V* = volume of the cube

$$pressure, P = \frac{force}{area} = \frac{Nm\overline{u^2}/l}{l^2} = \frac{Nm\overline{u^2}}{V}$$

...Then for the **General Equation** you need to think about **All 3 Directions** — x, y and z

A gas particle can move in **three dimensions** (i.e. the *x*, *y*, and *z* directions).

1) You can calculate its **velocity**, *c*, from Pythagoras' theorem:
   $c^2 = u^2 + v^2 + w^2$ where *u*, *v* and *w* are the components of the particle's velocity in the *x*, *y* and *z* directions.

2) If you treat all *N* particles in the same way, this gives an **overall** mean square speed of: $\overline{c^2} = \overline{u^2} + \overline{v^2} + \overline{w^2}$

3) Since the particles move **randomly**: $\overline{u^2} = \overline{v^2} = \overline{w^2}$ and so $\overline{c^2} = 3\overline{u^2}$

4) You can substitute this into the equation for pressure that you derived earlier to give:

$$pV = \frac{1}{3}Nm\overline{c^2}$$

A Useful Quantity is the **Root Mean Square Speed** $\sqrt{\overline{c^2}}$

$\overline{c^2}$ is the **mean square speed** and has **units** m^2s^{-2}.
In kinetic theory, it helps to think about the motion of a typical particle.

1) $\overline{c^2}$ is the **square** of the **speed** of an **average particle**, so the square root of it gives you the typical speed.

2) This is called the **root mean square speed** or, usually, the **r.m.s. speed**.

$$r.m.s.\ speed = \sqrt{mean\ square\ speed} = \sqrt{\overline{c^2}}$$

Finding the Pressure of an Ideal Gas

Lots of Simplifying Assumptions are Used in Kinetic Theory

In **kinetic theory**, physicists picture gas particles moving at **high speed** in **random directions**.
To get **equations** like the one you just derived though, some **simplifying assumptions** are needed:

1) The gas contains a **large number of particles**.
2) The particles **move rapidly** and **randomly**.
3) The motion of the particles follows **Newton's laws**.
4) **Collisions** between particles themselves or at the walls of a container are **perfectly elastic**.
5) There are **no attractive forces** between particles.
6) Any **forces** that act during collisions are **instantaneous**.
7) Particles have a **negligible volume** compared with the volume of the container.

A **gas obeying** these **assumptions** is called an **ideal** gas. Real gases behave like ideal gases as long as the **pressure isn't too big**, and the **temperature** is **reasonably high** (compared with absolute zero).

Brownian Motion Supports Kinetic Theory

Brownian motion is Edexcel only.

In 1827, the botanist **Robert Brown** was looking at pollen grains in water.
He noticed that they constantly moved with a zigzag, **random motion**.

Brownian Motion Experiment

You can **observe** Brownian motion in the lab.

Put some **smoke** in a **brightly illuminated** glass jar and observe the particles using a **microscope**.

The smoke particles appear as **bright specks** moving **haphazardly** from side to side, and up and down.

Brown couldn't explain this, but nearly 80 years later Einstein showed that this provided evidence for the existence of atoms or **molecules** in the air. The **randomly moving** air particles were hitting the smoke particles unevenly, causing this motion.

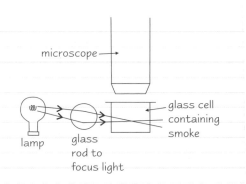

Practice Questions

Q1 What did Robert Brown observe?

Q2 Why do smoke particles show Brownian motion?

Q3 What are the seven assumptions made about ideal gas behaviour?

Q4 What is the definition of the mean square speed for *N* particles?

Exam Question

Q1 Some helium gas is contained in a flask of volume 7×10^{-5} m³. Each helium atom has a mass of 6.8×10^{-27} kg, and there are 2×10^{22} atoms present. The pressure of the gas is 1×10^5 Pa.

(a) What is the mean square speed of the atoms? [2 marks]

(b) What is the r.m.s. speed of a typical atom? [1 mark]

(c) If the absolute temperature of the gas is doubled, what will the r.m.s. speed of an atom become? [2 marks]

Brownian motion — girl guide in a tumble drier...

*Mean square speed is the average (mean) of the speeds squared. To find its value **square all the speeds** and then **find the average**. Don't make the mistake of finding the average speed first and then squaring. Cos that would be, like, soooo stupid.*

Internal Energy of a Gas

As every up and coming physicist knows, a gas is really a load of particles whizzing about and bumping into each other. So that means that it has energy of some kind — or the particles wouldn't move anywhere and it wouldn't be a gas at all, it'd be a solid at absolute zero. So... er... yeah... every gas has energy. That's what these pages are about.

Gas Particles Don't all Travel at the **Same Speed**

The **particles** in a **gas don't** all **travel** at the **same speed**.
Some particles will be moving fast but others much more slowly.
Most will travel around the average speed. The shape of the
speed distribution depends on the **temperature** of the gas.

As the temperature of the gas increases:

1) the average particle speed increases.

2) the maximum particle speed increases.

3) the distribution curve becomes more spread out.

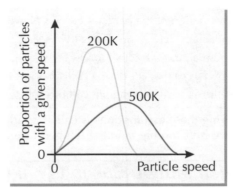

Energy Changes *Happen Between Particles*

The particles of a gas **collide** with each other **all the time**. Some of these will be '**head-on**' (particles moving in **opposite directions**) while others will be '**shunts from behind**' (particles moving in the **same direction**).

1) As a result of the collisions, **energy** will be **transferred** from one particle to another.

2) Some particles will **gain speed** in a collision and others will **slow down**.

3) **Between collisions**, the particles will travel at **constant speed**.

4) Although the energy of an individual particle changes at each collision,
the collisions **don't alter** the **total energy** of the **system**.

5) So, the **average** speed of the particles will stay the same provided the
temperature of the gas **stays the same**.

If you're doing Edexcel Salters Horners, you can skip straight to the questions now.

The **Average Kinetic Energy** of a Particle is **Proportional to T**

There are **two equations** for the **product pV** of a gas.
You can **equate these** to get an expression for the **average kinetic energy**.

1) The **ideal gas equation** is $pV = nRT$

2) The **pressure** of an **ideal gas** gives $pV = \frac{1}{3}Nm\overline{c^2}$

3) **Equating** these two gives: $\frac{1}{3}Nm\overline{c^2} = nRT$

4) **Multiplying** by **3/2** gives: $\frac{3}{2} \times \frac{1}{3}Nm\overline{c^2} = \frac{3nRT}{2}$

$$\frac{1}{2}m\overline{c^2} = \frac{3}{2}\frac{nRT}{N}$$

5) $\frac{1}{2}m\overline{c^2}$ is the **kinetic energy** of an **average individual particle**.

So the average kinetic energy of the gas particles is **proportional** to the **absolute temperature, T**.

Internal Energy of a Gas

Boltzmann's Constant k is Equal to R/N_A

One mole of any gas contains the same number of particles. This number is called
Avogadro's constant and is given the symbol N_A. The value of N_A is 6.02×10^{23}.

1) The number of particles in a mass of gas is given by the number of moles, *n*, multiplied by Avogadro's constant.
So the number of particles $N = nN_A$

2) This can be used to simplify the kinetic energy equation from page 66 to:

$$\frac{1}{2}m\overline{c^2} = \frac{3RT}{2N_A}$$

where *m* = mass
of one molecule

Boltzmann constant?
$\frac{R}{N_A}$, you say?

Hmmm...
That's not funny.

3) Boltzmann's constant, k is equivalent to R/N_A, so:

$$\frac{1}{2}m\overline{c^2} = \frac{3}{2}kT$$

4) The value of Boltzmann's constant is 1.38×10^{-23} JK^{-1}.

5) You can think of Boltzmann's constant as the gas constant for one particle of gas,
while R is the gas constant for one mole of gas.

Practice Questions

Q1 What happens to the r.m.s. speed of particles in a gas as the gas is heated?

Q2 Describe the changes in the distribution of gas particle speeds as the temperature of the gas is increased.

Q3 Explain how the speed of a gas particle can change even though the temperature of the gas stays constant.

Q4 What happens to the kinetic energy of an average particle if the temperature of a gas changes from 100 K to 200 K?

Exam Questions

Q1 The mass of one mole of nitrogen molecules is 2.8×10^{-2} kg. There are 6.02×10^{23} molecules in one mole.

  (a) What is the mass of one molecule? [1 mark]

  (b) Calculate the typical speed of a nitrogen molecule at 300 K. [3 marks]

Q2 Some air freshener is sprayed at one end of a room. The room is 8.0 m long and the temperature is 20 °C.

  (a) Assuming the average freshener molecule moves at 400 ms^{-1}, how long will it take for a particle to travel
directly to the other end of the room. [1 mark]

  (b) The perfume from the air freshener only slowly diffuses from one end of the room to the other.
Explain why this takes much longer than your answer to part (a). [2 marks]

  (c) What difference would you notice about the speed of diffusion for the air freshener if the temperature was 30 °C? [2 marks]

So that's why dustbins smell worse on a hot day...

Don't forget the speed of an average particle is the root mean square value.
For air particles, that's about 500 ms^{-1} at room temperature. If you're interested, like.

Thermodynamics and Engines

Here's another couple of Edexcel only pages.

These pages are all about using heat in different ways — e.g. in fridges. Sounds odd, I know, but bear with me...

The **First Law** of **Thermodynamics** is $Q = \Delta U - W$

There are **two** ways to raise the **temperature** of a system:

1) Put it in **thermal contact** with something **hotter** (i.e. supply heat energy)
2) **Do work** on it. E.g. you can raise the temperature of your arm by rubbing it, i.e. doing work against friction.

Temperature is a measure of how much **internal energy** a system has.

> The **first law** of thermodynamics says that the **change in internal energy** of a **system** is the **thermal energy put into the system** minus the **work done by the system** — it's just conservation of energy.

$$Q = \Delta U - W$$

1) **Q** is the **heat energy** supplied **to** the system.
2) Δ **U** is the **gain** in **internal energy** by the system.
3) **W** is the **work done on** the system.

You Need to Get Your **Signs** Right in the Equation

1) The flow of **heat energy**, **Q**, comes from **random interactions** between **objects** in **thermal contact**. The heat energy **always flows** from **hot to cold**. If heat is flowing **into** the system, **Q is positive**, if it's flowing **out** of the system, **Q is negative**.

2) The **internal energy**, **U**, is the **sum** of the **kinetic** and **potential** energies of all the particles. If the internal energy **rises**, ΔU **is positive**, and if it **falls**, ΔU **is negative**.

3) The **work done** is due to any process that's **independent** of the **temperature difference**. If work is done **on** the system, **W is positive**, if work is done **by** the system, **W is negative**.

Getting your signs right is generally a good idea.

Heat Engines Convert **Heat** Energy into **Work**

Heat engines absorb heat from a source, produce some **mechanical work** and **lose** some **heat** energy to an **exhaust.**

> An **example** of a heat engine is a **steam-driven turbine** in a power station:
>
> Water is heated under extremely high pressure to produce steam at about 500 °C.
>
> The steam enters the turbines, does work turning them, and leaves the turbines at a much lower temperature.
>
> Some of the internal energy of the steam is lost by doing work on the turbines, and the rest goes to heat the surroundings.

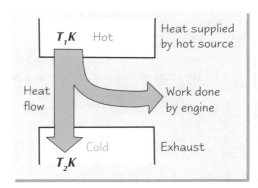

1) The **efficiency** of a **heat engine** is defined as:

$$\frac{\text{work done by the engine}}{\text{energy supplied to the engine}} \times 100\,\%$$

2) Some heat energy will **always** flow to the **exhaust**, so the **efficiency** of a heat engine can **never be 100%**.

3) The **maximum efficiency** is given by:

$$\text{maximum efficiency} = \frac{T_1 - T_2}{T_1} \times 100\,\%$$

You don't need to know where this equation comes from, you just need to learn it.

where temperatures T_1 and T_2 are measured on the **absolute** scale.

Thermodynamics and Engines

A *Thermopile* is an Example of a *Heat Engine*

A **thermopile** provides an **output voltage** when one side of it is **hotter** than the other. **Heat** flows from the **hot water** into the **thermopile**, which provides a voltage. The **other** side of the thermocouple has to be kept **cold**, so some heat also flows **into** the **cold water**.

1) The **voltage output** can make a **motor turn** to produce work.

2) The **maximum efficiency** is **limited** by the temperature of the water.

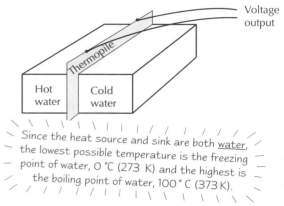

maximum efficiency = $\dfrac{373\ K - 273\ K}{373\ K} \times 100 = 26.8\ \%$

Since the heat source and sink are both <u>water</u>, the lowest possible temperature is the freezing point of water, 0 °C (273 K) and the highest is the boiling point of water, 100° C (373 K).

The *Heat Pump* is a *Heat Engine* in *Reverse*

Heat pumps take in **heat energy** at a **low temperature** and **exhaust** at a **higher temperature**.

1) Heat **naturally flows** from a **higher** to a **lower** temperature.

2) **Work** needs to be done on the system to make heat flow from a **lower temperature** T_2 to a **higher temperature** T_1.

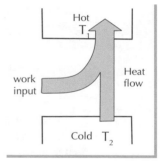

A fridge is an example of a heat pump.

A tube containing a volatile liquid runs inside and outside the fridge. Where the pipe enters the fridge, it narrows right down. The liquid evaporates and cools as it's forced through the tiny gap. The cool vapour absorbs heat from its surroundings. After leaving the fridge, it passes through a condenser where it gets compressed and heated. This heat is dissipated as it passes through cooling pipes on the back of the fridge.

Practice Questions

Q1 How is the internal energy of a system made up?

Q2 A system receives 20 J of heat energy. If the system does no work, what happens to this heat energy?

Q3 What is meant by the term 'heat engine'?

Q4 Why can't a heat engine ever be 100 % efficient?

Q5 A thermopile engine that uses water as its heat source and exhaust, has a maximum efficiency of 26.8 %. Why can't it have a higher efficiency than this?

Exam Questions

Q1 A quantity of helium gas is trapped inside an insulated container. 100 J of heat energy is supplied to the gas.

(a) Explain why the temperature of the gas will increase. [2 marks]

(b) If the gas then does 80 J of work, what will be the change in its internal energy compared with its original value? [2 marks]

Q2 A heat engine operates between an upper reservoir at 500 °C and exhausts at room temperature of 20 °C. When operating, the engine receives 4000 W from the upper reservoir and does work at a rate of 1.5 kW.

(a) What is the maximum efficiency of this heat engine? [2 marks]

(b) What is the actual efficiency the engine is operating at? [2 marks]

(c) Why is the actual efficiency of the engine less than the maximum value? [1 mark]

It'd be nice if you could convert heat energy into homework...

You see, if it was me, the first law of thermodynamics would be "run for your lives". But it isn't. *Sigh.* OK, here goes: In exams people usually mess up the +/− signs when they're using the $Q = \Delta U - W$ formula, especially with the W. So remember — think before you ... erm... substitute values into equations... *(hmm... not the most snappy advice I've ever come up with)*

The Nature of Waves

AQA A people only need to do pages 74 and 75, and if you're doing Edexcel you can skip the whole section. Slackers.

Aaaah... playing with slinky springs and waggling ropes about. It's all good clean fun as my mate Richard used to say...

A **Wave Transfers Energy** Away from its Source

Wave Experiments in the Classroom

1) Two pupils hold a **rope** — one at each end. The pupil at one end **shakes** the rope **up and down**. Point **A** on the rope is **dragged along** in the same up-and-down pattern as the **hand**, but **slightly later**. Point **B** moves slightly **later still**. So the **disturbance travels** along the length of the rope. Note that no actual bits of rope move from one end to the other, just the **wave profile**. It carries **energy** with it.

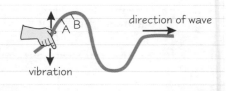

2) Now the two pupils make waves with a **slinky**. The pupil at one end shakes the slinky **parallel** to the direction of travel. In that case, the wave consists of **alternating compressions** and **stretched out bits** (rarefactions) travelling along the slinky. Again, no material is moved from one pupil to the other, just the **pattern**.

Vibrations in same direction

as wave is travelling

All three of the types of wave described above are progressive waves (moving waves). Not all waves are progressive, though — you get standing waves as well (see pages 84-85).

3) You can make water waves by **bobbing a plank** in a **ripple tank**. The **disturbance** in the water travels out from the **plank** to the **edge of the tank**.

Waves Can Be **Reflected** and **Refracted**

Reflection — the wave is **bounced back** when it **hits a boundary**. E.g. you can see the reflection of light in mirrors. The reflection of water waves can be demonstrated in a ripple tank.

Refraction — the wave **changes direction** as it enters a **different medium**. The change in direction is a result of the wave slowing down or speeding up (see page 74).

Here's all the **bits** of a **Wave** you Need to Know

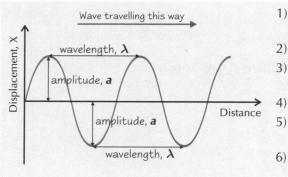

1) **Displacement**, X, metres — how far a **point** on the wave has **moved** from its **undisturbed position**.

2) **Amplitude**, **a**, metres — **maximum displacement**.

3) **Wavelength**, λ, metres — the **length** of **one whole wave**, from **crest** to **crest** or **trough** to **trough**.

4) **Period**, T, seconds — the **time taken** for a **whole vibration**.

5) **Frequency**, f, hertz — the **number** of **vibrations per second** passing a given **point**.

6) **Phase difference** — the amount by which **one wave lags behind another** wave. **Measured** in **degrees** or **radians**. See page 76.

A **louder** sound has **greater amplitude**.

A more **high-pitched** sound has a **higher frequency**.

A **brighter light** has **greater amplitude**.

Blue light has **higher frequency** than red light.

The Nature of Waves

The **Frequency** is the **Inverse** of the **Period**

$$\text{Frequency} = \frac{1}{\text{period}}$$

It's that simple.
Get the **units** straight: **1 Hz = 1s⁻¹**.

Wave Speed, Frequency and Wavelength are Linked by the Wave Equation

Wave speed can be measured just like the speed of anything else:

$$\text{Speed } (v) = \frac{\text{distance moved } (d)}{\text{time taken } (t)}$$

Remember, you're not measuring how fast a physical point (like one molecule of rope) moves. You're measuring how fast a point on the **wave pattern** moves.

Learn the **Wave Equation**...

$$\text{Speed of wave } (v) = \text{wavelength } (\lambda) \times \text{frequency } (f)$$

$$v = \lambda f$$

You need to be able to rearrange this equation for v, f or λ.

... and How to **Derive** it

You can work out the **wave equation** by imagining **how long** it takes for the **crest** of a wave to **move** across a **distance** of **one wavelength**. The **distance travelled** is λ. **By definition**, the **time taken** to travel **one whole wavelength** is the **period** of the wave, which is equal to **1/f**.

$$\text{Speed } (v) = \frac{\text{distance moved } (d)}{\text{time taken } (t)} \implies \text{Speed } (v) = \frac{\text{distance moved } (\lambda)}{\text{time taken } (1/f)}$$

Learn to recognise when to use **v = λf** and when to use **v = d/t**. Look at which variables are mentioned in the question.

Practice Questions

Q1 Give the units of frequency, displacement and amplitude.

Q2 Write down the equation connecting **v**, **λ** and **f**.

Q3 Does a wave carry matter **or** energy from one place to another?

Q4 Diffraction and interference are two wave properties. Write down two more.

Exam Questions

Q1 A buoy floating on the sea takes 6 seconds to rise and fall once (complete a full period of oscillation).
The difference in height between the buoy at its lowest and highest points is 1.2 m, and waves pass it at a speed of 3 m/s.

(a) How long are the waves? [2 marks]

(b) What is the amplitude of the waves? [1 mark]

Learn the wave equation and its derivation — pure poetry...

This isn't too difficult to start you off — most of it you'll have done at GCSE anyway. But once again, it's a whole bunch of equations to learn, and you won't get far without learning them. Ya de ya de ya.

Longitudinal and Transverse Waves

There are different types of wave — and the difference is easiest to see using a slinky.
You can move the end either left and right or forwards and backwards. Hours of fun.

In **Transverse Waves** the **Vibration** is at **Right Angles** to the **Direction** of Travel

All **electromagnetic waves** are **transverse**.
Other examples of transverse waves are **ripples**
on water and waves on **ropes**.

Vibrations from side to side
Wave travelling this way

There are Two Main Ways of **Showing Transverse Waves** on Paper

Transverse waves
can be shown as
graphs of
displacement
against **distance
travelled by the
wave**.

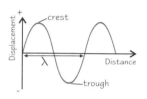

crest
Displacement
λ
Distance
trough

They can also
be shown as
graphs of
**displacement
against time**.

Displacement
Time

Both sorts of graph often give the **same shape**, so pay attention to the label on the **x-axis**.
Displacements **upwards** from the centre line are given a **+ sign**.
Displacements downwards are given a **– sign**.

Mr Harris is a
forward-thinking
physics teacher ...

Vibrations
Wave travelling this way

... showing how
transverse ...

In **Longitudinal Waves** the **Vibrations** are **Along** the Direction of Travel

The most **common** example of a **longitudinal wave** is **sound**. A sound
wave consists of alternate **compressions** and **rarefactions** of the
medium it's travelling through. (That's why sound can't go through
a vacuum.) Some types of **earthquake shock waves** are also longitudinal.

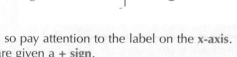

Compression   Rarefaction
One wavelength
Vibrations in same direction
as wave is travelling

It's hard to **represent** longitudinal waves **graphically**. You'll usually see them plotted as **displacement**
against **time**. These can be **confusing**, though, because they look like a **transverse wave**.

You can **Measure** the **Speed of Sound** in the **Laboratory**

You can use a **cathode ray oscilloscope (CRO)** to get an accurate measurement of the **speed of sound**.

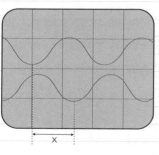

Vibrations in same direction

... and longitudinal
waves have exciting
real-world
applications.

Prat.

<u>Measuring the Speed of Sound</u>

1)   Connect a **loudspeaker** to a **signal generator** and set up a
microphone a known distance *d* from the loudspeaker.

2)   Connect the loudspeaker to one input of a **CRO**
and the microphone to the other.

3)   **Calibrate** the CRO so that its **time base** is known.

4)   The **traces** on the CRO screen from the loudspeaker
and microphone will look something like this:

x

5)   There is a **phase difference** between the signal from the
loudspeaker and the one from the microphone, corresponding
to the **time taken** for the sound to travel the distance, *d*.

6)   The time between the signal leaving the loudspeaker
and arriving at the microphone is given by:
t = separation of two signals on screen (X) × time base of CRO
Then use the equation $v = d / t$ to work out the speed of sound.

The speed of sound in air is approximately
330 ms^{-1}, depending on atmospheric
conditions. If your answer comes out
much bigger or smaller, check it again.

Longitudinal and Transverse Waves

Both *Longitudinal* and *Transverse* Waves Carry *Energy*

The greater the **amplitude**, the greater the **energy** carried by the wave.
Here are some ways you can tell waves carry energy:

1) Electromagnetic waves cause things to **heat up**.
2) **X-rays** and **gamma** rays knock electrons out of their orbits, causing **ionisation**.
3) Loud **sounds** make things **vibrate**.
4) **Wave power** can be used to **generate electricity**.
5) Since waves carry energy away, the **source** of the wave **loses energy**.

A *Polarised Wave* only *Oscillates* In One Direction

1) If you **shake a rope** to make a **wave** you can move your hand **up and down** or **side to side** or in a **mixture** of directions — it still makes a **transverse wave**.
2) But if you try to pass **waves in a rope** through a **vertical fence**, the wave will only get through if the **vibrations are vertical**. The fence filters out vibration in other directions. This is called **polarising** the wave.

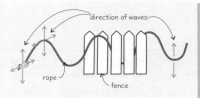

3) Ordinary **light waves** are a mixture of **different directions** of **vibration**. (The things vibrating are electric and magnetic fields.) A **polarising filter** only transmits vibrations in one direction.
4) If you have two polarising filters at **right angles** to each other, then **no** light will get through.
5) Polarisation **can only happen** for **transverse** waves. The fact that you can polarise light is one **proof** that it's a transverse wave.

Practice Questions

Q1 Give examples of a transverse wave and a longitudinal wave.

Q2 Sketch a graph of displacement against time, for an electromagnetic wave.

Q3 Write down two pieces of evidence that waves carry energy.

Q4 What do polarising sunglasses do to light?

Exam Questions

Q1 In an experiment, light is shone through a disc of a type of crystal called "Iceland Spar".
It is found that the beam of light that emerges from the other side is less bright.

Then a second identical disc of Iceland Spar is placed in front of the first. The first disc is held steady while the other is rotated (in the plane of the disc).
It is found that the amount of light emerging changes as the second disc rotates.
At one point in each rotation, no light gets through at all.

Explain the results of these experiments. Use diagrams if you wish. [5 marks]

Q2 An audio oscillator is set up to produce short bursts of sound and connected to a loudspeaker. Two microphones A and B are connected to a dual channel CRO with a time base of ten milliseconds per centimetre. Microphone A is placed near the loudspeaker and microphone B is placed 6.6 metres away. When a burst of sound is emitted it is found that the CRO shows the pulse from A as two centimetres to the left of the pulse from B.

(a) Describe how this set-up could be used to measure the speed of sound. [3 marks]

(b) Calculate the speed of sound in the room using the information given. [2 marks]

Ahhh — interesting...

The waves broadcast from TV or radio transmitters are polarised. So you have to line up the receiving aerial with the transmitting aerial to receive the signal properly. That's why the TV picture's lousy if the aerial gets knocked.

Refraction

This stuff explains why your legs look short in a swimming pool.

Refraction Happens when a Wave Changes Speed at a Boundary

When a ray of light meets a boundary between one medium and another, some of its energy is **reflected** back into the first medium and the rest of it is **transmitted** through into the second medium. The transmitted ray is bent or "**refracted**".

Light Slowing Down Makes it Change Direction

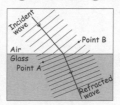

1) Light goes fastest in a **vacuum**. It **slows down** in other materials, because the wave **loses** some of its **energy** in **interactions** with particles.

2) The diagram shows a **wavefront** of a ray of light meeting an **air/glass boundary**. Point A reaches the boundary and **starts slowing down** before **point B** does. So the wavefront **bends** — that's refraction.

The more **optically dense** a material is, the more light slows down when it enters it.

The Refractive Index of a Material Measures How Much it Slows Down Light

The **absolute refractive index** of a material, **n**, is the **ratio** between the **speed of light** in a **vacuum**, **c**, to the speed of light in that **material**, **v**.

$$n = \frac{c}{v} \qquad c = 3 \times 10^8 \text{ ms}^{-1}$$

$$_1n_2 = \frac{v_1}{v_2}$$

The **relative refractive index** between two materials, $_1n_2$, is the ratio of the speed of light **in material 1** to the speed of light **in material 2**.

The speed of light in air is only a tiny bit smaller than c. So you can assume the refractive index of air is 1.

Combining the two equations gives: $\Longrightarrow$

$$_1n_2 = \frac{n_1}{n_2}$$

1) The **absolute refractive index** of a material is a **property** of that material only. But a **relative refractive index** is a property of the **interface** between two materials. It's different for **every possible pair**.

2) Because you can assume $n_{air} = 1$, you can assume the refractive index for an **air to glass boundary** equals the **absolute refractive index** of the glass.

Snell's Law uses Angles to Calculate the Refractive Index

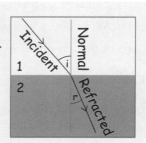

1) The angle the **incoming light** makes to the **normal** is called the **angle of incidence, i**. The angle the **refracted ray** makes with the **normal** is the **angle of refraction, r**.

2) When light enters an optically denser medium it is refracted **towards** the normal.

3) **n, i** and **r** are related by **Snell's Law**.

You don't need to know the geometry of why Snell's Law works, but you need to be able to use it in any of these three ways.

$$n_1 \sin i = n_2 \sin r$$

Light Leaving an Optically Denser Material is Refracted Away from the Normal

When light **leaves** an optically denser material and is refracted into an optically **less dense** material (e.g. glass to air) then angle **i** is **less** than **r** — and interesting things start to happen.

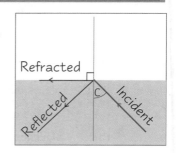

If you keep **increasing** the **angle of incidence** at a **glass to air** boundary, the angle of refraction gets closer and closer to **90°**. Eventually **i** reaches a **critical angle C** for which **r** = 90°. The light is **refracted** along the **boundary**. For light being refracted from glass into air at the **critical angle**, Snell's Law $n_{glass} \sin i = n_{air} \sin r$ becomes:

$$n \sin C = 1 \quad \text{so:} \quad n = \frac{1}{\sin C}$$

That's because the refractive index of air is 1 and sin 90 degrees = 1

You can use this formula to work out the **critical angle, C** of a material if you know **n**.

At angles of incidence **greater than C** refraction is **impossible**.

That means **all** the light is reflected back into the material. This effect is called **total internal reflection (TIR)**.

Refraction

Optical Fibres Use Total Internal Reflection

1)   An optical fibre is a very **thin flexible tube** of **glass fibre** that can carry **light signals** over long distances and round corners.

2)   The optical fibres themselves have a **high refractive index** but are surrounded by **cladding** with a lower refractive index.

3)   Light is shone in at **one end** of the fibre. The fibre is so **narrow** that the light always **hits the boundary** between fibre and cladding at an **angle bigger** than the **critical angle**.

4)   So all the light is **totally internally reflected** from wall to wall until it reaches the other end.

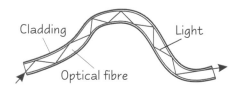

Optical Fibres are Useful for Medicine and Communications

Endoscopes made of optical fibres can see inside the human body, making **keyhole surgery** possible.

Light running through optical fibres is used to transmit **phone and cable TV signals**. It beats the **old system** of using **electricity** flowing through **copper cables** for several reasons.

1)   The signal carries **more information** because of the high frequency of visible light

2)   The light **doesn't heat up the fibre** — so energy is not lost as heat

3)   There is no electrical **interference**.

Multipath Dispersion is a Problem

Multipath dispersion happens because **not** all the **rays** that travel through the **fibre optic cable** follow exactly the **same path**. Light that goes **straight through** has the **shortest** path. Light that has **more bounces** with steeper zig-zags has a **longer journey**. Different **journey times** mean that what started off as a **single pulse of light** will be **spread out** by the time it reaches the other end.

Two solutions to Multipath Dispersion are:

1)   Use **narrow fibres** — minimising the difference between possible paths.

2)   Choose materials with values of *n* so that the **critical angle** is as **high as possible**.

Practice Questions

Q1   Why does light go fastest in a vacuum and slow down in other media?

Q2   What is the formula for the critical angle for a ray of light at a water/air boundary?

Q3   Which has a higher refractive index, an optical fibre or the cladding surrounding it?

Q4   What is multipath dispersion and how can you deal with it?

Exam Questions

Q1   (a)   Light travels in diamond at 1.241×10^8 ms^{-1}. What is the refractive index of diamond?   [1 mark]

   (b)   What is the angle of refraction if light strikes a facet of a diamond ring at an angle of 50° to the normal of the air/diamond boundary?   [2 marks]

Q2   An adjustable underwater spotlight is placed on the floor of an aquarium. When the light points upwards at a steep angle a faint beam comes through the surface of the water into the air, and the aquarium is dimly lit. When the spotlight is placed at a shallower angle, no light comes up through the water surface, but the aquarium is brightly lit.

   (a)   Explain what is happening.   [2 marks]

   (b)   It is found that the beam into the air disappears when the spotlight is pointed at any angle of less than 41.75° to the floor. Calculate the refractive index of water.   [2 marks]

I don't care about expensive things — all I care about is wave speed...

AS Physics examiners are always moaning about how candidates do worst in the optics bit of the exam. You'd hope they'd have something more important worry about — the Middle East crisis, the rise of the BNP, Posh & Becks... But no.

Superposition and Coherence

When two waves get together, it can be either really impressive or really disappointing.

Superposition *Happens When* Two *or* More *Waves* Pass Through *Each Other*

1) At the **instant** when the waves **cross**, the **displacements** due to each wave **combine**. Then **each wave** goes on its merry way. You can **see** this happening if **two pulses** are sent **simultaneously** from each end of a rope or slinky.

2) The **principle of superposition** says that when two or more **waves cross**, the **resultant** displacement equals the **vector sum** of the **individual** displacements.

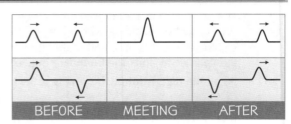

BEFORE   MEETING   AFTER

"Superposition" means "one thing on top of another thing." You can use the same idea in reverse — a complex wave can be separated out mathematically into several simple sine waves of various sizes.

Interference can be Constructive or Destructive

1) A **crest** plus a **crest** gives a **big crest**. A **trough** plus a **trough** gives a **big trough**. These are both examples of **constructive interference**.

2) A **crest** plus a **trough** of **equal size** gives... **nothing**. The two displacements **cancel each other out** completely. This is called **destructive interference**.

3) If the **crest** and the **trough** aren't the **same size**, then the destructive interference **isn't total**. For the interference to be **noticeable**, the two **amplitudes** should be **nearly equal**.

You Get Patterns of Loud and Quiet from Interference of Sound Waves

Set up **two speakers** attached to the **same sound source** at **either end** of a long bench. If you walk from one end of the bench to the other, you'll hear the sound getting **louder** then **quieter** then **louder** again.

What you're hearing is **bands** of **constructive** and **destructive** interference, depending on whether the waves are **in phase** or **out of phase**.

In Phase *Means In* Step

1) Two points on a wave are **in phase** if they are both at the **same point** in the **wave cycle**. Points in phase have the **same displacement** and **velocity**. In the graph below, points **A** and **B** are **in phase**; points **A** and **C** are **out of phase**.

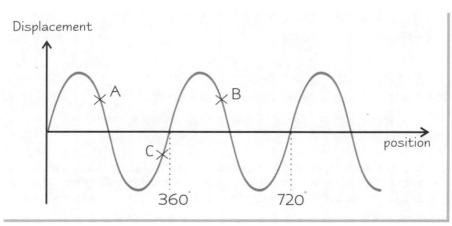

2) It's mathematically **handy** to show one **complete cycle** of a wave as an **angle of 360°**. **Two points** with a **phase difference** of **zero** or a **multiple of 360°** are **in phase**. Points with a **phase difference** of **odd-number multiples** of **180°** are **exactly out of phase**.

3) You can also talk about two **different waves** being **in phase**. **In practice**, this happens because **both** waves **originally** came from the **same oscillator**. In **other** situations, there will nearly always be a **phase difference** between the two waves.

Superposition and Coherence

To Get Interference Patterns The Two Sources Must Be Coherent

Interference **still happens** when you're observing waves of **different wavelength** and **frequency** — but it happens in a **jumble**. In order to get clear **interference patterns**, the two or more sources must be **coherent**.

Two sources are **coherent** if they have the **same wavelength** and **frequency** and a **fixed phase difference** between them.

In exam questions at AS level the 'fixed phase difference' is almost certainly going to be zero. The two sources will be in phase.

Constructive or Destructive Interference Depends on the Path Difference

1) Whether you get **constructive** or **destructive** interference at a **point** depends on how **much further one wave** has travelled than the **other wave** to get to that point.

2) The **amount** by which the path travelled by one wave is **longer** than the path travelled by the other wave is called the **path difference.**

3) At **any point an equal distance** from both sources you will get **constructive interference.** You also get constructive interference at any

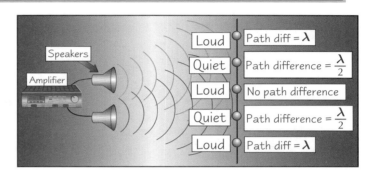

point where the **path difference** is a **whole number of wavelengths.** At these points the two waves are **in phase** and **reinforce** each other. But at points where the path difference is **half a wavelength, one and a half** wavelengths, **two and a half** wavelengths etc., the waves arrive **out of phase** and you get **destructive interference**.

Constructive interference occurs when: $\text{path difference} = n\lambda$ (where **n** is an integer)

Destructive interference occurs when: $\text{path difference} = \dfrac{(2n+1)\lambda}{2} = (n + \frac{1}{2})\lambda$

Practice Questions

Q1 Why does the principle of superposition deal with the **vector** sum of two displacements?

Q2 What happens when a crest meets a slightly smaller trough?

Q3 If two points on a wave have a phase difference of 1440°, are they in phase?

Q4 Does the phase difference between two sources have to be zero for them to be coherent?

Exam Questions

Q1 a) Two sources are coherent.
        What can you say about their frequencies, wavelengths and phase difference? [3 marks]

    b) Suggest why you might have difficulty in observing interference patterns in an area affected by
        two waves from two sources even though the two sources are coherent? [1 mark]

Q2 Two points on a wave are exactly out of phase.

    (a) What is the phase difference between them, expressed in degrees? [1 mark]

    (b) Compare the displacements and velocities of the two points. [2 marks]

Learn those pink box equations — oh go on, you know you want to...

You can't have interference between different types of wave like, say, sound and light for instance.
But I guess you probably knew that already. I'll get me coat.

Diffraction

Ripple tanks, ripple tanks — yeah.

Waves Go **Round Corners** and **Spread out** of **Gaps**

The way that **waves spread out** as they come through a **narrow gap**, or go round obstacles is called **diffraction**.   **All** waves diffract, but it's not always easy to observe.

To Show Diffraction of **Water Waves** Use a **Ripple Tank**
You can make diffraction patterns in ripple tanks.
The **amount** of diffraction depends on the **wavelength** of the wave compared with the **size of the gap**.

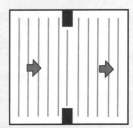

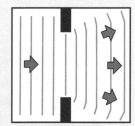

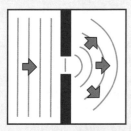

When the gap is **a lot bigger** than the **wavelength**, diffraction is **unnoticeable**.

You get **noticeable diffraction** through a gap **several** wavelengths wide.

You get the **most** diffraction when the gap is **the same** size as the **wavelength**.

If the gap is **smaller** than the wavelength, the waves are just **reflected back**.

When **sound** passes through a **doorway**, the **size of gap** and the **wavelength** are about **equal**, so the **maximum diffraction** occurs. That's why you have no trouble **hearing** someone through an **open door** to the next room, even if the other person is out of your **line of sight**. The reason that you can't **see** him or her is that when **light** passes through the doorway, it is passing through a **gap** around a **hundred million times bigger** than its wavelength — the amount of diffraction is **tiny**.

Demonstrate **Diffraction** in **Light** Using **Laser Light**

1) Diffraction in **light** can be demonstrated by shining a **laser light** through a very **narrow slit** onto a screen. You can alter the amount of diffraction by changing the width of the slit.

2) You can do a similar experiment using a **white light** source instead of the laser (which is monochromatic) and a set of **colour filters**. The size of the slit can be kept constant while the **wavelength** is varied by putting different **colour filters** over the slit.

Warning. Use of coloured filters may result in excessive fun.

Diffraction is Sometimes **Useful** and Sometimes a Pain...

1) For a **satellite transmission** you want a **narrow**, **targeted** beam, so satellite communications companies aim to **minimise** diffraction.

2) For a **loudspeaker** you want the sound to be heard as widely as possible, so you aim to **maximise** diffraction.

3) With a **microwave oven** you want to **stop** the **microwaves** diffracting out and frying your kidneys **and** you want to **let light through** so you can **see** your food. A **metal mesh** on the **door** has **gaps too small** for microwaves to diffract through, but **light** slips through because of its **tiny wavelength**.

Diffraction

With **Light Waves** you get a **Pattern** of **Light** and **Dark Fringes**

1) If the wavelength of a light wave is about the same size as the aperture, you get a diffraction pattern of light and dark fringes.

2) The pattern has a bright central fringe with alternating dark and bright fringes on either side of it.

3) The first set of dark fringes are produced at an angle θ to the direction of the incident light, where:

$$\sin\theta = \frac{\lambda}{a}$$

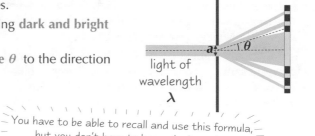

You have to be able to recall and use this formula, but you don't have to know why it works.

Diffraction Puts a **Limit** on How Much **Detail** You Can See

1) **Blurring** due to **diffraction** means that if you're looking at **two points** it can be hard to **resolve** one from the other. The **limit of resolution** is when you can't tell any more whether you're looking at **two sources** or **one**.

2) When the **wavelength** is **much smaller** than the **gap** (e.g. the lens of a telescope), there's hardly any **diffraction** and **resolution** is **good**. As the **wavelength** gets **closer** to the size of the gap, diffraction **increases** and resolution gets **worse**.

3) This is a **big problem** in **astronomy**. Even the **best** telescopes can't **resolve two stars** very close on the sky.

4) One solution is to make the "**gap**" **very large indeed** by building an **array** of telescopes that together make an aperture **several kilometres square**. Talk about extreme measures...

5) Diffraction also causes problems in **resolving details** in an **ultrasound** image. To minimise diffraction, it's best to have the **wavelength** as **small** as possible.

Practice Questions

Q1 What is diffraction?

Q2 Sketch what happens when plane waves meet an obstacle about as wide as one wavelength.

Q3 For a long time some scientists argued that light couldn't be a wave because it did not seem to diffract. Why did they get this impression?

Q4 Do all waves diffract?

Q5 If the wavelength of light causing a diffraction pattern gets bigger, does the pattern get wider or narrower?

Exam Questions

Q1 A mountain lies directly between you and a radio transmitter. Explain using diagrams why you can pick up longwave radio broadcasts from the transmitter but not shortwave. [4 marks]

Q2 A beam of coherent light of wavelength 6×10^{-7}m falls on a narrow slit of width 0.1mm producing a diffraction pattern on a screen some metres away.

(a) State qualitatively what would happen to the width of the pattern if the slit were halved in width. [1 mark]

(b) Calculate the angle θ the first dark fringe makes with the incident beam. [2 marks]

I always wondered how they stopped microwaves escaping...

By the way, blurring due to diffraction is completely separate from blurring due to atmospheric conditions. Diffraction blurring is a result of the wave nature of light. Atmospheric blurring is due to the air moving and distorting the image.

Two-Source Interference

Yeah, I know, fringe spacing doesn't really sound like a Physics topic — just trust me on this one, OK.

Demonstrating Two-Source Interference In **Water** and **Sound** is Easy

1) It's **easy** to demonstrate **two-source interference** for either **sound** or **water** because they've got **wavelengths** of a handy **size** that you can **measure**.

2) You need **coherent** sources, which means the **wavelength** and **frequency** have to be the **same**. The trick is to use the **same oscillator** to drive **both sources**. For **water**, one **vibrator drives two dippers**. For sound, **one oscillator** is connected to **two loudspeakers**. (See diagram on page 77.)

Demonstrating **Two-Source** Interference for **Light** is Harder

Young's Double Slit Experiment

1) You **can't** arrange **two separate coherent light sources** because **light** from **each source** is emitted in **random bursts**. Instead a **single** laser lamp is shone through **two slits**.

2) Light spreading out by **diffraction** from the slits is equivalent to **two coherent point sources**. Laser light is used so that there's only **one wavelength** present.

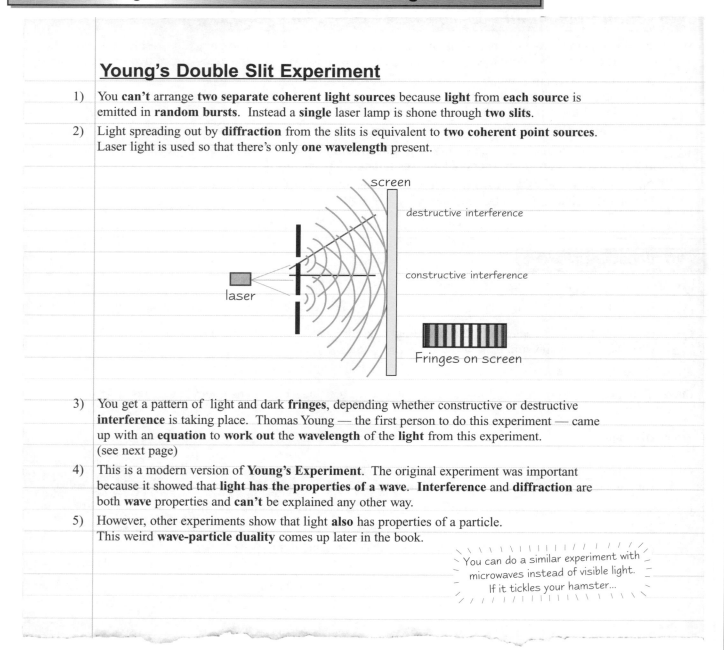

3) You get a pattern of light and dark **fringes**, depending whether constructive or destructive **interference** is taking place. Thomas Young — the first person to do this experiment — came up with an **equation** to **work out** the **wavelength** of the **light** from this experiment. (see next page)

4) This is a modern version of **Young's Experiment**. The original experiment was important because it showed that **light has the properties of a wave**. **Interference** and **diffraction** are both **wave** properties and **can't** be explained any other way.

5) However, other experiments show that light **also** has properties of a particle. This weird **wave-particle duality** comes up later in the book.

You can do a similar experiment with microwaves instead of visible light. If it tickles your hamster...

Two-Source Interference

Work Out the Wavelength with Young's Double Slit Formula

1) The fringe spacing, wavelength, spacing between slits (**d**) and the distance from slits to screen (**D**) are all related by **Young's double slit formula** which you need to know but not prove.

$$\text{Fringe spacing, } X = \frac{D\lambda}{d}$$

"Fringe spacing" means the distance from the centre of one minimum to the centre of the next minimum or from the centre of one maximum to the centre of the next maximum.

2) Since the wavelength is so small you can see from the formula that a high ratio of **D / d** is needed to make the fringe spacing **big enough to see**.

3) Rearranging you can use $\lambda = Xd / D$ to **calculate the wavelength** of light.

4) The fringes are **so tiny** that it's very hard to get an **accurate value of X**. It's easier to measure across **several** fringes then **divide** by the number of **fringe widths** between them.

Always check your fringe spacing.

You Can Also Get Interference Patterns Using a Partial Reflector

1) Light sent in at an **angle** is **partially transmitted** and **partially reflected** at the **half-silvered surface** of the **partial** reflector.

2) The reflected beam **bounces back** from the **left hand reflector** and the same thing happens **again** repeatedly.

3) The end result is **multiple parallel beams**, with each beam **out of phase** with the next by a **fixed amount**.

4) The beams can be focussed with a lens to produce an **interference pattern**.

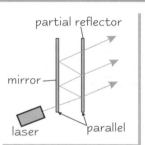

Practice Questions

Q1 In Young's experiment, why do you get a bright fringe at a point equidistant from both slits?

Q2 What does Young's experiment show about the nature of light?

Q3 Write down Young's double slit formula.

Exam Questions

Q1 (a) The diagram on the right shows waves from two coherent light sources S_1 and S_2. Sketch the interference pattern marking on constructive and destructive interference.
[2 marks]

(b) In practice if interference is to be observed S_1 and S_2 must be slits in a screen behind which there is a source of laser light. Why? [2 marks]

Q2 In an experiment to study sound interference, two loudspeakers are connected to an oscillator emitting sound at 1320 Hz and set up as shown in the diagram below. They are 1.5 m apart and 7 m away from the line AC. A listener moving from A to C hears minimum sound at A and C and maximum sound at B.

Oscillator — 1.5m — 7m — A / B / C

(a) Calculate the wavelength of the sound waves if the speed of sound in air is taken to be 330 ms⁻¹. [1 mark]

(b) Calculate the separation of points A and C. [2 marks]

Carry on Physics — this page is far too saucy...

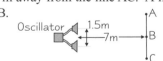

Be careful when you're calculating the fringe width by averaging over several fringes. Don't just divide by the number of bright lines. Ten bright lines will only have nine fringe-widths between them, not ten. It's an easy mistake to make, but you have been warned... mwa ha ha ha (felt necessary, sorry).

Diffraction Gratings and Intensity

Ay... starting to get into some pretty funky stuff now. I like light experiments.

Interference Patterns Get **Sharper** When You Diffract Through **More Slits**

1) You can repeat **Young's double slit** experiment (see p80) with **more than two equally spaced** slits. You get basically the **same shaped** pattern as for two slits — but the **bright bands** are **brighter** and **narrower** and the **dark areas** between are **darker**.

2) When **monochromatic light** (one wavelength) is passed through a **grating** with **hundreds** of slits per millimetre, the interference pattern is **really sharp** because there are so **many beams reinforcing** the **pattern**.

3) Sharper fringes make for more **accurate** measurements.

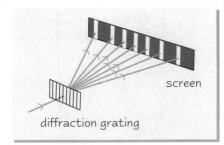

screen

diffraction grating

Monochromatic Light on a Diffraction Grating gives Sharp Lines

1) For **monochromatic** light, all the **maxima** are sharp lines. (It's different for white light, see below.)

2) There's a line of **maximum brightness** at the centre called the **zero order** line.

3) The lines just **either side** of the central one are called **first order lines**. The **next pair out** are called **second order** lines and so on.

4) For a grating with slits a distance **d** apart, the angle between the **incident beam** and **the nth order maximum** is given by:

$$d \sin \theta = n \lambda$$

5) So by observing **d**, **θ** and **n** you can **calculate the wavelength** of the light.

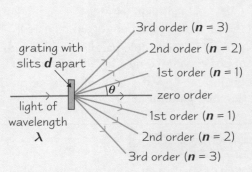

grating with slits **d** apart

light of wavelength λ

3rd order (**n** = 3)
2nd order (**n** = 2)
1st order (**n** = 1)
zero order
1st order (**n** = 1)
2nd order (**n** = 2)
3rd order (**n** = 3)

You can Draw **General Conclusions** from **d** sin θ = n λ

1) If λ is **bigger**, **sin θ** is **bigger**, and so **θ** is **bigger**. This means that the larger the **wavelength**, the more the pattern will **spread out**.

2) If **d** is **bigger**, **sin θ** is **smaller**. This means that the **coarser** the **grating**, the **less** the pattern will **spread out**.

3) Values of **sin θ** greater than **1** are **impossible**. Light **can't** be scattered by an angle of more than **90°**. If for a certain **n** you get a result of **more than 1** for **sin θ** you know that order **doesn't exist**.

Shining **White Light** Through a **Diffraction Grating** Produces **Spectra**

1) **White light** is really a **mixture** of **colours**. If you **diffract** white light through a **grating** then the patterns due to **different wavelengths** within the white light are **spread out** by **different** amounts.

2) Each **order** in the pattern becomes a **spectrum**, with **red** on the **outside** and **violet** on the **inside** (see p110). The **zero order maximum** stays **white** because there's **no path difference** between waves arriving there.

Astronomers and chemists often need to study spectra. They use diffraction gratings rather than prisms because they're more accurate.

Diffraction Gratings and Intensity

Intensity is a Measure of How Much Energy a Wave is Carrying

1) Sound, light and other waves all carry energy.

2) When you talk about "brightness" for light or "loudness" for sound, what you really want to know is how much light or sound energy is hitting your eyes or your ears per second.

3) The scientific measure of this is intensity.

> Intensity is the rate of flow of energy per unit area at right angles to the direction of travel of the wave. It's measured in Wm^{-2}.

Energy Spreading From a Point Source Forms a Sphere

1) The power P of a source is the energy it emits per second.

2) If you have waves radiating evenly from a point source, at a distance r from the source, P is spread out over a sphere of surface area $4\pi r^2$.

3) So intensity I at a distance r from the source is given by:

$$I = \frac{P}{4\pi r^2}$$

4) Notice that I is proportional to $1/r^2$. If you move twice as far from a light source the light is one quarter as intense. Three times further out the light is one ninth as intense.

5) Inverse square laws crop up all over the place in physics.

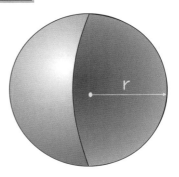

Intensity is Proportional to the Square of the Amplitude of the Wave

$$I \propto A^2$$

1) This comes from the fact that intensity is proportional to energy, and the energy of a wave depends on the square of the amplitude.

2) From this you can tell that for a vibrating source it takes four times as much energy to double the size of the vibrations.

Practice Questions

Q1 How is the diffraction grating pattern for white light different from the pattern for laser light?

Q2 What difference does it make to the pattern if you use a finer grating?

Q3 What are the SI units of intensity?

Q4 If P is the total energy emitted per second in all directions by a point source, what is the formula for the intensity at a distance r from the source?

Exam Questions

Q1 Yellow laser light of wavelength 600 nm (6×10^{-7} m) is transmitted through a diffraction grating of 4×10^5 lines per metre.

    (a)   At what angle to the normal are the first and second order bright lines seen?   [4 marks]

    (b)   Is there a fifth order line?   [1 mark]

Remember — monochromatic = one colour...

Woah woah woah — loads of information to take in. OK, to sum up: for monochromatic light you get sharper patterns the more slits you have, there's an equation $d \sin \theta = n\lambda$ to learn, for white light you get a pretty spectrum, and intensity is all about light energy and there are a couple of equations to learn for that too. Phew. Cuppa before I go any further I think.

Standing Waves

Standing waves are waves that... er... stand still... well, not still exactly... I mean, well...they don't go anywhere... um...

You get Standing Waves When a **Progressive Wave** is **Reflected** at a **Boundary**

A standing wave is the **superposition** of **two progressive waves** with the **same wavelength**, moving in **opposite directions**.

1) Unlike progressive waves, **no energy** is transmitted by a standing wave.

2) You can demonstrate standing waves by setting up a **driving oscillator** at one end of a **stretched string** with the other end fixed. The wave generated by the oscillator is **reflected** back and forth.

3) For most frequencies the resultant **pattern** is a **jumble**. However, if the oscillator happens to produce an **exact number of waves** in the time it takes for a wave to get to the **end** and **back again**, then the **original** and **reflected** waves **reinforce** each other.

4) At these **"resonant frequencies"** you get a **standing wave** where the **pattern doesn't move** — it just sits there, bobbing up and down. Happy, at peace with the world...

A sitting wave.

Standing Waves in **Strings** Form **Oscillating "Loops"** Separated by **Nodes**

1) Each particle vibrates at **right angles** to the string.
Nodes are where the **amplitude** of the vibration is **zero**.
Antinodes are points of **maximum amplitude**.

2) At resonant frequencies, an **exact number** of **half wavelengths** fits onto the string.

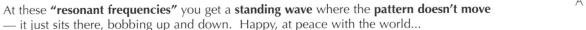

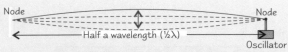

The standing wave above is vibrating at the **lowest possible** resonant frequency (the **fundamental frequency**). It has **one** "loop" with a **node at each end**.

This is the **second harmonic** (or **first overtone**). It is **twice** the fundamental frequency. There are two "loops" with a **node** in the **middle** and **one** at **each end**.

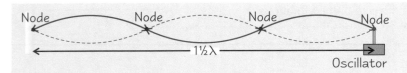

The **third harmonic** (or **second overtone**) is **three times** the fundamental frequency. **1½ wavelengths** fit on the string.

The **Notes** Played by **Stringed** and **Wind Instruments** Are Standing Waves

Transverse standing waves form on the strings of **stringed instruments** like **violins** and **guitars**. Your finger or the bow sets the **string vibrating** at the point of contact. Waves are sent out in **both directions** and **reflected** back at both ends.

Longitudinal Standing Waves Form in a **Wind Instrument** or Other **Air Column**

1) If a source of sound is placed at the open end of a flute, piccolo, oboe or other column of air, there will be some **frequencies** for which **resonance** occurs and a standing wave is set up.

2) If the instrument has a **closed end**, a **node** will form there. You get the lowest resonant frequency when the length of the pipe is a **quarter wavelength**.

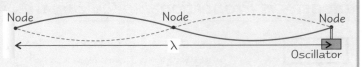

$$l = \frac{\lambda}{4}$$

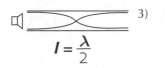

$$l = \frac{\lambda}{2}$$

3) **Antinodes** form at the **open ends** of pipes. If both ends are open, you get the lowest resonant frequency when the length of the pipe is a **half wavelength**.

Remember, the sound waves in wind instruments are longitudinal — they don't actually look like these diagrams.

Standing Waves

Fundamental Frequency of a String Depends on *Length*, *Weight* and *Tension*

1) The **longer** the string, the **lower** the note — because the **half-wavelength** at the natural frequency is longer.

2) The **heavier** (i.e. the more mass per length) the string, the **lower** the note — because waves travel more **slowly** down the string. For a given **length** a **lower** velocity, *v* makes a **lower** frequency, *f*.

3) The **looser** the string the **lower** the note — again because waves travel more **slowly** down a **loose** string.

You can Demonstrate Standing Waves with Microwaves and Sounds

Microwaves Reflected Off a Metal Plate Set Up a Standing Wave

Microwave standing wave apparatus ⟶
You can find the **nodes** and **antinodes** by moving the **probe** between **transmitter** and **reflecting** plate.

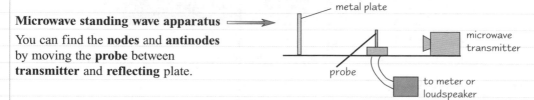

Powder can Show Standing Waves in a Tube of Air

Stationary sound waves are produced in the **glass tube**.

The **lycopodium powder** (don't worry, you don't need to know what that is) laid along the bottom of the tube is **shaken away** from the **antinodes** but left **undisturbed** at the **nodes**.

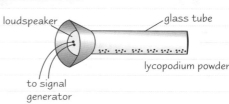

Practice Questions

Q1 How do standing waves form?

Q2 At four times the fundamental frequency, how many half wavelengths fit on a violin string?

Q3 Which factors affect the fundamental frequency of a guitar string?

Q4 Describe an experiment to investigate standing waves in a column of air.

Exam Questions

Q1 (a) A standing wave of three times the fundamental frequency is formed on a stretched string of length 1.2m. Sketch a diagram showing the form of the wave. [2 marks]

(b) What is the wavelength of the standing wave? [1 mark]

(c) Explain how the amplitude varies along the string. How is that different from the amplitude of a progressive wave? [2 marks]

(d) At a given moment, how does the displacement of a particle at one antinode compare to the displacement of a particle at the next antinode? [2 marks]

Just get hold of a guitar and try it out...

Exam questions often get you to compare standing waves to progressive waves.
Remember the fundamental (ho ho) difference is that standing waves don't transmit energy.

The Electromagnetic Spectrum

There's nothing really deep and meaningful to understand on this page — just a load of facts to learn I'm afraid.

All **Electromagnetic Waves** Have Some **Properties** In Common

1) They travel in a **vacuum** at a **speed** of **2.998 × 10^8 ms^{-1}**, and at slower speeds in other media.
2) They are **transverse** waves consisting of **vibrating electric** and **magnetic fields**.
   The **electric** and **magnetic** fields are at **right angles** to each other and the **direction of travel**.
3) Like all waves, EM waves can be **reflected**, **refracted**, **diffracted** and undergo **interference**.
4) Like all waves, EM waves obey $v = f\lambda$ (v = velocity, f = frequency, λ = wavelength).
5) Like all progressive waves, progressive EM waves **carry energy**.
6) Like all transverse waves, EM waves can be **polarised**.

Electromagnetic (EM) Waves Are Split Into **Seven** Categories

EM waves with different wavelengths behave differently in some respects.
The seven categories are **radio**, **microwaves**, **infrared**, **visible light**, **ultraviolet**, **X-rays**, and **gamma rays**.

The **Properties** of an **EM Wave** Change with **Wavelength**

Type	Approximate wavelength / m	Penetration	Uses
Radio waves	10^{-1} — 10^6	Pass through matter.	Radio transmissions.
Microwaves	10^{-3} — 10^{-1}	Mostly pass through matter, but cause some heating.	Radar. Microwave cookery. TV transmissions.
Infra-red (IR)	7×10^{-7} — 10^{-3}	Mostly absorbed by matter, causing it to heat up.	Heat detectors. Night vision cameras. TV remote controls. Optical fibres.
Visible light	4×10^{-7} — 7×10^{-7}	Absorbed by matter, causing some heating effect.	Human sight. Optical fibres.
Ultra-violet (UV)	10^{-8} — 4×10^{-7}	Absorbed by matter. Slight ionisation.	Sunbeds. Security markings that show up in UV light.
X-rays	10^{-13} — 10^{-8}	Mostly pass through matter, but cause ionisation as they pass.	To see damage to bones and teeth. Airport security scanners. To kill cancer cells.
Gamma rays	10^{-16} — 10^{-10}	Mostly pass through matter, but cause ionisation as they pass.	Irradiation of food. Sterilisation of medical instruments. To kill cancer cells.

X-rays and **gamma rays** overlap in terms of wavelength. The main difference between them is how they're produced. Gamma rays are produced in **radioactive decay** but X-rays are produced by **bombarding targets** with **fast-moving electrons**.

The Electromagnetic Spectrum

Some Properties Vary Across the EM Spectrum

1) The longer the wavelength, the more **obvious** the wave characteristics. E.g. long radio waves diffract round hills.

2) **Energy** is directly proportional to **frequency**. **Gamma rays** have the **highest energy**, **radio waves** the **lowest**.

3) The **higher** the **energy**, the more **dangerous** the wave.

4) The **lower the energy** of an EM wave, the **further from the nucleus** it comes from. **Gamma radiation** comes from inside the **nucleus**. **X-rays to visible light** come from energy-level transitions in **atoms** (see p110). **Infrared** radiation and **microwaves** are associated with **molecules**. **Radio waves** come from oscillations in **electric fields**.

Different Types of EM Wave Are Produced and Detected Differently

Type	Production	Detection	Effect on human body
Radio waves	Oscillating electrons in an aerial	Radio receivers.	No effect.
Microwaves	Electron tube oscillators. Masers.	Crystal detectors. Diodes.	Absorbed by water — danger of cooking human body*.
Infra-red (IR)	Natural and artificial heat sources.	Heat sensors in human skin. IR cameras.	Heating. Excess heat can harm the body's systems.
Visible light	Natural and artificial light sources.	Human eye. Photographic film.	Used for sight. Too bright a light can damage eyes.
Ultra-violet (UV)	e.g. the Sun.	Photographic film.	Tans the skin. Can cause skin cancer and eye damage.
X-rays	Bombarding metal with electrons.	Photographic film.	Cancer due to cell damage. Eye damage.
Gamma rays	Radioactive decay of the nucleus.	Geiger counter. Scintillation counter.	Cancer due to cell damage. Eye damage.

* Or small animals.

Practice Questions

Q1   What are the main practical uses of infrared radiation?

Q2   Which types of electromagnetic radiation have the highest and lowest energies?

Q3   What is the significance of the speed 2.998×10^8 ms^{-1}?

Q4   Why are microwaves dangerous?

Q5   How does the energy of an EM wave vary with frequency?

Exam Questions

Q1   In a vacuum, do X-rays travel faster, slower or at the same speed as visible light? Explain your answer.   [2 marks]

Q2   a)   How can X-rays be detected?   [1 mark]

   b)   Describe briefly the physics behind a practical use of X rays.   [2 marks]

   c)   What is the difference between gamma rays and X-rays?   [2 marks]

Q3   Give an example of a type of electromagnetic wave causing a hazard to health.   [2 marks]

I've got UV hair...

No really I have. It's great. It's purple. And it's got shiny glittery white bits in it.
Aaaanyway... moving swiftly on. Loads of facts to learn on this page. You probably know most of this from GCSE anyway, but make sure you know it well enough to answer a question on it in the exam. Not much fun, but... there you go.

Atomic Structure

You don't need any of this section if you're doing OCR (A or B). Bit of a shame really — it's got some funky stuff in it.

"So what did you do today Johnny?" "Nuclear and Particle Physics, Mum." "How nice dear — done with times tables then?"
*Yeah, well, it's not exactly the **easiest** topic in the world, but it's a darn sight more interesting than mechanics.*

Atoms are made up of Protons, Neutrons and Electrons

Inside **every atom**, there's a **nucleus** containing **protons** and **neutrons**.
Protons and **neutrons** are both known as **nucleons**.   **Orbiting** this core are the **electrons**.

This is the **nuclear model** of the atom.

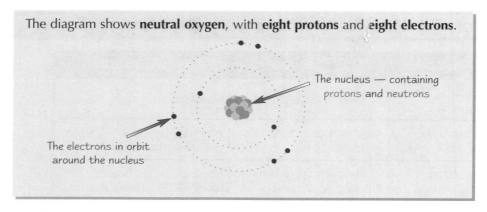

The diagram shows **neutral oxygen**, with **eight protons** and **eight electrons**.

The nucleus — containing protons and neutrons

The electrons in orbit around the nucleus

You have to know the **properties** of **electrons**, **protons** and **neutrons** for the exam — make sure you **learn this table**.

Particle	Charge	Relative Mass
Proton	Positive, +1	1
Neutron	Neutral, 0	1
Electron	Negative, −1	0.0005

Atoms are Really, Really Tiny

Each atom is about a **tenth of a nanometre (1×10^{-10} m)** in **diameter**. To give you that in context
— you'd need to line up **43 million iron atoms** side by side to give you a line **1 millimetre** long.
And if you think that's small…

1)   Although the **proton** and **neutron** are **2000 times** more **massive** than the **electron**, the nucleus
      only takes up a **tiny proportion** of the atom. The electrons orbit at relatively **vast distances**.

2)   The nucleus is only one **10 000th the size** of the whole atom — most of the atom is **empty space**.

3)   If we were to **shrink** the **solar system** so the **Sun** was the **size of a gold nucleus**, its furthest
      planet **Pluto** would only be **half as far** away as **gold's furthest electron**.

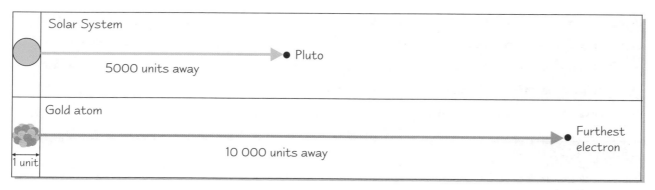

Solar System

● Pluto

5000 units away

Gold atom

1 unit

10 000 units away

● Furthest electron

ow, my head hurts

Atomic Structure

The **Proton Number** is the **Number** of **Protons** in the Nucleus   No... really.

The **proton number** is sometimes called the **atomic number**, and has the **symbol Z** (I'm sure it makes sense to someone). **Z** is just the **number of protons** in the nucleus.

It's the **proton number** that **defines** the element — **no two elements** will have the **same** number of protons.

In a **neutral atom**, the number of **electrons equals** the number of **protons**.
The element's **reactions** and **chemical behaviour** depend on the number of **electrons**.
So the **proton number** tells you a lot about its **chemical properties**.

The **Nucleon Number** is the **Total Number** of Protons and Neutrons

The **nucleon number** is also called the **mass number**, and has the **symbol A** (*shrug*).
It tells you how many **protons** and **neutrons** are in the nucleus. Since each **proton or neutron** has a **mass** of (approximately) **1** and the electrons weigh virtually nothing, the **number** of **nucleons** is the same as the **atom's mass**.

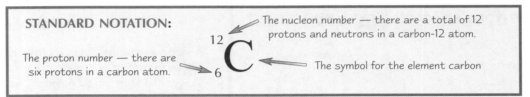

STANDARD NOTATION:

The nucleon number — there are a total of 12 protons and neutrons in a carbon-12 atom.

The proton number — there are six protons in a carbon atom.

$${}^{12}_{6}C$$

The symbol for the element carbon

Isotopes have the **Same Proton Number**, but **Different Nucleon Numbers**

Atoms with the **same number of protons** but **different numbers of neutrons** are called **isotopes**.

Example: Hydrogen has three isotopes — hydrogen, deuterium and tritium

Hydrogen has 1 proton and 0 neutrons.
Deuterium has 1 proton and 1 neutron.
Tritium has 1 proton and 2 neutrons.

Changing the number of **neutrons doesn't affect** the atom's **chemical** properties.

The **number of neutrons** affects the **stability** of the nucleus though.

In **general**, the **greater** the number of **neutrons** compared with the number of **protons**, the **more unstable** the nucleus.

Unstable nuclei may be **radioactive** (see p94).

Practice Questions

Q1   List the particles that make up the atom and give their charges and relative masses.

Q2   Define the proton number and nucleon number.

Q3   What is an isotope?

Exam Questions

Q1   Describe the nuclear model of the atom.   [3 marks]

Q2   Given the element oxygen: ${}^{16}_{8}O$
How many protons, neutrons and electrons are there in the neutral atom?   [2 marks]

Q3   Define the term 'isotope'. Describe the similarities and differences between the properties of two isotopes of the same element.   [3 marks]

"Proton no. = no. of protons" — not exactly nuclear physics is it... oh wait...

I dunno, I just can't get my head round that size of a nucleus stuff — it's just mindblowing. I have enough trouble imagining this huge Solar System, never mind something so small that, by rights, shouldn't even exist. It's like trying to imagine infinity or something. Still... in true Physicist fashion, I don't let that bother me — I just learn the powers of 10 and everything's OK.

Scattering to Determine Structure

These pages cover the history of the atom during the last century — from Thomson's plum pudding to Rutherford's nuclear model to protons and neutrons to up quarks and down quarks.

The **Thomson Model** was Popular in the **19th Century**

Until the early 20th century, physicists believed that the atom was a **positively charged globule** with **negatively charged electrons sprinkled** in it. This "**plum pudding**" model of the atom was known as the **Thomson Model**. This all changed in 1909 when the **Rutherford scattering experiment** was done.

In Rutherford's laboratory, **Hans Geiger** and **Ernest Marsden** studied the scattering of **alpha particles** by **thin metal foils**.

Rutherford's Experiment **Disproved** the **Thomson Model**

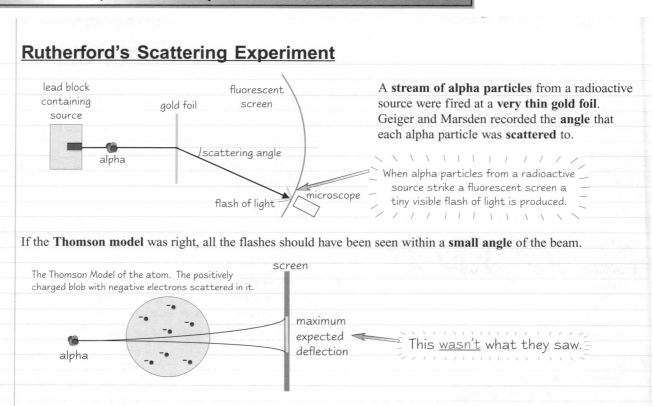

Rutherford's Scattering Experiment

A **stream of alpha particles** from a radioactive source were fired at a **very thin gold foil**. Geiger and Marsden recorded the **angle** that each alpha particle was **scattered** to.

When alpha particles from a radioactive source strike a fluorescent screen a tiny visible flash of light is produced.

If the **Thomson model** was right, all the flashes should have been seen within a **small angle** of the beam.

The Thomson Model of the atom. The positively charged blob with negative electrons scattered in it.

This wasn't what they saw.

Geiger and Marsden observed that alpha particles occasionally **scatter at angles greater than 90°**. This can only be possible if they're **striking something more massive** than themselves.

Rutherford's **Model** of the **Atom** — **The Nuclear Model**

This experiment led Rutherford to some **important conclusions**:

1)   Most of the **fast, charged alpha particles** went **straight though** the gold foil. Therefore the atom is **mostly empty space**.

2)   **Some** of the alpha particles are **deflected back** through **significant angles**, so the **centre** of the atom must be **tiny** but contain **a lot of mass**. Rutherford named this the **nucleus**.

3)   The **alpha particles** were **repelled**, so the **nucleus** must have **positive charge**.

4)   **Atoms** are **neutral overall** so the **electrons** must be on the outside of the atom — separating one atom from the next.

Scattering to Determine Structure

If you're doing AQA A, you can leave the rest of this and go to __p98__ — it's just for AQA B and Edexcel.

Deep Inelastic Scattering *Shows the* **Structure** *of the* **Nucleus**

The **electron**'s nearly **pin-point size** makes it an **excellent probe** of the **nucleus**.

In **'deep inelastic scattering'** experiments, **high energy electrons** are fired **into** the nucleus.

You don't need to know the **details** of these experiments, you just need to know the **findings**:

1) The fact that the electron **penetrates** the nucleus means the nucleus **can't be one particle**.

2) The electron is often **scattered** through **large angles**. This suggests that the electron is scattering off an **area** of **high charge** within the **nucleus** — the **proton**.

3) At **very high energy**, the nucleus **breaks apart**. You can then look at the bits it's made of...

Protons *and* Neutrons *Have* Deeper Structure

Now it's getting exciting...

If you fire extremely high-energy electrons at **protons** and **neutrons** they, in turn, show evidence of **internal structure**. The **electrons** are again **scattered** in **many directions**, showing that the nucleons contain **small, dense regions** of charge.

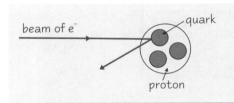

The **proton and neutron aren't fundamental particles**, but are composed of yet **smaller** constituents called **quarks** (see pages 102-103).

Fundamental particles can't be broken into smaller pieces.

The **internal structure** of the **proton** is believed to be **3 quarks**. (2 up and 1 down.)   (see pages 102-103)

The **internal structure** of the **neutron** is believed to be **3 quarks**. (2 down and 1 up.)

Practice Questions

Q1   Describe the Thomson model of the atom.

Q2   Describe the Rutherford Scattering experiment.

Q3   What does most of an atom consist of?

Q4   Is the proton a fundamental particle?

Exam Questions

Q1

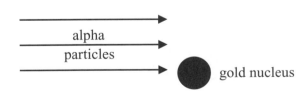

(a)   Complete the 3 paths of alpha particles meeting a gold nucleus.   [2 marks]

(b)   Give 3 properties of the nucleus that are demonstrated by this experiment.   [3 marks]

And lo — a quark was born...

Quarks are great. More about them later. You need to learn all the stuff about how physicists found out they existed. Yeah, OK, you know what the nuclear model looks like, but you still need to be able to explain in detail how they worked it out.

Radioactive Emissions

Some of this is revision from GCSE, but you need a few more details for AS level. As you'd expect.

Unstable Atoms Become Radioactive

If an atom is **unstable**, it will **break down** to **become** stable. This **instability** could be caused by having **too many neutrons**, **not enough neutrons**, or just **too much energy** in the nucleus.

The atom **decays** by **releasing energy** and/or **particles**, until it reaches a **stable form**.

This is called **radioactive decay**.

Radioactivity is **random** — it can't be predicted (see p96).

There are Four Types of Nuclear Radiation

Particle	Symbol	Constituent	Charge	Mass
Alpha	α	A helium nucleus — 2 protons & 2 neutrons	+2	4
Beta-minus (Beta)	β or β^-	Electron	-1	(negligible)
Beta-plus	β^+	Positron	+1	(negligible)
Gamma	γ	Short-wave, high-frequency electromagnetic wave.	0	0

Learn this table.

The Different Types of Radiation have Different Penetrations

When a radioactive particle **hits** an **atom** it can **knock off** the **outer electrons**, creating an **ion** — so, radioactive emissions are also known as **ionising radiation**.

Alpha, **beta** and **gamma** particles can be **fired** at a **variety of objects** with **detectors** placed the **other side** to see whether they **penetrate** the object.

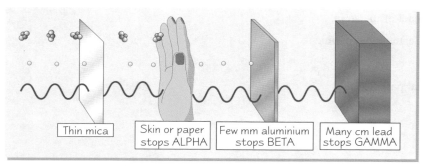

Thin mica | Skin or paper stops ALPHA | Few mm aluminium stops BETA | Many cm lead stops GAMMA

Particle	Symbol	Ionising	Speed	Penetrating power	Affected by magnetic field
Alpha	α	Strongly	Slow	Absorbed by paper or a few cm of air	Yes
Beta-minus (Beta)	β or β^-	Weakly	Fast	Absorbed by ~3 mm of aluminium	Yes
Beta-plus	β^+	Annihilated by electron — so zero range			
Gamma	γ	Very weakly	Speed of light	Absorbed by many cm of lead, or several m of concrete.	No

You've got to learn this table as well.

Radioactive Emissions

Alpha and Beta Particles have Different Ionising Properties

1) **Alpha** particles are **strongly positive** — so they can **easily pull electrons** off atoms.

2) Ionising atoms **transfers** some of the **energy** from the **alpha particle** to the **atom**. The alpha particle **quickly ionises** many atoms (10 000 ionisations per alpha particle) and **loses** all its **energy**.

3) That's why it has **low penetration** of **matter**.

4) Alpha's **strong ionisation** makes it **dangerous**. If you **breathe it in**, it can **damage** your lung tissue.

5) The **beta**-minus particle has **lower charge** than the alpha particle, but a **higher speed**. That means it can still **knock electrons** off atoms. Each **beta** particle will ionise about 100 atoms, **losing energy** at each interaction.

6) This **lower interaction** rate with matter means that it has **better penetration** than the alpha particle, and is less dangerous inside the body.

The Intensity of Gamma Radiation Obeys the Inverse Square Law

As gamma radiation **spreads out** from its **source**, its **intensity decreases** by the **square of the distance** from the source.

$$I \propto \frac{1}{d^2}$$

We're Surrounded by Background Radiation

Put a Geiger-Müller tube **anywhere** and the counter will click — it's detecting **background radiation**.

When you take a **reading** from a radioactive source, you need to **measure** the **background radiation** first and **subtract** it from your **measurement**.

There are Many Sources of Background Radiation

1) **Food:** All our food contains **carbon**, and some of this will be the radioactive **carbon-14**.

2) **The air:** Radioactive **radon gas** is released from **rocks**. It emits alpha radiation.

3) **The ground and buildings: All rock** contains radioactive isotopes.

4) **Cosmic radiation:** From **space**, mostly from the **sun**.

5) **Man-made radiation:** Radiation from **medical** or **industrial** sources — most of this is from medical **X-rays**.

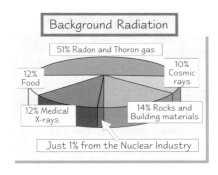

Background Radiation

51% Radon and Thoron gas
10% Cosmic rays
12% Food
12% Medical X-rays
14% Rocks and Building materials
Just 1% from the Nuclear Industry

Practice Questions

Q1   What makes an atom radioactive?

Q2   Name three types of nuclear radiation and give three properties of each.

Q3   Name 5 sources of background radiation.

Exam Questions

Q1   Draw a diagram showing the relative penetration of alpha, beta and gamma radiation.   [4 marks]

Q2   Explain the relative penetrations of alpha and beta radiation.   [3 marks]

Q3   Give the symbols and describe the constituents of alpha, beta and gamma radiation.   [3 marks]

Make the most of this — it gets much harder...

Whereas the average Joe on the street just thinks "woahh, radiation... dangerous innit..." the dedicated Physics AS student has more of an informed opinion. The dedicated Physics AS student will know how radiation occurs, exactly how dangerous it is, where it comes from, how to stop it, what it's used for and how many marks they'll get on it in the Exam.

Nuclear Decay

*Radioactive materials don't all do the same thing. And there's a whole load of **exciting facts to learn** about that,
girls and boys. Urgh. Sorry. I can't pretend, you'd just see straight through me. Just learn it, OK, it's not that bad.*

Some Nuclei are **More Stable** than Others

The nucleus is under the **influence** of the **two** most **powerful forces**
known to man* — the **strong nuclear force holding** it **together** and
the **electromagnetic force** trying to **push** the **protons apart**.

It's a very **delicate balance**, and it's easy
for a nucleus to become **unstable**.

> A nucleus will be **unstable** if it has:
>
> 1) **too many neutrons**
>
> 2) **too few neutrons**
>
> 3) **too many nucleons** altogether,
>   i.e. it's **too heavy**
>
> 4) **too much energy**

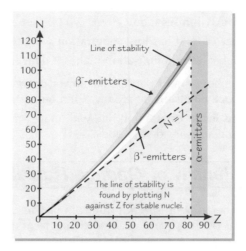

α Emission Happens in **Heavy Nuclei**

1) **Alpha emission** only happens in **very heavy** atoms
   (with more than 82 protons), like **uranium** and **radium**.

2) The **nuclei** of these atoms are **too massive** to be stable.

3) When an alpha particle is **emitted**:

> The **proton number decreases** by **two**,
> and the **nucleon number decreases** by **four**.

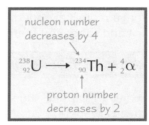

nucleon number
decreases by 4

$$^{238}_{92}U \longrightarrow {}^{234}_{90}Th + {}^4_2\alpha$$

proton number
decreases by 2

β⁻ Emission Happens in **Neutron Rich** Nuclei

1) **Beta-minus** (usually just called beta) decay is the emission
   of an **electron** from the **nucleus** along with an **antineutrino**.

2) Beta decay happens in isotopes that are **"neutron rich"** (i.e. have many
   more **neutrons** than **protons** in their nucleus). When a nucleus ejects a
   beta particle, one of the **neutrons** in the nucleus is **changed** into a **proton**.

> The **proton number increases** by **one**,
> and the **nucleon number stays the same**.

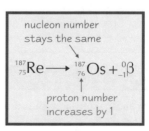

nucleon number
stays the same

$$^{187}_{75}Re \longrightarrow {}^{187}_{76}Os + {}^{\ 0}_{-1}\beta$$

proton number
increases by 1

3) In **beta-plus emission**, a **proton** gets **changed** into a **neutron**. The **proton
   number decreases** by **one**, and the **nucleon number stays the same**.

γ Radiation is Emitted from **Nuclei** with **Too Much Energy**

1) **After alpha** or **beta** decay, the **nucleus** often has **excess energy**.
   This energy is **lost** by emitting a **gamma ray**.

2) Remember that **most alpha** and **beta** emitters **also** emit **gamma** rays as part of their decay process.

3) You **never** get **just gamma** rays emitted.

> During **gamma emission**, there is **no change** to the nuclear **constituents**, the nucleus just **loses excess energy**.

* Except for the governor of California

Nuclear Decay

There are **Conservation Rules** in **Nuclear Reactions**

In every nuclear reaction **energy**, **momentum**, **proton number** and **nucleon number** must be conserved.

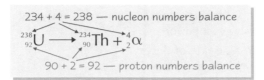

234 + 4 = 238 — nucleon numbers balance

$$^{238}_{92}U \longrightarrow \, ^{234}_{90}Th + ^{4}_{2}\alpha$$

90 + 2 = 92 — proton numbers balance

Mass *is* **Not Conserved**

1) The **mass** of the **alpha particle** is less than the **individual masses** of **two protons** and **two neutrons**. This is called the **mass defect**.

2) Mass **doesn't** have to be **conserved** because of **Einstein's equation**:

$$E = mc^2$$

3) This says that **mass and energy** are **equivalent**. The **energy released** when the nucleons **bonded together** accounts for the missing mass.

Okay, this is getting really hard now. Do your best to get your head round it, then just learn it.

The **Antineutrino Conserves Energy** in **Beta** Decay

You don't need this bit unless you're doing AQA B.

1) When a particle **decays**, the **energy emitted** is **equal** to the **energy equivalent** of the **mass defect** — that's just **conservation of energy**.

2) Because of this, **alpha particles** emitted from a **pure alpha source** (i.e. one that doesn't emit beta or gamma) **all** carry the **same amount of energy**.

3) You would **expect** the **same thing** from a **pure beta source**.

4) No such luck... the **energy** of beta particles **varies continuously** from **zero** up to the **predicted value**.

5) The **rest of the energy** must be **carried off** by **another neutral particle** — called the **antineutrino**.

Practice Questions

Q1 What makes a nucleus unstable?

Q2 Describe the changes that happen in the nucleus during alpha, beta and gamma decay.

Q3 Explain the circumstances in which gamma radiation may be emitted.

Q4 Define the mass defect.

Exam Questions

Q1

(a) Radium undergoes alpha decay to radon — complete a balanced nuclear equation for this reaction.　　　[3 marks]

$$^{226}_{88}Ra \longrightarrow \, Rn +$$

(b) Potassium (Z = 19, A = 40) undergoes beta decay to calcium.
Write a balanced nuclear equation for this reaction.　　　[3 marks]

Q2 Describe in terms of the energy carried by the particles how beta decay differs from alpha.　　　[5 marks]

The antineutrino conserves energy, don't you know — riveting stuff...

Learn what causes each type of radioactive decay and all the picky little details that go with each one... blah blah... conservation rules... blah blah... mass not conserved... blah blah... antineut.......

Activity and Half Life

Oooh look — some maths. Good.

Every Isotope Decays at a Different Rate

1) **Radioactive decay** is completely **random**. You **can't predict which** atom will decay **when**.

2) Although you can't predict the decay of an **individual atom**, if you take a **very large number of atoms**, their **overall behaviour** shows a **pattern**.

3) Any sample of a particular **isotope** has the **same rate of decay**, i.e. the same **proportion** of atoms will **decay** in a **given time**.

It could be you.

The Rate of Decay is Measured by the Decay Constant

The **activity** of a sample — the **number** of atoms that **decay each second** — is **proportional** to the **size of the sample**. For a **given isotope**, a sample **twice** as big would give **twice** the **number of decays** per second.

The **decay constant** (λ) measures how **quickly** something will **decay** — the **bigger** the value of λ, the faster the rate of decay. Its unit is s^{-1}.

Activity = Decay Constant × Number of atoms

Or in symbols: $A = \lambda N$ ◄— *Don't get λ confused with wavelength.*

Activity is measured in **becquerels** (Bq):

1 Bq = 1 decay per second (s^{-1})

You Need to Learn the Definition of Half-Life

The **half-life** ($T_{\frac{1}{2}}$) of an **element** is the **average time** it takes for the **number of undecayed atoms** to **halve**.

Measuring the **number of undecayed atoms** isn't the easiest job in the world. **In practice**, half-life isn't measured by counting atoms, but by measuring the **time it takes** the **activity** to **halve**.

The **longer** the **half-life** of an isotope, the **longer** it stays **radioactive**.

The Number of Undecayed Particles Decreases Exponentially

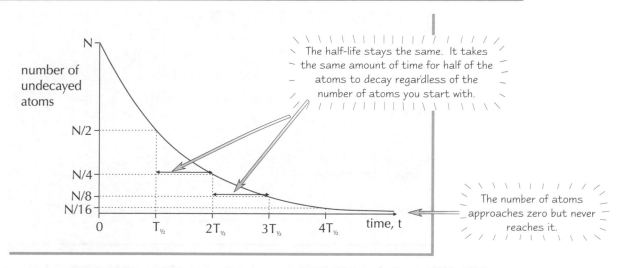

The half-life stays the same. It takes the same amount of time for half of the atoms to decay regardless of the number of atoms you start with.

The number of atoms approaches zero but never reaches it.

You'd be **more likely** to actually meet a **count rate-time graph** or an **activity-time graph**. They're both **exactly the same shape** as the graph above, but with different **y-axes**.

Activity and Half Life

You can *Find* the *Half-Life* of an *Isotope* from the *Graph*

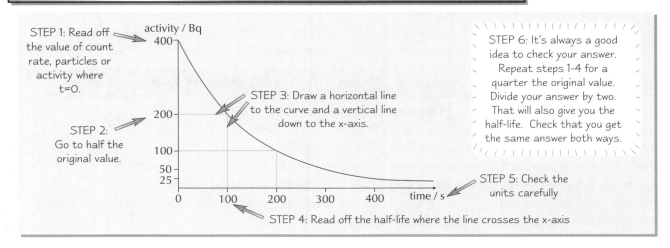

STEP 1: Read off the value of count rate, particles or activity where t=0.

STEP 2: Go to half the original value.

STEP 3: Draw a horizontal line to the curve and a vertical line down to the x-axis.

STEP 6: It's always a good idea to check your answer. Repeat steps 1-4 for a quarter the original value. Divide your answer by two. That will also give you the half-life. Check that you get the same answer both ways.

STEP 5: Check the units carefully

STEP 4: Read off the half-life where the line crosses the x-axis

You Need to *Take Background Radiation* into *Account*

When you're **measuring** the **activity** and **half-life** of a **source**, you've got to **remember background radiation**. The **background radiation** needs to be **subtracted** from the **activity readings** to give the **source activity**.

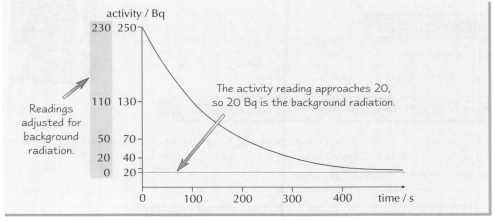

Readings adjusted for background radiation.

The activity reading approaches 20, so 20 Bq is the background radiation.

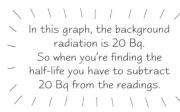

In this graph, the background radiation is 20 Bq. So when you're finding the half-life you have to subtract 20 Bq from the readings.

Practice Questions

Q1 Give the units of radioactive activity and the decay constant.

Q2 Sketch a general particle number-time decay graph.

Q3 Define half-life.

Exam Questions

Q1 (a) You take a reading of 750 Bq from a source. (Background activity in your lab is 50Bq.)
Given the number of atoms in your sample is 50 000, calculate the decay constant for your sample. [3 marks]

(b) In a second experiment in the same lab, you are given a different sample with a decay constant of 0.03 per second and measure the activity at 400 Bq. Calculate the number of atoms in the sample. [3 marks]

Radioactivity is a random process — just like revision shouldn't be...

Remember that shape of graph — whether it's count rate, activity or number of atoms plotted against time, the shape's always the same. This is all pretty straightforward mathsy-type stuff: plugging values in equations, reading off graphs, etc. Not very interesting, though. Ah well, once you get onto quantum physics you'll be longing for a bit of boredom.

Classification of Particles

The rest of this section's just for AQA A and B. If you're doing an Edexcel course, move directly to the bottom of p113.

There are loads of different types of particle, as well as the ones you get in normal matter (protons, neutrons, etc.). They only appear in cosmic rays and in particle accelerators, and they often decay very quickly so they're difficult to get a handle on. Nonetheless, you need to learn about a load of them and what their properties are.

You probably won't understand this (I don't) — but you only need to learn it. Stick with it — you'll get there.

Hadrons are Particles that Feel the Strong Interaction (e.g. Protons and Neutrons)

1) The **nucleus** of an atom is made up from **protons** and **neutrons** (déjà vu).

2) Since the **protons** are **positively charged** you might think that the nucleus would **fly apart** with all that repulsion — there has to be a strong **force** holding the **p**'s and **n**'s together.

3) That force is called the **strong interaction** (who said physicists lack imagination...)

4) **Not all particles** can **feel** the **strong interaction** — the ones that **can** are called **hadrons**.

(Leptons are an example of particles that <u>can't</u>. See p99.)

5) Hadrons aren't **fundamental** particles. They're made up of **smaller particles** called **quarks** (see pages 102-103).

6) There are **two** types of **hadron** — **baryons** and **mesons**.

Protons and Neutrons are Baryons

1) It's helpful to think of **protons** and **neutrons** as **two versions** of the **same particle** — the **nucleon**. They just have **different electric charges**.

2) As well as **protons** and **neutrons**, there are **other baryons** that you don't get in normal matter — like **sigmas** (Σ) — they're **short-lived** and you **don't** need to **know about them** for AS (woohoo!).

The Proton is the Only Stable Baryon

All baryons except protons decay to a **proton**.
Most physicists think that protons don't **decay**.

<u>Some theories</u> predict that protons <u>should</u> decay with a <u>very long half-life</u> but there's <u>no evidence</u> for it at the moment.

Baryon and Meson felt the strong interaction.

The Number of Baryons in a reaction is called the Baryon Number

Baryon number is the number of baryons. (A bit like **nucleon number** but including unusual baryons like Σ too.)
The **proton** and the **neutron** each have a baryon number **B = +1**.
The **total baryon number** in **any** particle reaction **never changes**.

The Mesons You Need to Know About are Pions and Kaons

1) **All mesons** are **unstable** and have **baryon number B = 0** (because they're not baryons).

2) **Pions** (π-mesons) are the **lightest mesons**. You get **three versions** with different **electric charges** — π^+, π^0 and π^-. Pions were **discovered** in **cosmic rays**. You get **loads** of them in **high energy particle collisions** like those studied at the **CERN** particle accelerator.

3) **Kaons** (K-mesons) are **heavier** and more **unstable** than **pions**. You get different ones like **K^+** and **K^0**.

4) Mesons **interact** with **baryons** via the **strong force**.

Pion interactions swap p's with n's and n's with p's, but leave the overall baryon number unchanged.

Summary of Hadron Properties

DON'T PANIC if you don't understand

all this yet. For now, just **learn** these properties.
You'll need to work through to the end of page 103
to see how it **all fits in**.

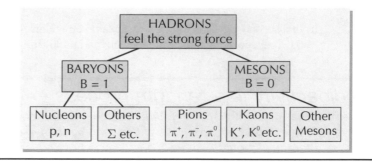

Classification of Particles

Leptons Don't feel the Strong Interaction (e.g. Electrons and Neutrinos)

1) **Leptons** are **fundamental particles** and they **don't** feel the **strong interaction**. The only way they can **interact** with other particles is via the **weak interaction** (and the electromagnetic force as well if they're charged).

2) **Electrons** (e⁻) are **stable** and very **familiar** but — you guessed it — there are also **two more leptons** called the **muon** (μ^-) and the **tau** (τ^-) that are just like **heavy electrons**.

3) **Muons** and **taus** are **unstable**, and **decay** eventually into **ordinary electrons**.

4) The **electron**, **muon** and **tau** leptons each come with their **own neutrino**, ν_e, ν_μ and ν_τ.

5) **Neutrinos** have **zero** or **almost zero mass** and **zero electric charge** — so they don't do much. **Neutrinos** only take part in **weak interactions** (see p103). In fact, a neutrino can **pass right through the Earth** without **anything** happening to it.

You Have to Count the Three Types of Lepton Separately

Each lepton is given a **lepton number** of **+1**, but the **electron**, **muon** and **tau** types of lepton have to be **counted separately**.

You get **three different** lepton numbers L_e, L_μ and L_τ.

Like the baryon number, the lepton number is just the number of leptons.

Name	Symbol	Charge	L_e	L_μ	L_τ
electron	e⁻	−1	+1	0	0
electron-neutrino	ν_e	0	+1	0	0
muon	μ^-	−1	0	+1	0
muon-neutrino	ν_μ	0	0	+1	0
tau	τ^-	−1	0	0	+1
tau-neutrino	ν_τ	0	0	0	+1

Neutrons Decay into Protons

The **neutron** is an **unstable particle** that **decays** into a **proton**.
It's really just an **example** of β^- decay which is caused by the **weak interaction**.

$$n \rightarrow p + e^- + \bar{\nu}_e$$

The antineutrino has $L_e = -1$ so the total lepton number is zero. Antineutrino? Yes, well I haven't mentioned antiparticles yet. Just wait for the next page ...

Practice Questions

Q1 List the differences between a hadron and a lepton.

Q2 Which is the only stable baryon?

Q3 A particle collision at CERN produces 2 protons, 3 pions and 1 neutron. What is the total baryon number of these particles?

Q4 Which two particles have lepton number $L_\tau = +1$?

Exam Questions

Q1 List all the decay products of the neutron. Explain why this decay cannot be due to the strong interaction. [3 marks]

Q2 Initially, the muon was incorrectly identified as a meson. Explain why the muon is not a meson. [3 marks]

Go back to the top of page 98 — do not pass GO, do not collect £200...

Do it. Go back and read it again. I promise — read these pages about 3 or 4 times and you'll start to see a pattern. There are hadrons that feel the force, leptons that don't. Hadrons are either baryons or mesons, and they're all weird except for those well-known baryons: protons and neutrons. There are loads of leptons, including good old electrons.

Antiparticles

This is becoming more like sci-fi by the minute. "Beam me up Scottie." "I cannae do that Cap'n — their electron-antineutrino ray gun's interfering with my antineutron positron reading. I'm afraid the ship's gonna blow..."

Antiparticles were Predicted Before they were Discovered

When **Paul Dirac** wrote down an equation obeyed by **electrons**, he found a kind of **mirror image** solution.

1) It predicted the existence of a particle like the **electron** but with **opposite electric charge**.

2) The **positron** turned up later in a cosmic ray experiment. Positrons are **antileptons** so $L_e = -1$ for them. They have **identical mass** to electrons but they carry a **positive** charge.

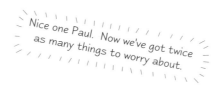
Nice one Paul. Now we've got twice as many things to worry about.

Every Particle has an Antiparticle

Each particle type has a **corresponding antiparticle** with the **same mass** but with **opposite charge**. For instance, an **antiproton** is a **negatively-charged** particle with the same mass as the **proton**.

Even the shadowy **neutrino** has an antiparticle version called the **antineutrino** — it doesn't do much either.

Particle	Symbol	Charge	B	L_e	Antiparticle	Symbol	Charge	B	L_e
proton	p	+1	+1	0	antiproton	$\bar{p}$	−1	−1	0
neutron	n	0	+1	0	antineutron	$\bar{n}$	0	−1	0
electron	e	−1	0	+1	positron	e^+	+1	0	−1
electron-neutrino	ν_e	0	0	+1	electron-antineutrino	$\bar{\nu}_e$	0	0	−1

You can Create Matter and Antimatter from Energy

You've probably heard about the **equivalence** of energy and mass. It all comes out of Einstein's Special Theory of Relativity. **Energy** can turn into **mass** and **mass** can turn into **energy** if you know how. You can work it all out using the formula $E = mc^2$ but you won't be expected to do the calculations for AS.

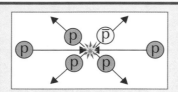

It's a good thing this doesn't randomly happen all the time or else you could end up with cute bunny rabbits popping up and exploding unexpectedly all over the place.
Oh, the horror...

As you've probably guessed, there's a bit **more to it** than that:

> When **energy** is converted into **mass** you have to make **equal amounts** of **matter** and **antimatter**.

Fire **two protons** at each other at high speed and you'll end up with a lot of **energy** at the point of impact. This energy can be used to make **more particles**.

If you create an extra **proton** you have to create an **antiproton** to go with it. It's called **pair production**.

Antiparticles

Each **Particle-Antiparticle Pair** is Produced from a **Single Photon**

Pair production only happens if **one gamma ray photon** has enough energy to produce that much mass. It also tends to happen near a **nucleus**, which helps conserve momentum.

You usually get **electron-positron** pairs produced (rather than any other pair) — because they have a relatively **low mass**.

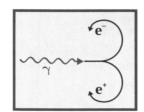

The particle tracks are curved because there's usually a magnetic field present in particle physics experiments (see p 104). They curve in opposite directions because of the opposite charges on the electron and positron.

The **Opposite** of **Pair-Production** is **Annihilation**

When a **particle** meets its **antiparticle** the result is **annihilation**. All the **mass** of the particle and antiparticle gets converted back to **energy**. Antiparticles can only exist for a fraction of a second before this happens, so you don't get them in ordinary matter.

The electron and positron annihilate and their mass is converted into the energy of a pair of gamma ray photons.

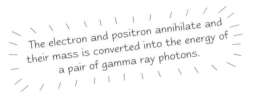

OR

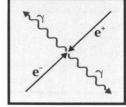

Mesons are Their **Own Antiparticles**   (If you don't know what a meson is, look back at page 98.)

Just before you leave this bit it's worth mentioning that the π^- meson is just the **antiparticle** of the π^+ meson, and the **antiparticle** of a π^0 meson is **itself**. You'll see why on p102. So we don't need any more particles here.....Phew.

Practice Questions

Q1   Which antiparticle has zero charge and a baryon number of –1?

Q2   Describe the properties of an electron-antineutrino.

Q3   What is pair production?

Q4   What happens when a proton collides with an antiproton?

Exam Questions

Q1   Write down an equation for the reaction between a positron and an electron
      and give the name for this type of reaction.   [2 marks]

Q2   According to Einstein, mass and energy are equivalent.
      Explain why the mass of a block of iron cannot be converted directly into energy.   [2 marks]

Q3   Give a reason why the reaction: $p + p \rightarrow p + p + n$ is not possible.   [1 mark]

This really is Physics at its ~~hardest~~ grooviest...

Inertial dampers are off-line Captain.........oops, no — it's just these false ears making me feel dizzy.
Anyway — you'd need to carry an awful lot of antimatter to provide enough energy to run a spaceship.
It's not easy to store, either. So it'd never work in real life.

Quarks

*If you haven't read pages 98 to 101, do it now! For the rest of you — here are the **juicy bits** you've been waiting for. Particle physics makes **a lot more sense** when you look at quarks. More sense than it did before anyway.*

Quarks are Fundamental Particles

If that first sentence doesn't make much sense to you, read pages 98-101 — you have been warned... twice.

Quarks are the **building blocks** for **hadrons** (baryons and mesons).

1) To make **protons** and **neutrons** you only need two types of quark — the **up** quark (**u**) and the **down** quark (**d**).

2) An extra one called the **strange** quark (**s**) lets you make more particles with a property called **strangeness**.

Antiparticles are made from **antiquarks**.

Particle physicists have found six different quarks altogether but you only need to know about three of them.

Quarks and Antiquarks have Opposite Properties

The **antiquarks** have **opposite properties** to the quarks — as you'd expect.

QUARKS

name	symbol	charge	baryon number	strangeness
up	u	$+\frac{2}{3}$	$+\frac{1}{3}$	0
down	d	$-\frac{1}{3}$	$+\frac{1}{3}$	0
strange	s	$-\frac{1}{3}$	$+\frac{1}{3}$	-1

ANTIQUARKS

name	symbol	charge	baryon number	strangeness
anti-up	$\bar{u}$	$-\frac{2}{3}$	$-\frac{1}{3}$	0
anti-down	$\bar{d}$	$+\frac{1}{3}$	$-\frac{1}{3}$	0
anti-strange	$\bar{s}$	$+\frac{1}{3}$	$-\frac{1}{3}$	$+1$

Baryons are Made from Three Quarks

Evidence for quarks came from **hitting protons** with **high energy electrons** (see page 91).
The way the **electrons scattered** showed that there were **three concentrations of charge** (quarks) **inside** the proton.

Proton = **uud**

Total charge
= 2/3 + 2/3 − 1/3 = 1
Baryon number
= 1/3 + 1/3 + 1/3 = 1

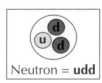

Neutron = **udd**

Total charge
= 2/3 − 1/3 − 1/3 = 0
Baryon number
= 1/3 + 1/3 + 1/3 = 1

Antiprotons are **u̅u̅d** and antineutrons are **u̅d̅d** — so no surprises there then.

Mesons are a Quark and an Antiquark

Pions are just made from **up** and **down** quarks and their **antiquarks**. **Kaons** have **strangeness** so you need to put in **s** quarks as well (remember that the **s** quark has a strangeness of S = −1).

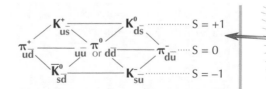

$$K^+_{us} \quad\quad K^0_{d\bar{s}} \quad\quad\quad S = +1$$
$$\pi^+_{u\bar{d}} \quad \pi^0_{u\bar{u}\ or\ d\bar{d}} \quad \pi^-_{d\bar{u}} \quad\quad S = 0$$
$$\bar{K}^0_{s\bar{d}} \quad\quad K^-_{s\bar{u}} \quad\quad\quad S = -1$$

Physicists love patterns. Gaps in patterns like this predicted the existence of particles that were actually found later in experiments. Great stuff.

There's no Such Thing as a Free Quark

What if you **blasted** a **proton** with **enough energy** — could you **separate out** the quarks? Nope.
Your energy just gets changed into more **quarks and antiquarks** — it's **pair production** again and you just make **mesons**. This is called **quark confinement**.

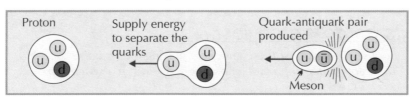

Proton

Supply energy to separate the quarks

Quark-antiquark pair produced

Meson

Quarks

The **Weak Interaction** is something that Changes the **Quark Type**

In β⁻ decay a **neutron** is changed into a **proton** — in other words **udd** changes into **uud**.
It means turning a **d** quark into a **u** quark. Only the weak interaction can do this.

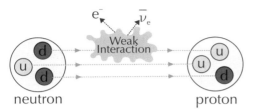

neutron → proton

Some unstable isotopes like **carbon-11** decay by β⁺ emission. In this case a **proton** changes to a **neutron**, so a **u** quark changes to a **d** quark and we get:

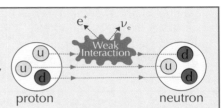

proton → neutron

Four Properties are **Conserved** in **Particle Reactions**

Charge and **Baryon Number** are **Always** Conserved

In **any** particle reaction, the **total charge** after the reaction must equal the total charge before the reaction. The same goes for **baryon number**.

Strangeness is Conserved in **Strong Interactions**

The **only** way to change the **type** of quark is with the **weak interaction**, so in strong interactions there has to be the same number of strange quarks at the beginning as at the end. The reaction $K^- + p \rightarrow n + \pi^0$ is fine for **charge** and **baryon number** but not for **strangeness** — so it won't happen. The negative kaon has an **s** quark in it.

Conservation of **Lepton Number** is a Bit More **Complicated**

The **three types** of lepton number have to be conserved **separately**.

1) For example, the reaction
    $\pi^- \rightarrow \mu^- + \bar{\nu}_\mu$ has $L_\mu = 0$ at the start and $L_\mu = 1 - 1 = 0$ at the end, so it's OK.

2) On the other hand, the reaction $\nu_\mu + \mu^- \rightarrow e^- + \nu_e$ can't happen.
    At the start $L_\mu = 2$ and $L_e = 0$ but at the end $L_\mu = 0$ and $L_e = 2$.

Practice Questions

Q1   What is a quark?

Q2   Which type of particle is made from a quark and an antiquark?

Q3   Describe how a neutron is made up from quarks.

Q4   List four quantities that are conserved in particle reactions.

Exam Questions

Q1   Give the quark composition of the π⁻ and explain how the charges of the quarks give rise to its charge.   [2 marks]

Q2   Explain how the quark composition is changed in the β⁻ decay of the neutron.   [2 marks]

Q3   Give two reasons why the reaction **p + p → p + K⁺** does not happen.   [2 marks]

A physical property called strangeness — how cool is that...

*True, there's a lot of information here, but this page really does **tie up** a lot of the stuff on the last few pages. Learn as much as you can from this double-page spread, then **go back** to page 98, and **work back** through to here. **Don't expect** to understand it all — but you will **definitely** find it **much easier to learn** when you can see how all the bits **fit in together**.*

Detecting Particles

These pages are AQA B only.

I know what you did last summer — you left a trail of ions for everyone to follow.

Charged Particles Leave Tracks

When a charged particle passes through a substance it causes **ionisation** — electrons are knocked out of atoms.
The particle leaves a **trail of ions** as it goes.

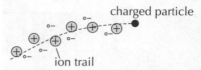

The easiest way to **detect** the particle is if you somehow make the **trail of ions show up** and then take a **photo**.

Cloud Chambers Work by Supercooling a Gas

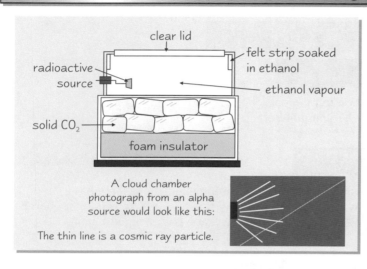

A cloud chamber photograph from an alpha source would look like this:

The thin line is a cosmic ray particle.

Cloud chambers work using a **supercooled vapour** — that's something that's still a gas below its condensation temperature. The ions left by particles make the vapour **condense** and you get "**vapour trails**" (a bit like the ones left by jet planes).

Only the **charged particles** show up.

A **magnetic field** makes the particles follow **curved tracks** — the larger the curve radius, the greater the particle's **momentum**. Positive and negative particles curve **opposite** ways — you can find out which is which using **Fleming's** left hand rule.

Cloud chambers are usually used to look at the products from **radioactive decay**:
Heavy, **short** tracks mean lots of ionisation, so those will be the α-**particles**. Fainter, **long** tracks are β-**particles**.

Bubble Chambers use a Superheated Liquid

Bubble chambers are a bit like cloud chambers in reverse. Hydrogen is kept as a **liquid** above its **boiling point** by putting it under **pressure**. If the pressure is suddenly **reduced**, **bubbles of gas** will start to form in the places where there is a trail of ions. You have to take the photo **quickly** before the bubbles grow too big.

Using **hydrogen** in a bubble chamber means you see collisions with **stationary proton targets** — hydrogen nuclei.

Neutral Particles Only Show up When They Decay

Remember that **neutral** particles **don't** make tracks.
You can only see them when they **decay**. If you see a **V**-shape starting in the middle of nowhere, it will be two oppositely charged particles from the decay of a neutral particle.

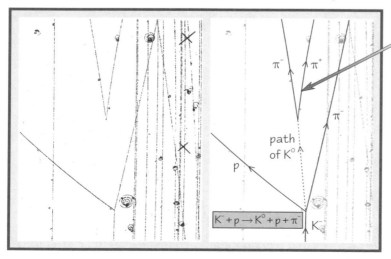

This V comes from the decay $K^0 \rightarrow \pi^+ + \pi^-$

The **distance** from the **interaction point** to the V depends on the **half-life** of the neutral particle. Longer-lived particles travel **further** before they decay — but you have to be careful.

The particles are travelling **close to the speed of light** so relativistic **time dilation** (aaarghhh — you'll do it next year) makes them survive for much longer than normal.

Here the particles have so much momentum that the tracks are almost straight.

Detecting Particles

Real Bubble Chamber Photographs can be a bit Intimidating

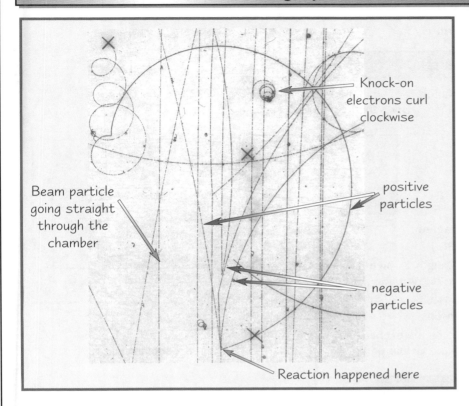

×

Knock-on electrons curl clockwise

Beam particle going straight through the chamber

positive particles

negative particles

Reaction happened here

At first sight the photo might look a bit of a mess with tracks everywhere. Don't panic — start by finding the incoming beam.

The **straight** lines are from the incoming beam. Several particles will go straight through without doing anything — you can just ignore them.

Look for a little spiral coming from one of the straight tracks. It shows a **knock-on electron** — an electron that's been kicked out of one of the hydrogen atoms. Knock-on electrons tell you **two** things — **which way** the particles are going and which way negative particles **curve**.

Here the particles are going **up** and **negative** ones curl **clockwise**.

Find a **point** with **several** curved tracks coming from it — that's a reaction. You can identify positively and negatively charged particles from the **way they curve**.

Cloud Chambers and Bubble Chambers aren't used any More

Nowadays, particle physicists use detectors that give out **electrical signals** that are sent **straight** to a **computer**. It's a bit easier than having a whole team of scientists squinting over thousands of photos. Modern detectors include **drift chambers**, **scintillation counters** and **solid state detectors**. You don't need to know any details about these for the exam.

Practice Questions

Q1 Describe how a cloud chamber works.

Q2 Explain the operation of a bubble chamber.

Q3 Which particles don't show up in bubble chamber photos?

Q4 How does the track of an electron show that the electron is losing energy?

Exam Questions

Q1 Explain how the charges of particles can be found from their tracks in bubble chamber photographs. [3 marks]

Q2 The reaction $p + p \rightarrow p + n + \pi^+ + \pi^0$ occurs in a bubble chamber.
Which tracks are formed by the products of this reaction? [1 mark]

Q3 A photon, travelling through a bubble chamber, is converted into an $e^- e^+$ pair.
Draw a sketch showing the tracks that would be formed by this reaction. [3 marks]

Look, there's one... ➞ ·

*Typical. They now have an easy way of detecting particles — but you have to learn the methods that are
a) harder, and b) now completely obsolete. *sigh* I suppose it's quite nice to actually see the pictures though.*

Exchange Particles and Feynman Diagrams

Here's a little pressie just for you AQA A lot — don't say I never give you anything.

*Having learnt about hadrons (baryons and mesons) and leptons, antiparticles and quarks, you now have the esteemed privilege of learning about yet another weirdy thing called a **gauge boson** (where did they get that name). To the casual observer this might not seem **entirely fair**. And I have to say, I'd be with them.*

Forces are Caused by Particle Exchange

You can't have **instantaneous action at a distance**. So, when two particles **interact**, something must **happen** to let one particle know that the other one's there. That's the idea behind **exchange particles**.

1) **Repulsion** — Each time the **ball** is **thrown or caught** the people get **pushed apart**. It happens because the ball carries **momentum**.

Particle exchange also explains **attraction** but you need a bit more imagination.

2) **Attraction** — Each time the **boomerang** is **thrown or caught** the people **get pushed together**. (In real life, you'd probably fall in first.)

←—REPULSION—→

→ATTRACTION←

These exchange particles are called **gauge bosons**.

The **repulsion** between two **protons** is caused by the **exchange** of **virtual photons** which are the gauge bosons of the **electromagnetic** force. Gauge bosons are **virtual** particles — they only exist for a **very short time**.

There are Four Fundamental Forces

All forces in nature are caused by these four **fundamental** forces.
Each one has its **own gauge boson** and you have to learn their names:

Type of Interaction	Gauge Boson	Particles Affected
strong	gluon	hadrons only
electromagnetic	photon (symbol, γ)	charged particles only
weak	W^+, W^-, Z^0	all types
gravity	graviton?	all types

Particle physicists never **bother** about **gravity** because it's so incredibly **feeble** compared with the other types of interaction. Gravity only really **matters** when you've got **big masses** like **stars and planets**.

The graviton **may** exist but there's **no evidence** for it.

The *Larger* the *Mass* of the *Gauge Boson*, the *Shorter* the *Range* of the *Force*

1) The **W bosons** have a **mass** of about **100 times that of a proton** so that gives the weak force a **very short range**. Creating a **virtual W particle** uses **so much energy** that they can only exist for a **very short time** and they **can't travel far**.

2) On the other hand, the **photon** has **zero mass** so that gives you a force with **infinite range**.

Feynman Diagrams Show What's *Going in* and What's *Coming Out*

Richard Feynman was a brilliant physicist who was famous for explaining complicated ideas in a fun way that actually made sense. He worked out a really **neat way** of **solving problems** by **drawing pictures** rather than doing **calculations**.

1) **Gauge bosons** are represented by **wiggly lines** (technical term).

2) **Particles** are represented by **straight lines**.

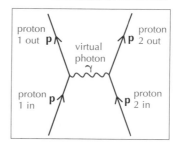

Exchange Particles and Feynman Diagrams

You can draw Feynman diagrams for **loads** of reactions but you **only** need to learn the ones on **this page** for your exam.

Beta-plus and Beta-minus Decay

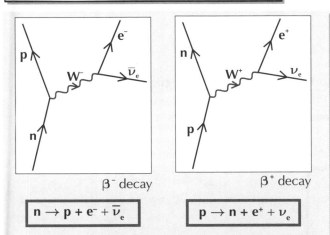

β^- decay β^+ decay

$$n \rightarrow p + e^- + \overline{\nu}_e$$ $$p \rightarrow n + e^+ + \nu_e$$

You get an **antineutrino** in β^- decay and a **neutrino** in β^+ decay so that **lepton number** is conserved.

RULES FOR DRAWING FEYNMAN DIAGRAMS:

1) **Incoming** particles start at the bottom of the diagram and move upwards.
2) The **baryons** stay on one side of the diagram, and the **leptons** stay on the other side.
3) The **W** bosons carry **charge** from one side of the diagram to the other — make sure charges balance.
4) A **W⁻** particle going to the **left** has the same effect as a **W⁺** particle going to the **right**.

A Proton Capturing an Electron

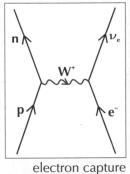

electron capture

Electrons and protons are of course attracted by the **electromagnetic interaction** between them, but if they **collide** the **weak interaction** can make this reaction happen.

$$p + e^- \rightarrow n + \nu_e$$

Neutrinos Interacting with Matter

There's a very **low probability** of a **neutrino interacting with matter**, but here's what happens when they do.

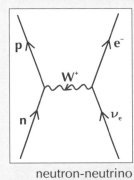
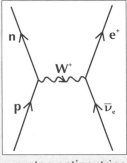

neutron-neutrino collision   proton-antineutrino collision

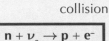

$$n + \nu_e \rightarrow p + e^-$$ $$p + \overline{\nu}_e \rightarrow n + e^+$$

Practice Questions

Q1   List the four fundamental forces in nature.

Q2   Explain what a virtual particle is.

Q3   Draw the Feynman diagram for a neutrino-neutron interaction.

Q4   Which gauge bosons are exchanged in weak interactions?

Exam Questions

Q1   How is the force of electromagnetic repulsion between two protons explained by particle exchange?   [2 marks]

Q2   Draw a Feynman diagram for the collision between an electron-antineutrino and a proton. Label the particles and state clearly which type of interaction is involved.   [3 marks]

I need a drink...

Urrrgghhhh... eyes... glazed... brain... melting... ears... bleeding... help me... help me...

help me...

The Photoelectric Effect

This double page is for AQA A and OCR only. If you're doing an Edexcel course, you don't need this section at all.
Quantum Theory doesn't really make much sense — to anyone. It works though, so it's hard to argue with.

Shining Light on a Metal can Release Electrons

If you shine **light** of a **high enough frequency** onto the **surface of a metal**,
it will **emit electrons**. For **most** metals, this **frequency** falls in the **U.V.** range.

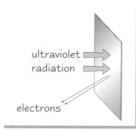
ultraviolet radiation
electrons

1) **Free electrons** on the **surface** of the metal **absorb energy** from the light, making them **vibrate**.

2) If an electron **absorbs enough** energy, the **bonds** holding it to the metal **break** and the electron is **released**.

3) This is called the **photoelectric effect** and the electrons emitted are called **photoelectrons**.

You don't need to know the details of any experiments on this, you just need to learn the three main conclusions:

Conclusion 1	For a given metal, **no photoelectrons are emitted** if the radiation has a frequency **below** a certain value — called the **threshold frequency**.
Conclusion 2	The photoelectrons are emitted with a variety of kinetic energies ranging from zero to some maximum value. This value of **maximum kinetic energy** increases with the **frequency** of the radiation, and is **unaffected** by the **intensity** of the radiation.
Conclusion 3	The **number** of photoelectrons emitted per second is **proportional** to the **intensity** of the radiation.

These are the two that had scientists puzzled. They can't be explained using wave theory.

The Photoelectric Effect Couldn't be Explained by Wave Theory

According to wave theory:

1) For a particular frequency of light, the **energy** carried is **proportional** to the **intensity** of the beam.
2) The energy carried by the light would be **spread evenly** over the wavefront.
3) **Each** free electron on the surface of the metal would gain a **bit of energy** from each incoming wave.
4) Gradually, each electron would gain **enough energy** to leave the metal.

SO... If the light had a **lower frequency** (i.e. was carrying less energy) it would take **longer** for the electrons to gain enough energy — but it would happen eventually. There is **no explanation** for the **threshold frequency**.

The **higher the intensity** of the wave, the **more energy** it should transfer to each electron — the kinetic energy should increase with **intensity**. There's **no explanation** for the **kinetic energy** depending only on the **frequency**.

Einstein came up with the Photon Model of Light

1) When Max Planck was investigating **black body radiation** (don't worry, you don't need to know about that just yet), he suggested that **EM waves** can **only** be **released** in **discrete packets**, or **quanta**.

2) The **energy carried** by one of these **wave-packets** had to be:

$$E = hf = \frac{hc}{\lambda}$$

where **h** = Planck's Constant = 6.63×10^{-34} Js
and **c** = speed of light in a vacuum = 3.00×10^8 ms^{-1}

3) **Einstein** went **further** by suggesting that **EM waves** (and the energy they carry) can only **exist** in discrete packets. He called these wave-packets **photons**.

4) He saw these photons of light as having a **one-on-one**, **particle-like** interaction with **an electron** in a **metal surface**. It would **transfer all** its **energy** to that **one**, **specific electron**.

The Photoelectric Effect

The Photon Model Explained the Photoelectric Effect Nicely

According to the photon model:
1) When light hits its surface, the metal is **bombarded** by photons.
2) If one of these photons **collides** with a free electron, the electron will gain energy equal to **hf**.

Before an electron can **leave** the surface of the metal, it needs enough energy to **break the bonds holding it there**. This energy is called the **work function energy** (symbol ϕ) and its **value** depends on the **metal**.

It Explains the Threshold Frequency...

1) If the energy **gained** from the photon is **greater** than the **work function energy**, the electron is **emitted**.
2) If it **isn't**, the electron will just **shake about a bit**, then release the energy as another photon. The metal will heat up, but **no electrons** will be emitted.
3) Since, for **electrons** to be released, **hf** $\geq \phi$, the **threshold frequency** must be:

$$f = \frac{\phi}{h}$$

In theory, if a second photon hit an electron before it released the energy from the first, it could gain enough to leave the metal. This would have to happen very quickly though. An electron releases any excess energy after about 10^{-8} s. That's 0.000 000 01 s — safe to say, the chances of that happening are pretty slim.

... and the Maximum Kinetic Energy

1) The **energy transferred** to an electron is **hf**.
2) The **kinetic energy** it will be carrying when it **leaves** the metal is **hf minus** any energy it's **lost** on the way out (there are loads of ways it can do that, which explains the **range** of energies).
3) The **minimum** amount of energy it can lose is the **work function energy**, so the **maximum kinetic energy** is given by the equation:

$$hf = \frac{1}{2}mv_{max}^2 + \phi$$

4) The **kinetic energy** of the electrons is **independent of the intensity**, because they can **only absorb one photon** at a time.

Practice Questions

Q1 Explain what the photoelectric effect is.
Q2 What three conclusions were drawn from detailed experimentation?
Q3 What is meant by the work function energy of a metal?
Q4 How is the maximum kinetic energy of a photoelectron calculated?

Exam Questions

Q1 An isolated zinc plate with neutral charge is exposed to high-frequency ultraviolet light. State and explain the effect of the ultraviolet light on the charge of the plate. [2 marks]

Q2 Explain why photoelectric emission from a metal surface only occurs when the frequency of the incident radiation exceeds a certain threshold value. [2 marks]

I'm so glad we got that all cleared up...

Well, that's about as hard as it gets at AS. The most important bits here are why wave theory doesn't explain the phenomenon, and why the photon theory does. A good way to learn conceptual stuff like this is to try and explain it to someone else. Make sure you can remember those formulae as well — you'll only be given them if you're doing AQA.

Energy Levels and Photon Emission

Right, bear with me a second. The bit on energy levels and fluorescent tubes is for AQA A (you need line spectra but ignore the rest); all the spectra stuff is for AQA B; the OCR bit's just the definition of the electronvolt. Got it? Good.

Electrons in Atoms Exist in Discrete Energy Levels

1) **Electrons** in an **atom** can **only exist** in certain **well-defined energy levels**. Each level is given a **number**, with **n = 1** representing the **ground state**.

2) Electrons can **move down** an energy level by **emitting** a **photon**.

3) Since these **transitions** are between **definite energy levels**, the **energy** of **each photon** emitted can **only** take a **certain allowed value**.

4) The diagram on the right shows the **energy levels** for **atomic hydrogen**.

5) The **energies involved** are **so tiny** that it makes sense to use a more **appropriate unit** than the **joule**. The **electronvolt (eV)** is defined as:

> The **kinetic energy carried** by an **electron** after it has been **accelerated** through a **potential difference** of **1 volt**.

> energy gained by electron (eV)
> = accelerating voltage (V)

> $1 \text{ eV} = 1.6 \times 10^{-19} \text{ J}$

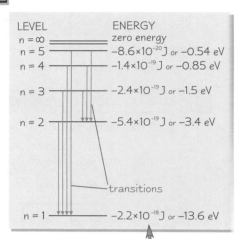

LEVEL   ENERGY
n = ∞   zero energy
n = 5 -8.6×10^{-20} J or -0.54 eV
n = 4 -1.4×10^{-19} J or -0.85 eV
n = 3 -2.4×10^{-19} J or -1.5 eV
n = 2 -5.4×10^{-19} J or -3.4 eV
transitions
n = 1 -2.2×10^{-18} J or -13.6 eV

6) On the diagram, energies are labelled in **both units** for **comparison's** sake.

7) The **energy** carried by each **photon** is **equal** to the **difference in energies** between the **two levels**. The equation below shows a **transition** between levels **n = 2** and **n = 1**:

$$\Delta E = E_2 - E_1 = hf = \frac{hc}{\lambda}$$

The energies are only negative because of how "zero energy" is defined. Just one of those silly convention things — don't worry about it.

Fluorescent Tubes use Excited Electrons to Produce Light

1) **Fluorescent tubes** contain **mercury vapour**, and have a **high voltage** across them.

2) When **electrons** in the **mercury collide** with **fast-moving free electrons** (accelerated by the **high voltage**), they're **excited** to a **higher energy level**.

3) When these **excited electrons** return to their **ground states**, they emit **photons** in the **UV** range.

4) A **phosphorus coating** on the **inside** of the tube **absorbs** these **photons**, exciting its **electrons** to **much higher orbits**. These electrons then **cascade** down the **energy levels**, emitting many **lower energy photons** in the form of **visible light**.

Fluorescent Tubes Produce Line Emission Spectra

1) If you **split** the light from a **fluorescent tube** with a **prism**, you get a **line spectrum**. A line spectrum is seen as a **series** of **bright lines** against a **black background**.

2) Each **line** corresponds to a **particular wavelength** of light **emitted** by the source.

3) Since only **certain photon energies** are **allowed** — you only see the **corresponding wavelengths**.

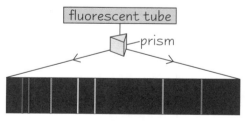

fluorescent tube
prism

Continuous Spectra Contain All Possible Wavelengths

1) The **spectrum** of **white light** is **continuous**.

2) If you **split** the **light** up with a **prism**, the **colours** all **merge** into each other — there **aren't** any **gaps** in the spectrum.

3) **Hot things** emit a **continuous spectrum** in the visible and infrared.

Decreasing wavelength ⟹

Energy Levels and Photon Emission

Shining *White Light* through a *Cool Gas* gives an *Absorption Spectrum*

1) You get a **line absorption spectrum** when **light** with a **continuous spectrum** of **energy** passes through a cool gas.

2) At **low temperatures**, **most** of the **electrons** in the **gas atoms** will be in their **ground states**.

3) **Photons** of the **correct wavelength** are **absorbed** by the **electrons** to **excite** them to **higher energy levels**.

4) These **wavelengths** are then **missing** from the **continuous spectrum** when it **comes out** the other side of the gas.

5) You see a **continuous spectrum** with **black lines** in it corresponding to the **absorbed wavelengths**.

6) If you **compare** the **absorption** and **emission spectra** of a **particular gas**, the **black lines** in the **absorption spectrum** **match up** to the **bright lines** in the **emission spectrum**.

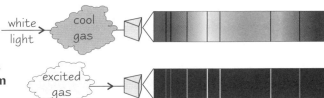

Excited *Molecules* Emit *Band Spectra*

1) You can **excite** a **molecule** by making the **electrons** in the **bond vibrate**.

2) The **energies** of these **vibrations** are in **levels** in the same way as the **electron levels** in atoms — so you get something like a **line spectrum**. The **energy levels** are in **groups** though, with **very similar** energies, so you get **loads** of **lines close together** on the **spectrum**.

3) The **fine lines** tend to **blur** together to make wide 'bands' in the spectrum.

Spectra are Useful to Astrophysicists

1) When **astronomers** view **stars**, they observe **absorption spectra** from the **atmosphere** of the **stars**. From the **continuous spectrum** they can work out the **temperature** of the star.

2) The **dark absorption lines** are **shifted** away from where they would **normally be** towards the **red end** of the spectrum. This is caused by the **Doppler effect**, and means that the object being viewed is **moving away** from us.

3) Its **velocity** is found from: $\Delta f = \dfrac{fv}{c}$ where Δf = change in frequency, f = frequency of the source, v = velocity and c = speed of light in a vacuum. (This only works if $v \ll c$)

Practice Questions

Q1 Describe line absorption and line emission spectra. How are these two types of spectra produced?

Q2 Use the size of the energy level transitions involved to explain how the coating on a fluorescent tube converts UV into visible light.

Exam Questions

Q1 An electron is accelerated through a potential difference of 12.1 V.

(a) How much kinetic energy has it gained in (i) eV and (ii) joules? [2 marks]

(b) This electron hits a hydrogen atom and excites it.
   (i) Explain what is meant by excitation. [1 mark]
   (ii) Using the energy values on the right, work out to which energy level the electron from the hydrogen atom is excited. [1 mark]
   (iii) Calculate the energies of the three photons that might be emitted as the electron returns to its ground state. [3 marks]

n = 5	− 0.54 eV
n = 4	− 0.85 eV
n = 3	− 1.5 eV
n = 2	− 3.4 eV
n = 1	− 13.6 eV

I can honestly say I've never got so excited that I've produced light...

...especially not where physics is concerned.
This is heavy stuff, it really is. Quite interesting though, as I was just saying to Dom a moment ago. He's doing a psychology book. Psychology's probably quite interesting too — and easier. But it won't help you become an astrophysicist.

Wave-Particle Duality

If you're not doing AQA A or OCR A skip to the bottom of page 113.

Is it a wave? Is it a particle? No, it's a wave. No, it's a particle. No it's not, it's a wave. No don't be daft, it's a particle. (etc)

Interference and Diffraction show Light as a Wave

1) Light produces **interference** and **diffraction** patterns — **alternating bands** of **dark** and **light**.

2) These can **only** be explained using **waves interfering constructively** (when two waves overlap in phase) or **interfering destructively** (when the two waves are out of phase). (See p80.)

The Photoelectric Effect Shows Light Behaving as a Particle

1) **Einstein** explained the results of **photoelectricity experiments** (see p108) by thinking of the **beam of light** as a series of **particle-like photons**.

2) If a **photon** of light is a **discrete** bundle of energy, then it can **interact** with an **electron** in a **one-to-one way**.

3) **All** the **energy** in the **photon** is **given** to one **electron**.

De Broglie Came up With the Wave-Particle Duality Theory

1) Louis de Broglie made a **bold suggestion** in his **PhD thesis**:

> If **'wave-like'** light showed **particle properties** (photons), **'particles'** like **electrons** should be expected to show **wave-like properties**.

2) The **de Broglie equation** relates a **wave property** (wavelength, λ) to a **moving particle property** (momentum, *mv*). **h** = Planck's constant = 6.63×10^{-34} Js.

$$\lambda = \frac{h}{mv}$$

I'm not impressed — this is just speculation. What do you think Dad?

3) Most physicists at the time **weren't very impressed** — his ideas were just **speculation**.

4) Later experiments **confirmed** the wave nature of electrons.

Electron Diffraction shows the Wave Nature of Electrons

1) **Diffraction patterns** are observed when **accelerated electrons** in a vacuum tube **interact** with the **spaces** in a graphite **crystal**.

2) This **confirms** that electrons show **wave-like** properties.

3) According to wave theory, the **spread** of the **lines** in the diffraction pattern **increases** if the **wavelength** of the wave is **greater**.

4) In electron diffraction experiments, a **smaller accelerating voltage**, i.e. **slower** electrons, gives **widely spaced** rings.

5) **Increase** the **electron speed** and the diffraction pattern circles **squash together** towards the **middle**. This fits in with the **de Broglie** equation above — if the **velocity** is **higher**, the **wavelength** is **shorter** and the **spread** of lines is **smaller**.

Electron diffraction patterns look like this.

> In general, λ for **electrons** accelerated in a **vacuum tube** is about the **same size** as **electromagnetic waves** in the **X-ray** part of the spectrum.

Wave-Particle Duality

Particles don't show Wave-Like Properties All the Time

You **only** get **diffraction** if a particle interacts with an object of about the **same size** as its **de Broglie wavelength**. A **tennis ball**, for example, with **mass 0.058 kg** and **speed 100 ms⁻¹** has a **de Broglie wavelength** of 10^{-34} m. That's 10^{19} **times smaller** than the **nucleus** of an **atom**! There's nothing that small for it to interact with.

> ### Example
>
> An electron of mass 9×10^{-31} kg is fired from an electron gun at 7×10^6 ms⁻¹. What size object will the electron need to interact with in order to diffract?
>
> Momentum of electron = $mv = 6.38 \times 10^{-24}$ kg ms⁻¹
>
> $\lambda = h/mv = 6.63 \times 10^{-34} / 6.38 \times 10^{-24} = \boxed{1 \times 10^{-10} \text{ m}}$
>
> Only crystals with atom layer spacing around this size are likely to cause the diffraction of this electron.

A **shorter wavelength** gives **less diffraction effects**. This fact is used in the **electron microscope**. **Diffraction** effects **blur detail** on an image. If you want to **resolve tiny detail** in an **image**, you need a **shorter wavelength**. **Light** blurs out detail more than '**electron-waves**' do, so an **electron microscope** can resolve **finer detail** than a **light microscope**. They can let you look at things as tiny as a single string of DNA... which is nice.

Practice Questions

Q1   Which observations show light to have a 'wave-like' character?

Q2   Which observations show light to have a 'particle' character?

Q3   What happens to the de Broglie wavelength of a particle if it is moving with a greater velocity?

Q4   Which observations show electrons to have a 'wave-like' character?

Exam Questions

$h = 6.63 \times 10^{-34}$ Js ; $c = 3.00 \times 10^8$ ms⁻¹ ; electron mass = 9.1×10^{-31} kg ; proton mass = $1840 \times$ electron mass

Q1   (a)   State what is meant by the wave-particle duality of electromagnetic radiation.   [1 mark]

       (b) (i) Calculate the energy in joules and in electronvolts of a photon of wavelength 590 nm.   [3 marks]
            (ii) Calculate the speed of an electron which will have the same wavelength as the photon in (b)(i).   [2 marks]

Q2   Electrons travelling at a speed of 3.5×10^6 ms⁻¹ exhibit wave properties

       (a)   Calculate the wavelength of these electrons.   [2 marks]

       (b)   Calculate the speed of protons which would have the same wavelength as these electrons.   [2 marks]

       (c)   Both electrons and protons were accelerated from rest by the same potential difference.
              Explain why they will have different wavelengths.
              (Hint: if they're accelerated by the same p.d., they have the same K.E.)   [3 marks]

Q3   (a)   An electron is accelerated through a potential difference of 6.0 kV.
              Calculate its kinetic energy in joules, assuming no energy is lost in the process.   [2 marks]

       (b)   Using the data above, calculate the speed of this electron.   [2 marks]

       (c)   Calculate the de Broglie wavelength of this electron.   [2 marks]

Don't look now, but... it's the ENDOFTHEBOOK — YAY...

Quantum phenomena, eh. What a whopper of a topic that is. Anyway, I don't care any more, because as of 2 cm ago, I'm officially finished. I'm only staying around to offer you a celebratory drink and show you politely but firmly towards the door.   (ps... Good luck with the exams...)

Answers

Section 1 — Mechanics
Page 3 — Scalars and Vectors
1) Start by drawing a diagram:

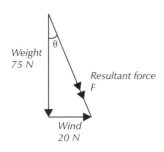

$F^2 = 20^2 + 75^2 = 6025$
So $F = 77.6 N$
$\tan \theta = 20 / 75 = 0.26$
So $\theta = 14.9°$
The resultant force on the rock is 77.6 N [1 mark]
at an angle of 14.9° [1 mark] to the vertical.
Make sure you know which angle you're finding — and label it on your diagram.

2) Again, start by drawing a diagram:

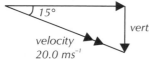

horizontal component $v_H = 20 \cos 15° = 19.3 ms^{-1}$ [1 mark]
vertical component $v_V = 20 \sin 15° = 5.2 ms^{-1}$ [1 mark]
Always draw a diagram.

Page 5 — Motion with Constant Acceleration
1)a) $a = -9.8 ms^{-2}, t = 5 s, u = 0 ms^{-1}, v = ?$
   use : $v = u + at$
   $v = 0 + 5 \times -9.8$ [1 mark for either step of working]
   $v = -49 ms^{-1}$ [1 mark]
   NB: It's negative because she's falling downwards and we took upwards as the positive direction.

b) Use $s = \left(\dfrac{u + v}{2}\right)t$ or $s = ut + \frac{1}{2} at^2$ [1 mark for either]

   $s = \dfrac{-49}{2} \times 5$ $\qquad s = 0 + \frac{1}{2} \times -9.8 \times 5^2$

   $s = -122.5 m$ $\qquad s = -122.5 m$
   So she fell 122.5 m [1 mark for answer]

2)a) $v = 0 ms^{-1}, t = 3.2 s, s = 40 m, u = ?$

   use: $s = \left(\dfrac{u + v}{2}\right)t$ [1 mark]

   $40 = 3.2u \div 2$

   $u = \dfrac{80}{3.2} = 25 ms^{-1}$ [1 mark]

b) use $v^2 = u^2 + 2as$ [1 mark]
   $0 = 25^2 + 80a$
   $-80a = 625$
   $a = -7.8 ms^{-2}$ [1 mark]

Page 7 — Displacement-Time Graphs
1) Split graph into four sections:

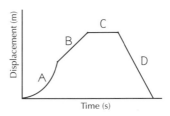

A: acceleration [1 mark]
B: constant velocity [1 mark]
C: stationary [1 mark]
D: constant velocity in opposite direction to A and B [1 mark]

2)a)

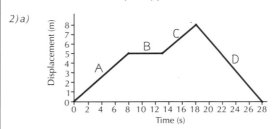

[4 marks]

b) At A: $v = \dfrac{\text{displacement}}{\text{time}} = \dfrac{5}{8} = 0.625 ms^{-1}$

At B: $v = 0$

At C: $v = \dfrac{\text{displacement}}{\text{time}} = \dfrac{3}{5} = 0.6 ms^{-1}$

At D: $v = \dfrac{\text{displacement}}{\text{time}} = \dfrac{-8}{10} = -0.8 ms^{-1}$

[2 marks for all correct or just 1 mark for 3 correct]

Page 9 — Velocity-Time and Acceleration-Time Graphs
1)a)

[2 marks]

b) use $s = \left(\dfrac{u + v}{2}\right)t$ [1 mark]

   $t = 1, s = 1$
   $t = 2, s = 4$
   $t = 3, s = 9$
   $t = 4, s = 16$
   $t = 5, s = 25$
   [2 marks for all correct or 1 mark for at least 3 pairs of values right]

Answers

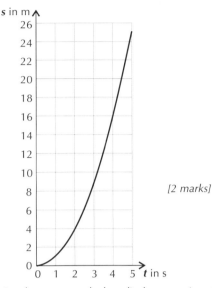

[2 marks]

c) Another way to calculate displacement is to find the area under the velocity-time graph. [1 mark]
E.g total displacement = ½ × 5 ×10 =25 m [1 mark]

Page 11 — Mass, Weight and Centre of Gravity

1)a) Density is a measure of 'compactness' of a material — its mass per unit volume. [1 mark]
b) $\rho = \dfrac{m}{V}$ [1 mark]
V of cylinder = $\pi r^2 h = \pi \times 4^2 \times 6 = 301.6$ cm³ [1 mark]
$\rho = 820 \div 301.6 = 2.7$ g cm⁻³ [1 mark]
c) $V = 5 \times 5 \times 5 = 125$ cm³
$m = \rho \times V = 2.7 \times 125 = 338$ g [1 mark]
2)a) The centre of gravity is the point through which the entire mass of a body can be considered to act. [1 mark]
b) If weight is higher up the centre of gravity is raised. [1 mark]
This makes the object less stable as it's easier for the weight to fall outside base area. [2 marks for diagrams]

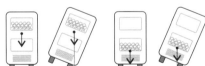

Page 13 — Forces and Equilibrium

1)

Weight = vertical component of tension × 2
80 × 9.8 = 2T sin50° [1 mark]
784 = 0.766 × 2T
1023.4 = 2T
T = 512 N [1 mark]

2)

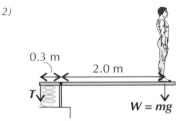

By Pythagoras:
$R = \sqrt{1000^2 + 600^2} = 1166$ N [1 mark]
$\tan \theta = \dfrac{600}{1000}$, so $\theta = \tan^{-1} 0.6 = 30.9°$ [1 mark]

Page 15 — Moments and Torques

1) Torque = Force × distance [1 mark]
60 = 0.4F, so F = 150 N [1 mark]

2)

clockwise moment = anticlockwise moment
W × 2.0 = T × 0.3 [1 mark for either line of working]
60 × 9.8 × 2.0 = T × 0.3
T = 3920 N anticlockwise [1 mark]
The tension in the spring is equal and opposite to the force exerted by the diver on the spring.

Page 17 — Momentum

1) Before / After

total momentum before collision = total momentum after collision [1 mark]
(0.6 × 5) + 0 = (0.6 × −2.4) + 2v (minus sign for change in direction)
3 + 1.44 = 2v [1 mark for either line of working]
v = 2.22 ms⁻¹ [1 mark]

2) Before / After

momentum before = momentum after
(0.7 × 0.3) + 0 = 1.1v [1 mark]
0.21 = 1.1v [1 mark]
v = 0.19 ms⁻¹ [1 mark]

Answers

Page 19 — Newton's Laws of Motion

1)a) (i)

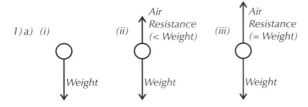

[1 mark each diagram]

b) A parachutist could wear clothes with 'flares' and under arm 'wings' to increase air resistance.
They could also change the position of their body, e.g. limbs spread out horizontally increases air resistance and reduces terminal velocity, (diving vertically reduces air resistance and increases terminal velocity.) [2 marks for any 2 sensible points]

Page 21 — Newton's Second Law

1)a) Force perpendicular to river flow = 500 − 100 = 400 N [1 mark]
Force parallel to river flow = 300 N

Resultant force = $\sqrt{400^2 + 300^2}$ = 500 N [1 mark]

b) $a = F/m$ (from $F = ma$) [1 mark]
= 500/250 = 2 ms^{-2} [1 mark]

2)a) The resultant force acting on each car [1 mark] and its mass [1 mark]

b) Michael is able to exert a greater force than Tom.
Michael is lighter than Tom. [1 mark each for 2 sensible points]

c) The only force acting on each of them is weight = mg [1 mark].
Since $F = ma$, this gives ma = mg, or a = g [1 mark]. Their acceleration doesn't depend on the mass — it's the same — so they reach the water at the same time. [1 mark]

Page 23 — Newton's Laws of Motion

1)a) The computer needs:-
the time for the first strip of card to pass through the beam [1 mark]
the time for the second strip of card to pass through the beam [1 mark]
the time between these events [1 mark]

b) Speed when first strip breaks the light beam =
    width of card strip/time to pass through beam [1 mark]
Speed when second strip breaks the light beam =
    width of card strip/time to pass through beam [1 mark]
Acceleration =
(second speed − first speed) ÷ time between measurements [1 mark]

2)a) You know s = 5 m, a = −g, v = 0
You need to find u, so use $v^2 = u^2 + 2as$
0 = u^2 − 2 × 9.81 × 5 [1 mark for either line of working]
u^2 = 98.1, so u = 9.9 ms^{-1} [1 mark]

b) You know a = −g, v = 0 at highest pt, u = 9.9 ms^{-1} from a)
You need to find t, so use $v = u + at$
0 = 9.9 − 9.81t [1 mark for either line of working]
t = 9.9/9.81 = 1.0 s [1 mark]

c) Her velocity as she lands back on the trampoline will be −9.9 ms^{-1} (same magnitude, opposite direction)
[2 marks — 1 for correct number, 1 for correct sign]

Page 25 — Terminal Velocity

1)a) The velocity increases at a steady rate, which means the acceleration is constant. [1 mark]
Constant acceleration means there must be no air resistance (air resistance changes with velocity so wouldn't be constant).
So there must be no air. [1 mark]

b)

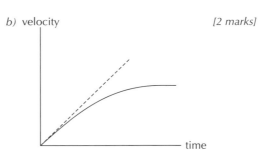

[2 marks]

Your graph must be a smooth curve which levels out. It must NOT go down at the end.

c) (The graph becomes less steep)
because the acceleration is decreasing [1 mark]
because air resistance increases with speed [1 mark]
(The graph levels out)
because air resistance has become equal to weight [1 mark]
If the question says 'explain', you won't get marks for just describing what the graph shows, you have to say <u>why</u> it is that shape.

Page 27 — Work and Power

1)a)

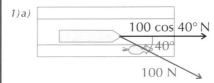

Force in direction of travel = 100 cos40° = 76.6 N [1 mark]
$W = Fs$ = 76.6 × 1500 = 114 900 J [1 mark]

b) Use $P = Fv$ [1 mark]
= 100cos40° × 0.8 = 61.3 W [1 mark]

2)a) Use $W = Fs$ [1 mark]
= 20 × 9.81 × 3 = 588.6 J [1 mark]
Remember that 20 kg is not the force, it's the mass. So you need to multiply it by 9.81 Nkg^{-1} to get the weight.

b) Use $P = Fv$ [1 mark]
= 20 × 9.81 × 0.25 = 49.05 W [1 mark]

Page 29 — Conservation of Energy

1)a) Use $KE = \frac{1}{2}mv^2$ and $PE = mgh$ [1 mark]
$\frac{1}{2}mv^2 = mgh$
$\frac{1}{2}v^2 = gh$
$v^2 = 2gh = 2 × 9.81 × 2 = 39.24$ [1 mark]
$v = 6.26$ ms^{-1} [1 mark]
'No friction' allows you to say that the changes in kinetic and potential energy will be the same.

b) 2 m — no friction means the kinetic energy will all change back into potential so he will rise back up to the same height as he started. [1 mark]

c) Put in some more energy by actively 'skating'. [1 mark]

Answers

2)

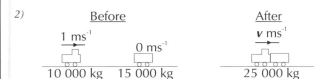

a) The kinetic energy will be less after the collision. [1 mark]
b) total momentum before = total momentum after
   $10\,000 \times 1 = 25\,000v$ [1 mark]
   so $v = 0.4$ ms^{-1} [1 mark]
c) Before: KE = $0.5 \times 10\,000 \times 1^2 = 5000$ J [1 mark]
   After: KE = $0.5 \times 25\,000 \times 0.4^2 = 2000$ J [1 mark]

Page 31 — Forces on Vehicles and Car Safety
1)a) reaction time is 0.5 s, speed is 20 ms^{-1}
   $s = vt$ [1 mark]
   $= 0.5 \times 20 = 10$ m [1 mark]
 b) Use $F = ma$ to get a: $a = -10\,000/850 = -11.76$ ms^{-2} [1 mark]

   Use $v^2 = u^2 + 2as$, and rearrange to get $s = \dfrac{v^2 - u^2}{2a}$

   Put in the values: $s = (0 - 400) \div (2 \times -11.76)$ [1 mark]
   $= 17$ m [1 mark]
   Remember that a force against the direction of motion should be
   negative.
 c) Total stopping distance = 10 + 17 = 27 m
   She stops 3 m before the cow. [1 mark]
2)a) Car: use $v = u + at$ to get acceleration:
   $a = 0 - 20/0.1 = -200$ ms^{-2} [1 mark]
   Use $F = ma$:
   $F = 900 \times -200 = -180\,000$ N [1 mark]
   Same for dummy:
   $a = 0 - 18/0.1 = -180$ ms^{-2} [1 mark]
   $F = 50 \times -180 = -9000$ N [1 mark]
 b) Crumple zones will increase the collision time for the car and
   dummy;
   this reduces forces on car and dummy;
   the air bag will keep the dummy in its seat;
   and increase the collision time further for the dummy;
   reducing the force on it.
   [3 marks for any three points]

Section 2 — Elastic Properties of Solids
Page 33 — Hooke's Law
1)a) Force is proportional to extension.
   The force is 1.5 times as great, so the extension will also be 1.5
   times the original value.
   Extension = 1.5×4.0 mm = 6.0 mm [1 mark]
 b) $F = ke$ and so $k = F/e$ [1 mark]
   $k = 10 \div 4.0 \times 10^{-3} = 2500$ Nm^{-1} [1 mark]
   There is one mark for rearranging the equation and another for getting
   the right numerical answer.
 c) One mark for any sensible point e.g.
   The string now stretches much further for small increases in force.
   When the string is loosened it is longer than at the start. [1 mark]
2) The rubber band does not obey Hooke's law [1 mark]
   because when the force is doubled from 2.5 N to 5 N, the
   extension increases by a factor of 2.3 from 4.4 cm to 10.2 cm.
   [1 mark]

Page 35 — Stress and Strain
1)a) Area = $\pi d^2/4$ or πr^2.
   So area = $\pi \times (1 \times 10^{-3})^2/4 = 7.85 \times 10^{-7}$ m^2 [1 mark]
 b) Stress = force/area = $300/7.85 \times 10^{-7} = 3.82 \times 10^8$ Nm^{-2} [1 mark]
 c) Strain = extension/length = $4 \times 10^{-3}/2.00 = 2 \times 10^{-3}$ [1 mark]
2)a) $F = ke$ and so rearranging $k = F/e$ [1 mark]
   So $k = 50/3.0 \times 10^{-3} = 1.67 \times 10^4$ Nm^{-1} [1 mark]
 b) Elastic strain energy = ½Fe
   Giving the elastic strain energy as
   ½ $\times 50 \times 3 \times 10^{-3} = 7.5 \times 10^{-2}$ J [1 mark]

Page 37 — The Young Modulus
1)a) Cross sectional area = $\pi d^2/4$ or πr^2.
   So the cross sectional area = $\pi \times (0.6 \times 10^{-3})^2/4 = 2.83 \times 10^{-7}$ m^2
   [1 mark]
 b) Stress = force/area = $80/2.83 \times 10^{-7} = 2.83 \times 10^8$ Nm^{-2} [1 mark]
 c) Strain = extension/length = $3.6 \times 10^{-3}/2.5 = 1.44 \times 10^{-3}$ [1 mark]
 d) The Young modulus for steel = stress/strain
   $= 2.83 \times 10^8/1.44 \times 10^{-3} = 1.96 \times 10^{11}$ Nm^{-2} [1 mark]
2)a) The Young modulus, E = stress/strain and so strain = stress/E
   [1 mark]
   Strain on copper = $2.6 \times 10^8/1.3 \times 10^{11} = 2 \times 10^{-3}$ [1 mark]
   There's one mark for rearranging the equation and another for using it
   properly.
 b) Stress = force/area and so area = force/stress
   Area of the wire = $100/2.6 \times 10^8 = 3.85 \times 10^{-7}$ m^2 [1 mark]
 c) Strain energy per unit volume = ½ $\times$ stress $\times$ strain
   $= ½ \times 2.6 \times 10^8 \times 2 \times 10^{-3}$
   $= 2.6 \times 10^5$ Jm^{-3} [1 mark]
   Give the mark if answer is consistent with the value calculated for
   strain in part a).

Page 39 — Interpreting Graphs for Different Materials
1)a) A brittle material is one which fractures at its elastic limit.
   It shows no plastic behaviour.
 b) k is the gradient of the tension-extension graph [1 mark]
   (i) $k_{(i)}$ = change in force-extension = $5.3 (\pm 0.2) \times 10^4$ Nm^{-1}
   [1 mark]
   (ii) $k_{(ii)}$ = change in force-extension = $4.2 (\pm 0.2) \times 10^4$ Nm^{-1}
   [1 mark]
 c) The higher the breaking stress of a material, the stronger the
   material [1 mark]. Material (ii) is stronger. [1 mark]

Section 3 — Electricity
Page 41 — Charge, Current and Potential Difference
1) Time in seconds = $10 \times 60 = 600$s.
   Use the formula $I = Q / t$ [1 mark]
   which gives you
   $I = 4500 / 600 = 7.5$ A [1 mark]
   Write down the formula first. Don't forget the unit in your answer.
2) Rearrange the formula $I = nAvq$ and you get $v = I / nAq$ [1 mark]
   which gives you
   $$v = \frac{13}{(1.0 \times 10^{29}) \times (5.0 \times 10^{-6}) \times (1.6 \times 10^{-19})} \quad \text{[1 mark]}$$
   $v = 1.63 \times 10^{-4}$ ms^{-1} [1 mark]
3) Work done = $0.75 \times$ electrical energy input
   so the energy input will be $90 / 0.75 = 120$ J. [1 mark]
   Rearrange the formula $V = W / Q$ to give $Q = W / V$ [1 mark]
   so you get $Q = 120 / 12 = 10$ C. [1 mark]
   The electrical energy input to a motor has to be greater than the work
   it does because motors are less than 100% efficient.

Answers

Page 43 — Resistance and Resistivity

1) a) Area = $\pi(d/2)^2$
  $d = 1.0 \times 10^{-3}\,m$
  so Area = $\pi \times (0.5 \times 10^{-3})^2$
       = $7.85 \times 10^{-7}\,m^2$ [1 mark for correct evaluation of area]

  $$R = \frac{\rho l}{A}$$

  $$= \frac{2.8 \times 10^{-8} \times 4}{7.85 \times 10^{-7}}$$

  $= 0.14\,\Omega$
  [1 mark for use of correct equation or correct working,
  1 mark for answer and unit.]

 b) Resistance will now be zero [1 mark]
  Because aluminium is a superconductor below its transition
  temperature of 1.2K [1 mark]

2) a) $R = V / I$

  $$= \frac{2}{2.67 \times 10^{-3}}$$

  $= 749\,\Omega$
  [1 mark for either step of working, 1 mark for correct answer
  and units.]

 b) Two further resistance calculations give $750\,\Omega$ for each answer
  [1 mark]
  No significant change in resistance for different potential
  differences [1 mark]
  Component is an ohmic conductor because its resistance is
  constant for different potential differences. [1 mark]

Page 45 — I/V Characteristics

1) a)

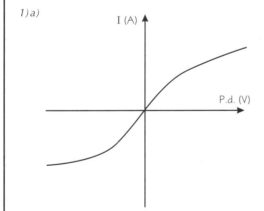

  [1 mark]
 b) Resistance increases as the temperature increases [1 mark]
 c) Increase in temperature makes metal ions vibrate more
  [1 mark]
  Increased collisions with ions impedes electrons [1 mark]

Page 47 — Electrical Energy and Power

1) a) Current = power/p.d.
       = 920/230 [1 mark for either step of working]
       = 4 A [1 mark]
 b) Current = p.d./resistance
       = 230/190 [1 mark for either step of working]
       = 1.21 A [1 mark]

 c) Motor power = p.d. × current
       = 230 × 1.21 [1 mark for either step of working]
       = 278 W [1 mark]
  Total power = motor power + heater power
       = 278 + 920
       = 1198 W which is approx. 1.2 kW [1 mark]
 d) Energy = power × time
       = 1.2 × 0.25 [1 mark for either step of working]
       = 0.3 kWh. [1 mark]

2) a) Energy supplied = p.d. × current × time
       = 12 × 48 × 2 [1 mark for either step of working]
       = 1152 J [1 mark]
 b) Energy lost = $current^2$ × resistance × time
       = 48^2 × 0.01 × 2 [1 mark for either step of working]
       = 46 J [1 mark]

Page 49 — E.m.f. and Internal Resistance

1) a) Total resistance = $R + r$ = 4 + 0.8 = $4.8\,\Omega$ [1 mark]
  Current = e.m.f./total resistance
       = 24/4.8
       = 5A [1 mark]
 b) $V = E - Ir$
       = 24 − 5 × 0.8
       = 20V [1 mark]

2) a) $E = I (R + r)$
  $500 = 50 \times 10^{-3} (10 + r)$ [1 mark]
  $10 + r = 500/(50 \times 10^{-3}) = 1 \times 10^4\,\Omega$ [1 mark]
  $r = 9990\,\Omega$ [1 mark]
 b) This is a very high internal resistance [1 mark]
  So only small currents can be drawn, reducing the risk to the user
  [1 mark]

Page 51 — Conservation of Energy and Charge in Circuits

1) a) Resistance of parallel resistors:
  $1/R_{parallel} = 1/6 + 1/3 = 1/2$
  $R_{parallel} = 2\,\Omega$ [1 mark]
  Total resistance:
  $R_{total} = 4 + R_{parallel}$ [1 mark]
  $R_{total} = 4 + 2 = 6\,\Omega$
 b) I_3 = p.d. / total resistance
       = 12 / 6 = 2 A [1 mark]
 c) $V = IR$
       = 2 × 4 = 8V [1 mark]
 d) E.m.f. = sum of p.d.s in circuit
  so $12 = 8 + V_{parallel}$
  $V_{parallel} = 12 − 8 = 4$ V [1 mark]
 e) Current = p.d. / resistance
  $I_1 = 4 / 3 = 1.33$ A [1 mark]
  $I_2 = 4 / 6 = 0.67$ A [1 mark]

Page 53 — The Potential Divider

1) Parallel circuit, so p.d. across both sets of resistors is 12V.
 a) $V_{AB} = ½ \times 12 = 6V$ [1 mark]
 b) $V_{AC} = 2/3 \times 12 = 8V$ [1 mark]
 c) $V_{BC} = V_{AC} - V_{AB} = 8 − 6 = 2V$ [1 mark]
2) a) $V_{AB} = 50/80 \times 12 = 7.5V$ (ignore the $10\,\Omega$, no current flows that
  way) [1 mark]
 b) Total resistance of the parallel circuit:
  $1/R_T = 1/50 + 1/(10 + 40) = 1/25$
  $R_T = 25\,\Omega$ [1 mark]
  p.d. over the whole parallel arrangement = 25/55 × 12 = 5.45V
  [1 mark]
  p.d. across AB = 40/50 × 5.45 = 4.36V [1 mark]
  current through $40\,\Omega$ = V / R = 4.36 / 40 = 0.11A [1 mark]

Answers

Page 55 — Alternating Current

1) $T = 1 / f = 1/100 = 0.01s$ (10ms) [1 mark]

Length of wave on screen = T / time base
= 10 ms / 2ms cm^{-1} = 5 cm.

So, one wave occupies 5cm horizontally and two waves take up the whole screen. [1 mark]

Height of wave on screen = peak voltage / voltage sensitivity
= 2V / 0.5 Vcm^{-1} = 4 cm.

Therefore the height is 4cm up and 4cm down from the zero line. [1 mark]

[Plus 1 mark for drawing the diagram correctly]

2)a) A dc signal with a time base produces a horizontal straight line. [1 mark]

Trace is a straight line 2cm above the zero line. [1 mark]

b) f = 50Hz so T = 1 / 50 = 20ms. [1 mark]

20ms / 5 ms div^{-1} = 4 divs

So, one wave occupies 4 divisions : 2½ waves occupy the whole screen (10 divs) [1 mark]

The height is 1½ divs above and below, vertically. [1 mark]

3)a) $T = 1/2500 = 4 \times 10^{-4}$ s = 0.4 ms

b) One complete wave must occupy 2 divisions if five waves are seen on the whole screen. [1 mark]

2 divisions represents a time of 0.4 ms.

So the time-base setting is 0.2 ms div^{-1} or 2×10^{-4} s div^{-1} [1 mark]

Page 57 — Magnetic Effects of Current

1) $F = BIl$ so $I = F / Bl$

$I = 0.03 / (0.02 \times 0.3) = 5$ A [1 mark]

Using Fleming's Left Hand Rule, the current flows from P to Q. [1 mark]

2)a) A current must flow at right angles to the magnetic field. [1 mark]

b) The current needs to have a component at right angles to the magnetic field. This wire is parallel to the field and so there is no force. [1 mark]

c) $F = BIl = 0.15 \times 10 \times 0.2$ [1 mark]
= 0.3N [1 mark for answer and unit]

d) The currents in the two wires produce magnetic fields [1 mark]
The left hand wire cuts the field produced by the right hand wire at right angles and experiences a force towards the right. [1 mark]
The right hand wire cuts the field produced by the left hand wire at right angles and experiences a force towards the left, so the two wires are attracted to each other. [1 mark]

Section 4 — Thermal Physics
Page 59 — Specific Heat Capacity and Specific Latent Heat

1) Electrical energy supplied:
$\Delta Q = VI\Delta t = 12 \times 7.5 \times 180 = 16200$ J [1 mark]
The temperature rise is 12.7 – 4.5 = 8.2 °C

Specific heat capacity: $c = \dfrac{\Delta Q}{m\Delta\theta}$ [1 mark]

= $\dfrac{16200}{2 \times 8.2}$ = 988 J kg^{-1} °C^{-1} [1 mark]

Remember to put the time in seconds.
You need to use the right unit to get the third mark — J kg^{-1} K^{-1} would be right too.

2) Total amount of energy needed to boil all the water:
$\Delta Q = l\Delta m$
= $2.26 \times 10^6 \times 0.5 = 1.13 \times 10^6$ J [1 mark]
3 kW means you get 3000 J in a second, so
Time in seconds = 1.13×10^6 / 3000 [1 mark]
= 377 s [1 mark]

We've assumed that the kettle doesn't have one of those helpful switchy things to turn itself off when it boils.

Page 61 — Pressure in Fluids

1) Total mass = 65.5 kg
Weight = mg = 65.5 × 9.8 = 641.9 N [1 mark]
Area = weight / pressure
= 641.9 / 310 × 10^3 = 2.1×10^{-3} m^2 [1 mark]
Check that the answer makes sense. It's 21 cm^2.

2) Pressure of oil = force of slave / area of slave
= $3000 / 5.5 \times 10^{-3}$
= 5.45×10^5 Pa [1 mark]
Force of master = pressure × area of master
= $5.45 \times 10^5 \times 4.2 \times 10^{-4}$
= 229 N [1 mark]

Remember the pressure is the same in both cylinders.
Check that you've got it the right way round — the force input should be less than the force output.

Page 63 — The Ideal Gas Equation

1)a) Number of moles = $\dfrac{\text{mass of gas}}{\text{molar mass}}$ = $\dfrac{0.014}{0.028}$ = 0.5 [1 mark]

b) $pV = nRT$
So $p = \dfrac{nRT}{V}$ [1 mark]

$p = \dfrac{0.5 \times 8.31 \times 300}{0.01}$ = 124 650 Pa [1 mark]

There's one mark for rearranging the equation and another for calculating the answer.

2)a) $\dfrac{pV}{T}$ = constant

At ground level, $\dfrac{pV}{T} = \dfrac{1 \times 10^5 \times 10}{293}$ = 3410 JK^{-1} [1 mark]

Higher up, the new values of p, V and T will equal this same constant. [1 mark]

So higher up, $p = \dfrac{\text{constant} \times T}{V} = \dfrac{3410 \times 260}{25}$

p = 35 500 Pa [1 mark]

b) Any two reasonable assumptions
e.g. no helium gas is lost from the balloon — the mass stays fixed, the helium behaves like an ideal gas (or a suitable property of ideal gases is given). [2 marks]

Page 65 — Pressure of an Ideal Gas

1)a) $pV = \dfrac{1}{3}Nm\overline{c^2}$

Mean square speed, $\overline{c^2} = \dfrac{3pV}{Nm}$ [1 mark]

$\overline{c^2} = \dfrac{3 \times 1 \times 10^5 \times 7 \times 10^{-5}}{2 \times 10^{22} \times 6.8 \times 10^{-27}} = 154\,000$ m^{2}s^{-2} [1 mark]

b) r.m.s. speed = $\sqrt{154\,000}$ = 392 ms^{-1} [1 mark]

c) Doubling the temperature, doubles the pressure if the volume stays fixed, so doubling the pressure doubles the mean square speed. [1 mark]

New r.m.s. speed = $\sqrt{2\overline{c^2}}$ = 555 ms^{-1} [1 mark]

Page 67 — Internal Energy of a Gas

1)a) Mass of 1 molecule = $\dfrac{\text{mass of 1 mole}}{N_A}$ = $\dfrac{2.8 \times 10^{-2}}{6.02 \times 10^{23}}$ = 4.65×10^{-26} kg [1 mark]

b) $\dfrac{1}{2}m\overline{c^2} = \dfrac{3kT}{2}$

Rearranging gives:

$\overline{c^2} = \dfrac{3kT}{m} = \dfrac{3 \times 1.38 \times 10^{-23} \times 300}{4.65 \times 10^{-26}} = 2.67 \times 10^5$ m^{2}s^{-2} [2 marks]

Typical speed = r.m.s. speed = $\sqrt{2.67 \times 10^5}$ = 517 ms^{-1} [1 mark]
There's one mark for rearranging the formula, one mark for using it and the third for realising that the answer was the r.m.s. speed.

Answers

2)a) Speed = $\dfrac{distance}{time}$ so   time = $\dfrac{distance}{speed}$

The time = $\dfrac{8.0\ m}{400\ ms^{-1}}$ = 0.02 s   [1 mark]

b) Although the particles are moving at 400 ms⁻¹, they are frequently colliding with other particles. [1 mark]
This means their forward motion is limited and so they only slowly move from one end of the room to the other. [1 mark]

c) At 30 ºC the average speed of the particles will be slightly faster [1 mark] since the absolute temperature has risen from 293 K to 303 K and the temperature determines the average speed. [1 mark]

Page 69 — Thermodynamics and Engines

1)a) From $Q = \Delta U - W$, if heat energy is supplied and no work is done on or by the gas, its internal energy must increase. [1 mark] This means the particles have more kinetic energy, which is equivalent to raising the temperature. So the temperature rises. [1 mark]

b) Using $Q = \Delta U - W$, $\Delta U = Q + W$ [1 mark]
W = work done on system. Since work is being done by system, W is negative, i.e. $W = -80\ J$.
So $\Delta U = +100\ J + (-80\ J) = +20\ J$
The internal energy increases by 20 J. [1 mark]

2)a) Maximum efficiency = $\dfrac{T_1 - T_2}{T_1} \times 100\%$ [1 mark]

The temperature must all be on the absolute scale.
Maximum efficiency = $\dfrac{773 - 293}{773} \times 100 = \dfrac{480}{773} \times 100 = 62\%$

[1 mark]

b) Actual efficiency = $\dfrac{work\ done\ by\ engine}{energy\ supplied\ to\ engine} \times 100\ \%$ [1 mark]
Energy supplied each second is 4000 J.
Work done each second is the power 1.5 kW i.e. 1500 Js⁻¹.
Actual efficiency = $\dfrac{1500\ J}{4000\ J} \times 100 = 37.5\ \%$ [1 mark]

c) There will always be energy losses from an engine because of friction, heat losses to the surroundings etc. Any sensible statements about this or a correct example would obtain the mark. [1 mark]

Section 5 — Waves
Page 71 — The Nature of Waves

1)a) Use $v = \lambda f$ and $f = 1 / T$
So $v = \lambda / T$ so $\lambda = vT$ [1 mark]
$\lambda = 3\ ms^{-1} \times 6\ s = 18\ m$ [1 mark]
The vertical movement of the buoy is irrelevant to this part of the question.

b) The trough to peak distance is twice the amplitude, so the amplitude is 0.6m [1 mark]

Page 73 — Longitudinal and Transverse Waves

1) [This question could equally well be answered using diagrams.]
For ordinary light, the EM field vibrates in all planes at right angles to the direction of travel. [1 mark]
Iceland Spar acts as a polariser. [1 mark]
When light is shone through a polariser it only allows through vibrations in one particular plane. [1 mark]
As the two crystals are rotated relative to each other there comes a point when the allowed planes are at right angles to each other. [1 mark]
So all the light is blocked. [1 mark]
Try to remember to say that for light and other EM waves it's the electric and magnetic fields that vibrate.

2)a) Measure the horizontal distance on the screen between the two pulses. [1 mark]
Use a known time base to calculate the time between the pulses. [1 mark]
Use speed = distance between microphones / time   [1 mark]

b) time between pulses = 2 cm × 10 ms cm⁻¹ = 20 ms = 0.02s [1 mark]
v = 6.6 m/ 0.02 s = 330 ms⁻¹ [1 mark]
In this version of the experiment the CRO is connected to microphone A rather than directly to the loudspeaker. Don't let it worry you. The principle's the same.

Page 75 — Refraction

1)a) $n_{diamond} = c / v_{diamond} = (3 \times 10^8) / (1.241 \times 10^8) = 2.417$ [1 mark]

b) $n_{air} \sin i = n_2 \sin r$, $n_{air} = 1$
So, $n_2 = \sin i / \sin r$ [1 mark]
$2.417 = \sin 50° / \sin r$
$2.417 = 0.766 / \sin r$
$\sin r = 0.766 / 2.417 = 0.317$
$r = 18.5°$ [1 mark]
You can assume the refractive index of air is 1, and don't forget to write the degree sign for your answer.

2)a) When the light is pointing steeply upwards some of it is refracted and some reflected — the faint beam emerging from the surface is the refracted part. [1 mark]
However when the beam hits the surface at more than the critical angle (to the normal to the boundary) refraction does not occur. All the beam is totally internally reflected to light the aquarium, hence its brightness. [1 mark]

b) The critical angle is 90° − 41.25° = 48.75°. [1 mark]
$n_{water} = 1 / \sin C$
$= 1 / \sin 48.75°$
$= 1 / 0.752 = 1.330$ [1 mark]
The question talks about the angle between the light beam and the floor of the aquarium. This angle is 90° minus the incident angle — measured from a normal to the surface of the water.

Page 77 — Superposition and Coherence

1)a) The frequencies and wavelengths of the two sources must be equal [2 marks] and the phase difference must be constant. [1 mark]

b) Interference will only be noticeable if the amplitudes of the two waves are approximately equal. [1 mark]

2)a) 180° (or 180° + 360n°). [1 mark]

b) The displacements and velocities of the two points are equal in size [1 mark] but in opposite directions. [1 mark]

Page 79 — Diffraction

1) When a wavefront meets an obstacle, the waves will diffract round the corners of the obstacle. When the obstacle is much bigger than the wavelength, little diffraction occurs. In this case, the mountain is much bigger than the wavelength of shortwave radio. So the "shadow" where you cannot pick up shortwave is very long.

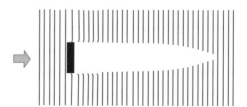

[2 marks]

Answers

When the obstacle is comparable in size to the wavelength, as it is for the longwave radio waves, more diffraction occurs. The wavefront re-forms after a shorter distance, leaving a shorter "shadow".

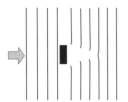

[2 marks]

2) a) The pattern would get wider. *[1 mark]*
   (Because $\sin \theta = \lambda / a$, and if a decreases θ increases.)
   b) $\sin \theta = \lambda / a$ *[1 mark]*
   $\sin \theta = 6 \times 10^{-7}$ m $/ 0.1 \times 10^{-3}$ m
   $\sin \theta = 6 \times 10^{-3}$
   $\theta = 0.344°$ *[1 mark]*

Page 81 — Two-Source Interference

1) a)

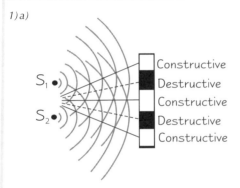

Constructive
Destructive
Constructive
Destructive
Constructive

[2 marks]
   b) Light waves from separate sources are not coherent, as light is emitted in random bursts of energy. To get coherent light the two sets of waves must emerge from one source. *[1 mark]* Then the light diffracts out of the slits which become secondary sources. A laser is used because it emits coherent light that is all of one wavelength.
   [1 mark]
2) a) $\lambda = v / f = 330 / 1320 = 0.25$m. *[1 mark]*
   b) Separation $= X = \lambda D / a$ *[1 mark]*
   $= 0.25$ m $\times 7$ m $/ 1.5$ m $= 1.167$ m. *[1 mark]*

Page 83 — Diffraction Gratings and Intensity

1) a) Use $\sin \theta = n \lambda / d$
   For the first order, $n = 1$
   So, $\sin \theta = \lambda / d$ *[1 mark]*
   No need to actually work out d. The number of lines per metre is $1 / d$. So you can simply multiply the wavelength by that.
   $\sin \theta = 600 \times 10^{-9} \times 4 \times 10^5 = 0.24$
   $\theta = 13.9°$ *[1 mark]*
   For the second order, $n = 2$ and $\sin \theta = 2\lambda / d$. *[1 mark]*
   You already have a value for λ / d. Just double it to get $\sin \theta$ for the second order.
   $\sin \theta = 0.48$
   $\theta = 28.7°$ *[1 mark]*
   b) No. Putting $n = 5$ into the equation gives value of $\sin \theta$ of 1.2, which is impossible. *[1 mark]*

Page 85 — Standing Waves

1) a)

[2 marks]
   b) For a string vibrating at three times the fundamental frequency, length $= 3\lambda / 2$
   1.2 m $= 3\lambda / 2$
   $\lambda = 0.8$ m
   [1 mark]
   c) In a standing wave amplitude varies from a maximum at the antinodes to zero at the nodes. *[1 mark]* In a progressive wave all the points have the same amplitude. *[1 mark]*
   d) The displacements in successive antinodes are of equal size *[1 mark]* but opposite directions. *[1 mark]*
   Remember that displacement is how "far out" the vibrating particle is at a particular time. Amplitude is the maximum displacement the particle *ever* reaches.

Page 87 — The Electromagnetic Spectrum

1) At the same speed. *[1 mark]*
   Both are electromagnetic waves and hence travel at c in a vacuum. *[1 mark]*
2) a) X-rays can be detected using photographic film. *[1 mark]*
   b) Medical X-rays *[1 mark]* rely on the fact that X-rays penetrate the body well but are blocked by bone. *[1 mark]*
   OR
   Security scanners at airports *[1 mark]* rely on the fact that they penetrate suitcases and clothes but are blocked by metal e.g. of a weapon. *[1 mark]*
   c) The main difference between gamma rays and X-rays is that gamma rays arise from nuclear decay *[1 mark]* but X-rays are generated when metals are bombarded with electrons. *[1 mark]*
3) Any of: unshielded microwaves, excess heat, damage to eyes from too bright light, sunburn or skin cancer from UV, cancer or eye damage due to ionisation by X-rays or gamma rays.
   [1 mark for the type of EM wave, 1 mark for the danger to health]

Section 6 — Nuclear and Particle Physics
Page 89 — Atomic Structure

1) Inside every atom there is a nucleus which contains protons and neutrons. *[1 mark]*
   Orbiting this core are the electrons. *[1 mark]*
   The tiny electrons orbit at comparatively vast distances, so most of the atom is empty space. *[1 mark]*
2) Proton number is 8, so there are 8 protons and 8 electrons.
   [1 mark]
   The nucleon number is 16. This is the total number of protons and neutrons.
   Subtract the 8 protons and that leaves 8 neutrons. *[1 mark]*
3) Atoms with the same number of protons but different numbers of neutrons are called isotopes. *[1 mark for definition]*
   Isotopes have the same chemical reactions and behaviour.
   The nuclei have different stabilities.
   Isotopes have different physical properties.
   [2 marks for any 2 sensible points]

Answers

Page 91 — Scattering to Determine Structure

1)a) [2 marks]

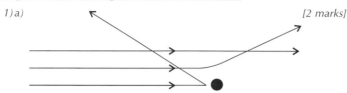

b) The nucleus is small compared to the size of the atom as a whole.
The nucleus contains most of the mass of the atom.
The nucleus is positively charged. *[3 marks, 1 mark per point]*

Page 93 — Radioactive Emissions

1)

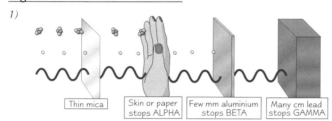

| Thin mica | Skin or paper stops ALPHA | Few mm aluminium stops BETA | Many cm lead stops GAMMA |

[1 mark for each material stopping correct radiation, total 4 marks.]

2) Beta radiation is more penetrative than alpha. *[1 mark]*
The alpha particle shows strong ionisation. The alpha particle quickly ionises many atoms and loses all its energy. This is why it has low penetration of matter. *[1 mark]*
The beta-minus particle has lower ionisation. Its lower interaction rate with matter means that it has better penetration than the alpha particle. *[1 mark]*

3)

Particle	Symbol	Constituent
Alpha	α	A helium nucleus: 2 protons & 2 neutrons
Beta-minus	β or β^-	Electron
Beta-plus	β^+	Positron
Gamma	γ	Short-wave, high-frequency electromagnetic wave.

[3 marks available — 1 mark for one or two rows correct, 2 marks for three rows correct, 3 marks for all correct.]

Page 95 — Nuclear Decay

1)a) $^{226}_{88}\text{Ra} \longrightarrow \, ^{222}_{86}\text{Rn} + \, ^{4}_{2}\alpha$

[3 marks available — 1 mark for alpha particle, 1 mark each for proton number and nucleon number of radon]

b) $^{40}_{19}\text{K} \longrightarrow \, ^{40}_{20}\text{Ca} + \, ^{0}_{-1}\beta$

[3 marks available — 1 mark for beta particle, 1 mark each for proton number and nucleon number of calcium]

2) In alpha decay, the energy carried by the particle corresponds to one or more set energy values.
In beta emission most of the particles emitted have less than the maximum energy available.
Beta energy varies continuously over a range.
From zero to the maximum for a source.
The energy of the antineutrino accounts for the energy difference in beta emission. *[1 mark for each point, 5 marks in total]*

Page 97 — Activity and Half-Life

1)a) Activity, **A** = measured activity − background activity
= 750 − 50 = 700 Bq *[1 mark]*
Use **A** = λ**N** to give 700 = 50 000 λ *[1 mark]*
So λ = 0.014 s^{-1} *[1 mark]*

b) Activity, **A** = measured activity − background activity
= 400 − 50 = 350 Bq *[1 mark]*
Use **A** = λ**N** to give 350 = 0.03 **N** *[1 mark]*
So **N** = 11670 *[1 mark]*

Page 99 — Classification of Particles

1) Proton, electron and electron-antineutrino. *[1 mark]*
The electron and the electron-antineutrino are leptons. *[1 mark]*
Leptons are not affected by the strong interaction, so the decay can't be due to the strong interaction. *[1 mark]*
Remember that this is really just the same as beta decay. Some books might leave out the antineutrino so don't be misled.

2) Mesons are hadrons but the muon is a lepton. *[1 mark]*
The muon is a fundamental particle but mesons are not.
Mesons are built up from simpler particles. *[1 mark]*
Mesons interact via the strong interaction but the muon does not. *[1 mark]*
You need to <u>classify</u> the muon correctly first and then say why it's different from a meson because of <u>what it's like</u> and <u>what it does</u>.

Page 101 — Antiparticles

1) $e^+ + e^- \rightarrow \gamma + \gamma$ *[1 mark]*
This is called annihilation. *[1 mark]*
Remember that there are two photons and they go off in opposite directions, just like two bits from an explosion.

2) The protons, neutrons and electrons which make up the iron atoms would need to annihilate with their antiparticles. *[1 mark]*
No antiparticles are available for this to happen in the iron block. *[1 mark]*

3) The creation of a particle of matter also requires the creation of its antiparticle. In this case no antineutron has been produced. *[1 mark]*
Also note that the total baryon number would have increased from 2 to 3 and that's not allowed.

Page 103 — Quarks

1) $\pi^- = d\bar{u}$ *[1 mark]*
Charge of down quark = −1/3 unit.
Charge of anti-up quark = −2/3 unit
Total charge = −1 unit *[1 mark]*

2) The weak interaction converts a down quark into an up quark plus an electron and an electron-antineutrino. *[1 mark]*
The neutron (udd) becomes a proton (uud). *[1 mark]*
The lepton number L_e is conserved in this reaction.

3) The baryon number changes from 2 to 1 so baryon number is not conserved.
OR
The strangeness changes from 0 to 1 so strangeness is not conserved. *[1 mark]*

Page 105 — Detecting Particles

1) Charged particles follow curved tracks in a magnetic field. *[1 mark]*
Positive and negative particle tracks curve in opposite directions *[1 mark]*
Identify the direction of curvature for negative particles by looking for knock-on electrons — OR — apply Fleming's left hand rule. *[1 mark]*

Answers

2) The proton and the positive pion give tracks but the neutron and the neutral pion do not. [1 mark]

3)

[1 mark for two tracks going in opposite directions, 1 mark for <u>not</u> showing a track for the photon, 1 mark for tracks spiralling inwards.]
The tracks spiral inwards as the particles lose energy through ionisation.

Page 107 — Exchange Particles and Feynman Diagrams

1) The electrostatic force is due to the exchange of virtual photons that only exist for a very short time. [1 mark]
The force is due to the momentum gained or lost by the photons as they are emitted or absorbed by a proton. [1 mark]

2)

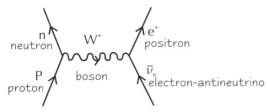

[2 marks]
This is a weak interaction. [1 mark]
Don't forget to put the arrows on your Feynman diagram.
Remember that only the weak interaction can change protons into neutrons or neutrons into protons.

Section 7 — Quantum Phenomena
Page 109 — The Photoelectric Effect

1) The plate becomes positively charged [1 mark]
Negative electrons in the metal absorb energy from the UV light and leave the surface [1 mark].
There's one mark for saying <u>what</u> happens, and a second mark for saying <u>why</u>.

2) An electron needs to gain a certain amount of energy (the work function energy) before it can leave the surface of the metal [1 mark]
If the energy carried by each photon is less than this work function energy, no electrons will be emitted [1 mark].

Page 111 — Energy Levels and Photon Emission

1) a) i) $E = V = 12.1$ eV [1 mark]
   ii) $E = V \times 1.6 \times 10^{-19} = 12.1 \times 1.6 \times 10^{-19} = 1.9 \times 10^{-18}$ J [1 mark]
  b) i) Excitation occurs when an electron moves from a lower energy to a higher energy level by absorbing energy. [1 mark]
   ii) $-13.6 + 12.1 = -1.5$ eV This corresponds to $n = 3$. [1 mark]
   iii) $n = 3 \rightarrow n = 2$: $3.4 - 1.5 = 1.9$ eV   [1 mark]
      $n = 2 \rightarrow n = 1$: $13.6 - 3.4 = 10.2$ eV   [1 mark]
      $n = 3 \rightarrow n = 1$: $13.6 - 1.5 = 12.1$ eV   [1 mark]

Page 113 — Wave-Particle Duality

1) a) Electromagnetic radiation can show characteristics of both a particle and a wave. [1 mark]

  b) i) $E_{photon} = \dfrac{hc}{\lambda} = \dfrac{6.63 \times 10^{-34} \times 3.00 \times 10^8}{590 \times 10^{-9}}$ [1 mark]
  $= 3.37 \times 10^{-19}$ J   [1 mark]

  $E \text{ (in eV)} = \dfrac{E \text{ (in J)}}{1.6 \times 10^{-19}} = \dfrac{3.37 \times 10^{-19}}{1.6 \times 10^{-19}} = 2.11$ eV   [1 mark]

   ii) $\lambda = \dfrac{h}{mv}$
   $\therefore v = \dfrac{h}{m\lambda} = \dfrac{6.63 \times 10^{-34}}{9.1 \times 10^{-31} \times 590 \times 10^{-9}} = 1230$ ms^{-1}
   [2 marks]

2) a) $\lambda = \dfrac{h}{mv} = \dfrac{6.63 \times 10^{-34}}{9.1 \times 10^{-31} \times 3.5 \times 10^6} = 2.08 \times 10^{-10}$ m   [2 marks]

  b) <u>Either</u> $v = \dfrac{h}{m\lambda}$ with $m_{proton} = 1840 \times m_{electron}$
   <u>or</u> momentum of protons = momentum of electrons
   $1840 \times \cancel{m_e} \times v_p = \cancel{m_e} \times 3.5 \times 10^6$
   $v_p = 1900$ ms^{-1}
   [2 marks]

  c) The two have the same kinetic energy if the voltages are the same. The proton has a larger mass, so it will have a smaller speed.
   [1 mark] Kinetic energy is proportional to the square of the speed, while momentum is proportional to the speed, so they will have different momenta. [1 mark]
   Wavelength depends on the momentum, so the wavelengths are different. [1 mark]
   This is a really hard question. If you didn't get it right, make sure you understand the answer fully. Do the algebra if it helps.

3) a) $E_k = 6 \times 10^3$ eV [1 mark]
   $= 6000 \times 1.6 \times 10^{-19} = 9.6 \times 10^{-16}$ J [1 mark]

  b) $E_k = \dfrac{1}{2}mv^2$
   $9.6 \times 10^{-16} = \dfrac{1}{2} \times 9.1 \times 10^{-31} \times v^2$
   $v = \sqrt{\dfrac{2 \times 9.6 \times 10^{-16}}{9.1 \times 10^{-31}}} = 4.6 \times 10^7$ ms^{-1}
   [2 marks]

  c) $\lambda = \dfrac{h}{mv} = \dfrac{6.63 \times 10^{-34}}{9.1 \times 10^{-31} \times 4.6 \times 10^7} = 1.58 \times 10^{-11}$ m
   [2 marks]

Index

Index

Index